Thomas Edward Bridgett

Ritual of the New Testament

Third Edition

Thomas Edward Bridgett

Ritual of the New Testament
Third Edition

ISBN/EAN: 9783337332822

Printed in Europe, USA, Canada, Australia, Japan

Cover: Foto ©Lupo / pixelio.de

More available books at **www.hansebooks.com**

THE

RITUAL OF THE NEW TESTAMENT.

AN ESSAY

ON THE

PRINCIPLES AND ORIGIN OF CATHOLIC RITUAL IN
REFERENCE TO THE NEW TESTAMENT.

BY THE

REV. T. E. BRIDGETT,
Of the Congregation of the Most Holy Redeemer.

THIRD EDITION.

𝔓ermissu 𝔖uperiorum.

LONDON: BURNS AND OATES, Limited.
NEW YORK: CATHOLIC PUBLICATION SOCIETY CO.
1887.

Nihil obstat.
✠ GUILELMUS WEATHERS,
Episc. Amycl.

Imprimatur.
✠ HENRICUS EDUARDUS,
Archiep. Westmonast.

NOTICE TO SECOND EDITION.

THE first edition of this Essay was entitled 'In Spirit and in Truth: an Essay on the Ritual of the New Testament.' In the present edition the first part of this title has been omitted. This requires a word of explanation.

Though the book has been recast and almost rewritten, with the addition of more than a hundred pages of new matter, yet I have not altered the title in order to give my Essay the appearance of a new book. I have done so because, since its publication, a translation into English has been made of the ascetic treatise of Father Nieremberg, called 'Of Adoration in Spirit and in Truth.' The similarity of titles between two books, in the very limited literature of Catholic England, had given rise to several mistakes, even though the books were issued by different publishers; and now that they are in the hands of the same publisher, the precaution was necessary to avoid confusion. I have therefore thought it better to yield to the prior claims of Father Nieremberg.

T. E. BRIDGETT, C.SS.R.

NOTICE TO THIRD EDITION.

MANY verbal corrections have been made, and about twenty pages of somewhat irrelevant matter omitted.

APPROBATIONS OF THE FIRST EDITION.

From the Most Rev. Henry Edward Manning, Archbishop of Westminster.

'Your book is sound, solid, and most useful. I hear approval of it from every one.'

From the Most Rev. Patrick Leahy, Archbishop of Cashel.

'Having looked through your Essay, and read some portions of it attentively, I have no manner of doubt but it will do much good with every class of readers.'

From the Most Rev. Peter Richard Kenrick, Archbishop of St. Louis.

'I do not remember to have met with any work for a long time which gave me greater satisfaction. I have suggested its republication here.'

From the Most Rev. Martin Spalding, Archbishop of Baltimore.

'Having carefully examined the work entitled "In Spirit and in Truth," we are pleased to be able to bear testimony to its numerous merits, both as to matter and manner, and to commend it to the faithful of the archdiocese, as a mine of useful sacred learning, and a creditable specimen of terse, moderate, and conclusive reasoning on a most interesting subject.'

From the Most Rev. William Vaughan, Bishop of Plymouth.

'I am reading your book with *much* satisfaction. I like it exceedingly, and think it may prove a help to many souls searching after rest and peace.'

ANALYSIS OF CONTENTS.

INTRODUCTION.

Scope of the Essay—For whom intended—Remarks on the Tone of certain Writers on Ritual—The Method adopted is an Appeal to the New Testament—Not for Construction but for Verification—The proper Spirit for such an Inquiry . . . . . *pp.* 1-19

PART I.
THE PRINCIPLES OF CATHOLIC RITUAL RECOGNISED IN THE NEW TESTAMENT.

CHAPTER I. A GENERAL VIEW.

Two preliminary Objections: 1. There is no Code of Ritual in the New Testament as in the Old—Catholic Reply—Difference between the two Dispensations—No Code of Morals, yet much Morality; 2. There is little said about Ritual—Reply—Further Reply: The Objection proves too much, and would overthrow the Sabbath or Sunday —Corollaries . . . . *pp.* 21-37

CHAPTER II. SPIRIT AND TRUTH.

Meaning of the words Spirit and Truth—Are they opposed to Ritual?—Catholic View stated—Our Lord's Maxims—Quakers' Views—Logical Issue in Rationalism . . . . . . *pp.* 38-51

CHAPTER III. IMPRESSIVE RITUAL.

Section I. Divine Pageantry.

Splendour not essential to Ritual, yet eminently Christian—This is proved from a Review of the supernatural Phenomena which accompanied the Birth, Baptism, Transfiguration, Death, Resurrection, and Ascension of Jesus Christ, and the Descent of the Holy Ghost—This was God's own Ritual, and the Model on which Catholic Ritual has been formed . . . . *pp.* 52-62

Section II. Apostolic Worship.

Apostolic Worship not splendid—Protestant Argument from this—Catholic Explanation in the Poverty and Persecution of the Early Church—Proofs that absence of Splendour was not the Result of Principle—Protestants misinterpret the Accounts of our Lord's 'Simplicity' in the New Testament, as the Jews misinterpreted the Prophecies of the Messiah's 'Magnificence'—Some Contrasts of Holy Scripture that explain each other . . . . *pp.* 62-67

Section III. Supposed Danger of Abuse.

Not so great as of the Splendour of Nature—Illustrations from Travellers and Poets—Protestants misjudge the Effect of Ritual on Catholics: 1. Because they do not understand the absorbing nature of Catholic Faith ; 2. Because to Protestants Ritual is strange and perplexing, not to Catholics ; 3. Because modern Controversies have given Ritual an unnatural Prominence—Is Protestant Simplicity always Spiritual ? —Testimonies of Menzel, Hamilton, Wilson . . . *pp.* 67-77

CHAPTER IV. SYMBOLIC RITUAL.

Section I. The Teaching of our Lord.

Strange Mistakes of some regarding the Effect of Ritual in the Conversion of the Heathen, and on Catholic Populations—Splendour is a rare Feature in Catholic Worship—Symbolism is an ordinary Characteristic—Objections stated to a multiplied, minute, and symbolic Ceremonial—No Analogy between Ritualism and Pharisaism—List of minute Ceremonies used by Jesus Christ and His Apostles—Symbolism of Ceremonies in all Religions . . . . *pp.* 78-90

Section II. Symbolism of Vestments.

Ridicule of 'Ecclesiastical Millinery'—Use of Colours justified—Mr. Marriott's sophistical Appeal to Antiquity—Milton's Attack on Vestments—Symbolism of Vestments abundantly recognised in New Testament . . . . *pp.* 90-97

Section III. Symbolic Language.

Images may be presented to the Mind by Rites as well as by Words— Verbal Imagery derived from Ritual—Nature made typical by our Lord's Parables—So also Christian Churches and Ritual recall Divine Teaching . . . . *pp.* 97-104

Section IV. Multitude and Obscurity.

Two Objections of the Anglican Reformers: 1. Multiplicity—Catholic Ceremonial not a Burden—Some Words of St. Peter explained ; 2. Obscurity—Catholic Worship not theatrical—In what Sense, to what Extent, and for what Purpose, Ritual is obscure—It is obscure like Holy Scripture . . . . *pp.* 104-110

Section V. On the Use of Dead Languages.

Past and present Discipline with regard to Dead Languages—Catholic Theory of Action and Prayer in Worship—Reasons for using Dead Languages—Catholic Discipline compared with the Doctrine of St. Paul . . . . *pp.* 110-119

Analysis of Contents. vii

CHAPTER V. EFFICIENT RITUAL NOT MAGICAL.

Sacramental Influences—Objection about Magic answered: 1. From Language of New Testament; 2. from History of Simon the Magician; 3. from Miracles worked at Ephesus to destroy Heathen Magic—Use of Relics . . . . . . *pp.* 120-130

CHAPTER VI. THE REAL PRESENCE AS REGARDS RITUAL.

Section I. Protestant View of the Real Presence.
Macaulay's Proof Charge—Dr. Vaughan's conceited Ignorance
pp. 131-136

Section II. An Argument from Analogy.
History of the sensible Presence of God on Earth, from the Creation of Man to the Incarnation—God's Presence in the Incarnation: 1. More Real; 2. More Hidden; 3. More Loving—Protestant View on the Disappearance of the *Shechinah*, and Catholic View on its Permanence contrasted . . . . *pp.* 136-147

Section III. Objections and their Results.
The Real Presence neither unspiritual nor too spiritual—The Mystery of Faith—The Protestant Mode of Thought destroys Belief in Scripture—Progress in Negation exemplified in Milton and Wordsworth—Harmonious Development of God's Providence in the Catholic View —Real Source of Opposition to God's sensible Presence . *pp.* 147-157

CHAPTER VII. COMPENSATION AND REPARATION.

Reparation a natural Instinct, which has peculiar Scope in the 'Religion of Jesus Christ—Singular Reasoning of some—The Wise Men at Bethlehem—Magdalen's Worship—The Procession of Palms—Application to Catholic Worship—Christian Chivalry . *pp.* 158-166

CHAPTER VIII. THE PATTERN ON THE MOUNT.

How Catholic Ritual grew up—The Pattern on the Mount is the Life of Jesus Christ—The Church is able to create Ritual—Answer to Objections—Catholic Ritual results from the Love of Jesus Christ
pp. 167-174

PART II.
THE ORIGIN OF CATHOLIC RITUAL JUSTIFIED BY THE NEW TESTAMENT.

CHAPTER I. RITUAL CONSIDERED AS TRADITION.

Scope of the Second Part is to show the Testimony of the New Testament to Traditional Ritual—" Unwritten " Tradition does not exclude Literature—Tradition not collected from ancient Books—It is living —The Publication of the Canon of the New Testament could not displace Tradition, even if they were Coextensive—Institutions must speak—Ritual Institutions of Divine Origin contain and proclaim Clusters of Doctrines—A supernatural Ritual does not admit Interruption — Therefore the assumption 'Bible alone' rejects such a Ritual *à priori*, and is inconsistent with free inquiry . *pp.* 175-186

Analysis of Contents.

CHAPTER II. SCRIPTURE SENDS US TO RITUAL AND TRADITION.

What Traditions our Lord condemned—Some Protestant Traditions—Tradition necessary for Ignorant and for Learned—Unanimity through Tradition—Our Lord and the Apostles both send us to Tradition—Living Tradition and Scripture both Instruments of the Holy Ghost—Tradition never superseded . . . . . *pp.* 187-199

CHAPTER III. RITUAL A KEY TO SCRIPTURE.

Section I. *How Ritual helped to edit the New Testament.*

Whately's Sophism about the Church as an ignorant Letter-Carrier—A true Analogy of Church as Guardian of Scripture—She alone could *edit* the Apostolic Writings . . . . . *pp.* 200-205

Section II. *What Key will open the New Testament.*

Historico-Grammatical Method not sufficient for understanding New Testament—Locke's Defence of Diversity a *Reductio ad absurdum*—Cause of Obscurity of New Testament—Providentially thus inspired lest the Casket should be opened without the Key of Unity and Charity . . . . *pp.* 205-212

Section III. *Baptism and Communion.*

The Notices of divinely instituted Rites in the New Testament presuppose the Knowledge of the Rites : 1. Notices of Baptism ; 2. Notices of Communion—Those for whom the New Testament was written had the Key in their Ritual 212-222

Section IV. *Other Rites.*

Other Rites considered—Feet-Washing—Anointing—Need of some Rule to determine the relative Importance and Permanency of Ritual—Rites may be justified but not derived from Scriptural Notices
pp. 222-229

CHAPTER IV. THE CANON AND THE CODE.

Traditions sifted like Scripture, by the Church only—The Canon of Scripture and Code of Ritual—Is Scripture incomplete ?—Plan of Inspiration—Well-known Doctrines and permanent Facts not prominent—. This is no Difficulty to those who possess Tradition, but Cause of Embarrassment and Error to Protestants . . . . *pp.* 230-240

CHAPTER V. VIEWS OF HISTORY.

The Protestant View makes Religious History an Anti-Climax—Passage from Milton—Grandeur of Catholic View—Recapitulation—The Tradition here defended not sub-Apostolic, but now living—The Catholic Church is always Apostolic—Illustration of Protestant, Anglican, and Catholic Views from a Building—The Church is God's Building—*Circumspice* . . . . *pp.* 241-250

THE RITUAL

OF

THE NEW TESTAMENT

———◆———

INTRODUCTION.

BEFORE entering directly into the matter of this Essay, I wish to let my reader know my scope in writing it, the class of persons to whom it is addressed, and the method it adopts.

I. It is now about half a century since Wordsworth, in one of his ecclesiastical sonnets, gave expression to his regrets at the destructive work of the Protestant Reformers:

> 'Would that our scrupulous sires had dared to leave
> Less scanty measure of those graceful rites
> And usages, whose due return invites
> A stir of mind too natural to deceive!'

These regrets are becoming every day more common, and those who share them seem determined that they shall no longer remain inefficacious.

But the recent endeavours which have been made within the Anglican Church to restore somewhat of the variety and splendour of the ancient Ritual have awakened a powerful opposition, and given rise to an active controversy regarding the nature of religious worship.

A Catholic can scarcely remain an indifferent spectator of a controversy in which the principles and practice of the Catholic Church are the main topic of dispute.

The modern controversy regarding Ritualism comprises two distinct questions.

First, Is that theory of worship in itself true or false?

Secondly, Is it in or out of place in the Anglican Church?

From the latter of these two questions I hold myself entirely aloof. By Ritualism is popularly meant that use of religious ceremonial which obtains in the Catholic Church; and it is loudly and repeatedly asserted by innumerable voices, that the principles of Catholic Ritualism are not of Christian origin, but are derived from Jewish and from heathen sources. The truth of these assertions is what I have undertaken to discuss.

A limitation must, however, here be made.

The word Ritualism is taken in several, perhaps in most, of the books which have been written against it, to mean that whole system of religion which recognises a priesthood, a sacrifice, sacraments, and the use of symbolism. I admit readily enough that the question of the use of external ceremonies, of art, and splendour, and wealth, in divine worship, is not merely æsthetical. I admit, and will show in the proper place, that not only great doctrines are in question, but that the very mode of revealing to the world almost all doctrines is involved in the Catholic system of worship. There is a close connection in fact, and perhaps even in logic, between Ritual and certain very fundamental principles of religion; such as, for instance, the visible nature of the Church, the supernatural character of the priesthood, and the efficacy of the sacraments. Yet it by no means follows that we cannot treat of the use of ceremonial without treating at the same time of all subjects connected with it. It is not my intention, therefore, to follow the example of some writers, who announce a Treatise on Ritualism, and then, touching only incidentally on the principles of worship, give long dissertations against the obligation of confession, the efficacy of absolution, and the lawfulness of the invocation of saints. The discussion shall be confined to Ritualism proper, and the topics immediately connected with it.

In order to avoid confusion, I will venture to make a threefold division of the subjects involved in this controversy.

1. It is well known that the Catholic Church teaches the supernatural character and efficacy of certain rites, which she believes to be of divine institution. This doctrine, and the practice resulting from it, have been sometimes called the Sacramental System. This is, no doubt, in itself by far the most important aspect of Ritualism. Yet comparatively little will be said about it in this Essay; partly because of the many doctrinal mattters that it would be necessary to discuss, and partly because the whole question has been so fully and frequently treated by other writers.

2. In the second place, the Catholic Church makes use of many symbolic ceremonies, some of which she believes to be of divine, others of ecclesiastical, origin; and this is a frequent subject of accusation against her. Sometimes the principle itself of *Symbolism* is objected to; sometimes, while the principle is admitted, either the variety or the minuteness of Catholic Symbolism is attacked.

These are matters which I shall enter into fully.

3. Lastly, there is a phase of Ritualism not considered essential by the Catholic Church. She can easily dispense with it: but she readily admits it. It is the natural development of her principles, when no obstacle hinders their development. This is *magnificence or splendour*. It is far less important in the eyes of Catholics than the two other forms of Ritualism I have just mentioned; yet, as it attracts the attention of Protestants more easily, it is considered peculiarly characteristic of the worship of Catholics: it will, therefore, occupy a prominent place in this Essay.

I shall not suppose in my reader a familiar acquaintance with Catholic rites. The opposition encountered by the Church is in respect of certain general characteristics of her worship. It is these features, common to all or to many of her rites, rather than the particular rites themselves, that we are to discuss.

II. Let me next explain for what class of readers my Essay is intended.

I trust that it may not be without interest and profit to my fellow Catholics. They do not indeed need the proofs that I shall adduce on behalf of the divine character of Catholic Ritual. The Catholic Church is the mother who has taught them to know God. They have knelt, if I may so say, like little children by their mother's side, with hands joined, and with eyes raised to their mother's face. They have seen her inspired and unearthly gaze fixed on the Invisible; and they have learnt from her to believe, to hope, to reverence, and love. Strangers may need proofs that such a mother is devout; it would be an insult to offer them to the child. Yet the child, too, may love to hear his mother's piety defended against detractors; and he may listen willingly to one who speaks to him of its sublimity, and traces it to its divine origin.

But this Essay is not written primarily for Catholics. It is intended as a help towards the removal of the prejudices of ordinary Protestants. 'We owe,' says Cardinal Manning, 'an especial duty to the class of the English people in which descends the mid-stream of traditional hostility to the Catholic Church, that is, the middle class of educated and industrious men, the heart of English national life, vigorous, quiet, intelligent, and benevolent, though darkened by inherited prejudices and narrowed by anti-Catholic faults. To this class, above all, we have a mission of charity, that is, to preach the truth in patience and to wait till they will listen.'[1]

If I may be allowed to say so, I have a more personal reason for this course. I have long made my own a prayer with which St. Augustine concludes one of his theological treatises, written against an error of the sect to which in his youth he had been attached: 'O great God, O God Almighty and of infinite bounty, O Thou, One God in three persons, whom the Catholic Church adores, I humbly beseech Thee, having experienced Thy mercy towards myself, that Thou wilt not permit that those with whom I have lived from my childhood upwards

[1] *The Reunion of Christendom*, p. 14.

in the closest union, should be separated from me in matters that regard Thy worship.'[2]

I was not altogether unacquainted with the writings of the older school of Puritans. I knew that with intense prejudices against the Catholic Church and a spirit of reckless vituperation, they often combined much erudition and vigorous reasoning. I had hoped that time would have removed prejudices, and that modern habits would have softened some of the asperities of language in those who now represent English Puritanism. In order to become better acquainted with the views of this class of Protestants, I have deemed it a duty to read several recent works against Ritualism, amongst others that *On Ritualism*, by the Rev. S. Malan; *Ritualism in the English Church*, by Dr. Robert Vaughan; Dr. White's *Ritualism and New Testament Christianity*, and Dr. Cumming's lectures entitled *Ritualism the Highway to Rome*. I will merely say that I have been greatly disappointed both as to matter and manner. Opponents are not treated even with the ordinary decency of civilised intercourse. The language of insult has grown so familiar to some, from familiarity with the older school of Protestant writers, that they have come to use it with an apparent unconsciousness of its nature. I know not how else to account charitably for what I meet with on every side. I open, for instance, Dr. Hessey's *Bampton Lectures* on 'The Origin and History of Sunday.' In Lecture VI. he is finding fault with the Continental Reformers for going farther than their Anglican fellow-labourers. This is his language: 'The low views entertained by several foreign Protestant communions of the grace of Baptism and of the Holy Eucharist are cases painfully in point. *If the Church of Rome had made the former of these a charm and condensed the latter into an idol*, there were those who, in their reforming zeal, and in the not unnatural reaction produced by a sense of liberty, reduced the one to a rite of initiation, the other to a mere metaphor.'

These lectures were delivered before the University of Ox-

---

[2] *Lib. de dua. Animabus*, n. 24: 'Supplex oro, expertus in me misericordiam tuam, ne homines, cum quibus mihi a pueritia in omni convictu fuit summa consensio, in tuo cultu a me dissentire permittas.'

ford. Yet the lecturer is so far from feeling that he has said anything in a tone unbefitting his audience or his subject, that he speaks, in the preface to the first edition, of the great care he has taken to offend no one; and in the postscript to the second edition is grateful because 'he has received the same *courteous* and candid treatment of his views, which he endeavoured to maintain throughout his lectures in speaking of opinions with which his subject brought him into contact.' I have no doubt that Dr. Hessey did intend to be courteous, and when he is opposing his fellow Protestants he uses the language of a liberal education. But it does not seem to have occurred to him that Catholics are within the pale of civilisation, or that his reverend and learned audience would expect the ancient founders of their colleges and churches to be treated with as much forbearance as Calvinists and Zwinglians.

To take another instance, Dr. Vaughan complains, I know not with what justice, of the 'haughty and censorious temper in which the majority of "Ritualists" indulge towards Protestant Christendom;' and yet he not only himself brings the most sweeping, disdainful, and odious accusations against Catholic Christendom, but even defends the virulence of his language. 'Some people,' he says, 'expect us to speak of the Ritual movement in terms of gentle courtesy, of tender forbearance, being studious of excuses in its favour. Souls of Wickliffe and of Knox, come back again and let us hear your tones on this theme!'

I have been anxious to state the views of our opponents as fairly and even as strongly as possible. I have therefore generally preferred to let them speak for themselves; and when it was possible, I have quoted from writers famous in literature, such as Milton and Locke, rather than from mere divines little known beyond their own sect.

I have studiously omitted to notice mere railing accusations, and the passages I have selected for quotation were such as contained the clearest statements or most specious reasonings of the writers, yet I fear that even these passages will jar on my readers' feelings as they did on my own. Yet what could I do? I had to quote from authors like Dr. Cumming, who conceive that they are doing God service in denouncing with all the energy of their souls 'the three unclean spirits, Rationalism, Romanism, and Ritualism :'[3] the fault was not mine if I could not find passages free from the taint of fanaticism.

Then, why quote from them at all? it may naturally be asked. Why enter into controversy with such writers? I reply, that their assertions, boldly made and continually repeated, have influenced and prejudiced against us men very different from themselves. There are some who think evil of Catholic worship, not because they wish to think evil, but because they have ever heard it spoken of as an evil thing. It is no pleasure to them to believe that the Christian Church throughout the world has apostatised for ages from the purity of the faith, and from 'worship in spirit and in truth.' They have reluctantly believed this to be the case; but the thought of it has lain on their souls with the oppression of a nightmare. They would willingly be relieved from it, if this could be done without treason to historic or religious truth. They have little or no intercourse with Catholics; they know the Catholic religion but from the lips of its enemies. There is an enormous prejudice instilled into their souls in early years, sedulously fostered by their teachers as they grow older, regarded as a first principle in the society into which they were born, which is a bar both to the arguments of reason and to the sympathies of noble instincts, until it is surmounted,—the prejudice that, however philosophy, art, or poetry, may approve of Catholic worship, yet that the Gospel is its enemy, that on the Gospel it is not based, and to the Gospel it dares not appeal.

It is to the removal of this prejudice my efforts are directed. I speak to the prejudiced, but I speak not to the obstinate. If there is any one who 'rejoiceth not in iniquity, but rejoiceth with the truth,' to him I address myself. As for men who are determined to think evil of us, on them argument would be thrown away.

I enter, therefore, once for all, my protest against the insulting and calumnious tone of controversy that so many of our opponents have thought proper to adopt; but as a Catholic, writing in defence of the Church, and venturing to speak in her

---

[3] *Ritualism the Highway to Rome.*

name, I can give but one answer to such language—the pathetic and dignified complaint of our divine Redeemer, when the Jews insulted Him as one possessed by a devil: 'I have not a devil, but I honour My Father, and you have dishonoured Me' (John viii. 49).[4]

I would not be understood to condemn an earnest, and even indignant language, when the subject demands it. I have not attempted myself to disguise the feelings with which I regard the indecent and outrageous attacks made on the Catholic Church, and the absurd pretence set up by some to a monopoly of reason and good sense. The distinction is well drawn by Lord Bacon, and I commend his words to all those who continue to invoke the shades of Wickliffe and of Knox. 'It is more than time,' says the Lord Chancellor, 'that there were an end and surcease made of this immodest and deformed manner of writing lately entertained, whereby matter of religion is handled in the style of the stage. Indeed, bitter and earnest writing must not hastily be condemned; for men cannot contend coldly and without affection about things which they hold dear and precious. A politic man may write from his brain without touch and sense of his heart, as in a speculation that appertaineth not unto him, but a feeling Christian will express in his words a character of zeal and love—the latter of which, as I could wish rather embraced, being more proper for these times, yet is the former warranted also by great examples. But to leave all reverent and religious compassion toward evils, or indignation towards faults, and to turn religion into a comedy or satire—to search and rip up wounds with a laughing countenance, to intermix Scripture and scurrility sometimes in one sentence, is a thing far from the devout reverence of a Christian, and scant beseeming the honest regard of a sober man.'[5]

I believe that I may say in sincerity, that these are the principles that have guided me in the present controversy. I

---

[4] As in none of the passages of Scripture that I shall quote, is there any important difference between the ordinary Protestant version and the translation in common use among English-speaking Catholics, I shall make use of the latter throughout the following Essay.

[5] Bacon, *Of Church Controversies.*

am sure that I shall neither rouse the anger nor wound the feelings of any sincere Protestant by ridicule of his belief. If I have now and then repelled unseemly attacks with warmth, or treated with scorn the arrogant pretensions of self-conceited men, I offer no apology. St. Augustine and St. Francis of Sales, the meekest and humblest of men, did the same.

III. It remains now to explain the method that I intend to pursue; for the subject is wide, and various modes of discussing it present themselves. An appeal might be made to reason, or to experience, or to tradition; to the Scriptures of the Old Testament, or to those of the New Dispensation. I shall confine myself in these pages to those proofs of the Catholic theory which may be found in the books of the New Testament. I am led to do so from having observed the peculiar tone of triumph with which our opponents appeal to the New Testament for the overthrow of ceremonial worship. Let us listen to the challenge.

A writer during the recent controversy states clearly enough, though in coarse and angry language, what seems to be the general impression among Protestants on the subject. 'I think it very lamentable,' he says, 'that so many of our countrymen should so persistently ransack the Bible in order to obtain what they consider a precedent or excuse for their absurd and irritating manner of worship. If the Jews wore particular dresses and used particular ceremonies by Divine command, is that a justifiable reason why the so-called ministers of God's Word should do so at this present time? We are not Jews; we have nothing in common with them; their whole ceremonial was different to what ours should be. It is the New Testament we should let guide us; and surely, in the name of common sense, we can find nothing in it to countenance the blasphemous antics of some of our present Ritualists. We should look at the highest authority in such cases. Our Lord's whole life on earth was conducted in the very simplest and plainest manner. Should we not try to imitate His walk if we are really anxious for religion's sake to act rightly? Without being irreverent, I may ask how would St. Peter or St. Paul have looked if dressed up in the gorgeous costume of the modern Ritualist? The very thought is monstrous. It is very sad to think that the plain and beautiful Gospel of God should be so perverted and smothered by all this wicked, useless, and ridiculous ceremonial.'[6] In a similar strain, Dr. Vaughan, after developing what he considers the testimony of the New Testament against Ritualism, exclaims triumphantly, 'Great, visibly great is the distress of the Ritualists on finding so much in the New Testament opposed to their tastes, and so little that can be construed, by any process, so as to seem to be in their favour.' 'Ritualists talk of the fathers,' says Dr. White, 'and carry us back to the third and fourth centuries; *we* talk of the apostles and of our Lord, and carry them back farther still, to the apostolic age, to the apostolic precedent, and the inspired apostolic rule.'[7]

Thus is the gauntlet confidently cast down, and with equal confidence I take it up. I do not admit that a question such as this has been left by God to be decided by each man's private opinion; neither do I think that the appeal should be made to the Holy Scriptures alone, before whatever tribunal it is made; nevertheless, I believe it will be a work of peace and charity to accept the appeal as it is proposed by Protestants.

Let not my design, however, be misunderstood. I shall not attempt to collect a system of Ritual from the pages of the New Testament. Mine will be an Essay of verification, not one of construction. Were true Christianity, like the Poles of the Earth, known indeed to exist but as yet undiscovered, I for one should not have the inclination or the hardihood to set out on a voyage of exploration. Many have already done this, and either perished in the attempt, or brought back little to repay their toil or to encourage new enterprise. Less modest, however, than Arctic navigators, each of these spiritual adventurers thinks he has solved the great riddle, and in emphatic language gives us the account of his discoveries. Milton was so dissatisfied with all the Protestant treatises that he had read, that

---

[6] A Correspondent in *Public Opinion*.
[7] *Ritualism and New Testament Christianity*, by the Rev. Dr. White—a work in which, strange to say, no use whatever is made of the New Testament.

'he dared not trust his creed nor his hopes of salvation to them,'[8] and believing that 'God's promises are made not to indolent credulity, but to constant diligence and unwearied research,' he fitted out a private expedition to explore the mysterious and unfathomed ocean of Scripture, disdaining the use of chart or compass. He has given us the results in his *Treatise on Christian Doctrine*. Arianism, divorce, polygamy, are only some of the strange lands which he has marked down on his new chart, and on which he would fain have set up the Christian flag.

Later on Locke made the same voyage, with different results, indeed, but for the same reason. 'The little satisfaction and consistency that is to be found in most of the systems of divinity I have met with,' he tells us, 'made me betake myself to the sole reading of the Scriptures for the understanding of the Christian religion. What from thence, by an attentive and unbiassed search, I have received, reader, I have delivered to thee.'[9] His principal discovery seems to have been, that in those regions there are few lands of which the position can be fixed with any accuracy, but rather an 'open Polar sea,' on which the hardy mariner may sail at liberty.

Readers, however, were not satisfied with his account, and few years have since passed which have not brought with them a new system or treatise 'compiled from Scripture alone.'

I am very far from thinking that by these and similar attempts no truths have been illustrated, no souls enlightened. But that this is the method ordained by God for the discovery of Christian faith and morals, Church government or ritual, I do not believe. Arctic navigators have made progress, and their perseverance may soon be crowned by entire success. But I see no general and admitted progress from the labours —able and indefatigable labours, certainly—of those who undertake to explore Scripture without tradition. *Magni passus sed extra viam!* Great strides, indeed, but on a wrong road.

I decline, therefore, to follow the example of Milton and

[8] Milton, Preface to *Treatise on Christian Doctrine*.
[9] Locke, Preface to *Reasonableness of Christianity*.

[handwritten: The true use of using Scriptures. — For Verification, not Construction.]

Locke and the rest, and to set out on a voyage of discovery. Catholic worship is a great historic fact, demanding some explanation, and claiming a purely Christian origin. It appeals to the records of the New Testament as giving an explanation of its existence and character. Our search will be to see whether this claim can be justified. The legitimacy of this method has often been defended. Cardinal Newman, while still an Anglican, wrote: 'It is nothing to the purpose whether or not we should have been able to draw the following view of the doctrine' (of the Blessed Trinity) 'from the Scriptures, had it never been suggested to us in the Creeds. For it has been (providentially) so suggested to all of us; and the question is not, What we should have done had we never had external assistance? but, taking things as we find them, Whether, the clue to the meaning of Scripture being given (as it ever has been given), we may not deduce the doctrine thence, by as argumentative a process as that which enables us to verify the recorded theory of gravitation, which perhaps we could never have discovered for ourselves, though possessed of the data from which the inventor drew his conclusions?'[10]

More will be said later on as to this method of using Scripture. I will here merely observe, that the 'texts' commonly relied on by Protestants to justify their view of the use of the Bible authorise at most a search of verification, not one of discovery or of construction. When our Lord said to the Pharisees, 'Search the Scriptures, . . . they give testimony of Me,' He meant His hearers to verify His claims, to compare the prophecies with that fulfilment of them which He indicated —the description of the Messiah with Him who was present before them. He did not intend that they should put away from their sight and thoughts all external facts, and, 'by letting their consciousness work freely,' like modern rationalists, or by relying on the interior teacher, like another school of Protestants, try to elicit the meaning of the Old Testament from the analysis or combination of its varied utterances. Nor did our Lord mean that any search through the Old Testament would tell them all that should be known about Him. He

---

[10] Newman, *The Arians of the Fourth Century*, ch. ii. sect. 2.

could only mean that a search diligently pursued, with proper dispositions, and in such circumstances, with the advantage of His own presence, and His appeal to and fulfilment of prophecy, would be sufficient, together with the other proofs they had, such as His holy life, wisdom, and miracles, to convince them that He was the Teacher promised to them by God, and to whom they should listen.

So again when St. Paul preached to the Bereans, the Acts of the Apostles inform us that 'they daily searched the Scriptures whether these things were so,' and they are praised for their nobility of character, because to this search they were prompted, and in it they were guided, by an ardent love of truth, and a resolve to embrace it at any cost (Acts xvii. 11). But this earnest toil of the Bereans was evidently one of verification, not one of construction. They did not think to find the truth by reading Scripture 'without note or comment,' and building up each for himself a system of faith, morals, and worship. They went to the Scriptures full of what they had just heard. They searched diligently to see whether matters really stood as St. Paul had represented them in his sermon, whether he had quoted the Scriptures correctly, and whether the interpretation he had given was a plausible, a probable, a convincing one.

Similarly, we are to compare together that system of Ritual which obtains in the Roman Catholic Church, and in the great Oriental bodies now separated from it and from one another, but which is generally repudiated by the various sections of Protestants, with those Scriptures generally admitted by these contending parties. The Church says to her Protestant assailants, 'Search the Scriptures, for in them ye think ye have eternal life: and they are they which testify of me.' But she says this only as Jesus Christ said it. He did not consider this the only or the best way of gaining disciples. Many admitted His authority without this search. They followed other processes, less laborious, equally convincing, and often such as proved a more docile and enlightened soul. But when the Pharisees rejected Him as an impostor, and in doing so talked much of Scripture, our Divine Master took them at their word, suffered or even approved of the appeal, though in that particular case He predicted its inutility.

The Catholic Church also does not recommend the method I am about to adopt as the sole or the best way in all cases of winning men to her allegiance. There are certainly shorter and simpler methods. But I have the example of too many of her Doctors and Apologists to doubt that it is a legitimate method. It is also in my opinion one adapted to the state of many minds among us at the present day. That it will be thrown away on men like the Pharisees, I know; but I have good hope that it may be useful to men like the Bereans.

IV. I may, perhaps, be allowed to say a word regarding the spirit in which our inquiry should be conducted. We have a warning in the words of our divine Lord Jesus Christ, 'Search the Scriptures, for you think in them to have life everlasting: and the same are they that give testimony of Me. But you will not come to Me that you may have life' (John v. 39, 40). It is not necessary to inquire whether these words are a counsel or a reproach.[11] One thing is beyond controversy. It is that men may be great students of Scripture, like the Pharisees; that they may have so much love and veneration for the Word of God as to think to find in it everlasting life; yet, at the same time, they may be so much under the dominion of prejudice and passion as utterly to misunderstand the teaching of Scripture, and to find arguments in it for opposing Him to whom it points. They thus find death where they think to find life.

In the particular case of the Pharisees our blessed Lord revealed the evil dispositions which prevented the searching of Scripture from leading to any good result. They 'had not the love of God in them,' and they 'received glory one from another' (John v. 42, 44). What then is the preparation necessary for a fruitful study? I know that I have no right to preach a sermon

---

[11] Different interpretations are given to our Lord's words. The Greek may be either the imperative or the indicative. St. Chrysostom prefers the former, St. Cyril the latter. Both Catholic and Protestant interpreters are divided in opinion. The Revised Version of 1881 has "Ye search," and "Search" in the margin.

while promising an essay, so I will borrow the homily from the pen of Dr. Cumming, and content myself with its application.

'That we may receive the truth,' says the preacher, 'that we may reject the error that is often intermixed, in all its destructive and deadly influences, let us pray that the Holy Spirit of God would remove from our minds every cloud of prejudice, and scatter from our hearts every corrupt appetite and desire. And let us never forget that a pure heart has more to do with a true creed than a vigorous or powerful mind. It is not logic, it is not argument, it is not evidence that men need, for they have abundance of all that; but it is the removal of the film from the mind's eye, the correction of the disturbing and distorting influence of the heart; and when that heart is made right, and the eye of the mind is made pure, then all things will be seen in their just and beautiful proportions; the truth will be received in all its purity; it will be unfolded in all its practical excellence.'

Beautiful words and most true! Alas, that the preacher should have exhibited in his own person the 'film' rather than the 'pure eye'! That this is the case whenever the Catholic Church is the object of his vision, is but too certain. An example will illustrate what I mean. In the preface to a book called *Voices of the Day*, he invites his readers to retire a little from the noises of the world, the din of party conflict, the clamour of infuriate disputants, and to hear in meditation and in peace 'the Voices of the Day.' Thus invited, I began to turn over the pages of his book, when to my surprise, at its very outset, I came upon the following passage : 'In the great Western Apostasy there is evidence of night, deep, dark, impenetrable, lying on head and heart, and overshadowing both with baleful delusion! A system is there in which truth is neutralised by error, in which the light is admitted only to be extinguished by darkness, or to be divided and distorted; in which Jesus is recognised in order to be betrayed, as of old, with a kiss; a system where the minister of the Gospel is perverted into the priest; where one sacrament is made a god, and the other an exorcism; in which worship is pantomime, the church a sepulchre, and Christianity a gigantic parody.'

I read on and found much more in the same strain. I was reflecting what 'the clamour of infuriate disputants' could mean, in the mind of Dr. Cumming, if this was 'peaceful meditation,' when, consulting other volumes by the same author, I found that this was his habitual language whenever ' Romanism ' was his topic. 'How,' I asked myself, 'can Dr. Cumming see things so perversely?' The thing was a perplexity to me until I read his Lectures on Ritualism, and there found the key to the mystery, and detected the workings of his mind.

In the fourth of these lectures, entitled, ' Should we confess to God or to man?' Dr. Cumming said to his hearers:

'In a beautiful poem by Longfellow, the confessional is so justly described, that I will trouble you by reading it.'

He then read the following lines:

> 'Here sits the priest, and faint and low,
> Like the sighing of an evening breeze,
> Comes through these painted lattices
> The ceaseless sound of human woe.
> Here, while her bosom aches and throbs
> With deep and agonising sobs,
> That half are passion, half contrition,
> The luckless daughter of perdition
> Slowly confesses her secret shame,
> The time, the place, the lover's name.
> Here the grim murderer, with a groan,
> From his bruised conscience rolls the stone ;
> Thinking that thus he can atone
> For ravages of sword and flame.
> Indeed I marvel, and marvel greatly,
> How a priest can sit here so sedately,
> Reading the whole year out and in
> Naught but a catalogue of sin,
> And still keep any faith whatever
> In human virtue—never, never.'

It is quite evident, from the words by which Dr. Cumming introduced these lines, that he wished his auditors to understand that he was quoting Longfellow's own sentiments, and that he had the authority of the celebrated American poet against the morality of the confessional. Did he believe this himself? Charity would make us wish to think that he was quoting at second-hand, and that he had never read the context. Yet if he had not read this poem, how could he call it beautiful? If he had read it, how should he not have remarked that the words that he quotes are put by Longfellow in the mouth of the *devil;* and that they in no way express the poet's own estimate of the confessional?

The poem is dramatic. In the lines which immediately precede those quoted, we have the beautiful soliloquy of the priest who has just risen from the confessional, which I will transcribe, both for its own sake and because it contains the contrast, intended by the author, to the diabolical view of the sacrament of penance, given in the lines which moved the admiration of Dr. Cumming:

> 'O blessed Lord! how much I need
> Thy light to guide me on my way!
> So many hands, that, without heed,
> Still touch Thy wounds, and make them bleed!
> So many feet, that, day by day,
> Still wander from Thy fold astray;
> Unless Thou fill me with Thy light,
> I cannot lead Thy flock aright.
> Nor, without Thy support, can bear
> The burden of so great a care,
> But am myself a castaway!
> The day is drawing to its close;
> And what good deeds, since first it rose,
> Have I presented, Lord, to Thee,
> As offerings of my ministry?
> What wrong repress'd, what right maintain'd,
> What struggle pass'd, what victory gain'd,
> What good attempted and attain'd?
> Feeble, at best, is my endeavour!
> I see, but cannot reach the height
> That lies for ever in the light,
> And yet for ever and for ever,
> When seeming just within my grasp,
> I feel my feeble hands unclasp,
> And sink discouraged into night!
> For Thine own purpose Thou hast sent
> The strife and the discouragement!'

Longfellow here clearly tells us what *he* thinks of the morality of the confessional. He may not hold its divine origin, yet he believes that a zealous pure-minded priest may labour there sincerely for the good of souls. He believes that a priest may hear all those details of human crime, and yet, not only 'keep faith in human virtue,' but aspire himself to the very ideal of perfection. And then, as if to give force to this view of his own, and no doubt indirectly to rebuke the bigots who think evil of things most divine, he puts *their* sentiments into the mouth of the devil, who, with all his cunning, pronounces a judgment both false and malicious. To find a parallel to this procedure of Dr. Cumming, we must imagine a preacher first quoting with approval the devil's opinion as to the virtue of Job, and then attributing it to Moses.[13]

Yet I am convinced that the quotation was rather a blunder than a conscious and deliberate perversion. It is, however, the more instructive on that account. For, how came a minister of religion to quote with approbation the sentiments of the devil? I will not suppose that he remarked whose sentiments they were. No; he read the beautiful words which Longfellow has put in the mouth of the confessor, but as in them there was nothing in harmony with his tone of mind, they made no impression upon him; he read on till he came to the devil's speech, and he found his own thoughts and sentiments so exactly echoed that he eagerly marked the passage for future quotation, and pronounced the poem 'beautiful.'

An example like this teaches us as clearly as a whole treatise written on the subject, how necessary is the 'removal of the film from the mind's eye' (as Dr. Cumming most truly said), before it can read Scripture aright. The Pharisees, to whom our blessed Lord said, 'Search the Scriptures, but you will not come to Me,' read the Old Testament just as Dr. Cumming read Longfellow, and as he read and saw everything that relates to the Catholic Church.

In contrast with this unhappy spirit of prejudice and hate, the Holy Scripture points to the noble spirit of the Bereans. With one remark founded on this example, I will conclude this Introduction. When St. Paul announced in the synagogue of the Jews that the carpenter's son of Nazareth, crucified at Jerusalem, was the long-expected Messiah, the proposition

---

[12] After this specimen of Dr. Cumming's candour, the reader can appreciate the good taste with which he says (Lect. ix.), 'I have never met with any man tainted with Romish doctrine who was not also very little reliable in his speaking truth.'

seemed to the Bereans strange in the last degree and almost incredible. It contradicted all their previous conceptions. Yet when they heard the Apostle appealing to the very Scriptures with which they were familiar, and giving to them an interpretation which had never occurred to their minds before, they determined to give him a patient hearing, and to weigh the matter calmly. The result was, that they found that St. Paul was right, and that till then 'a veil had been over their eyes when Moses was read.'

Let me suppose, then, that my reader is just as firmly convinced that the New Testament is opposed to Ritualism as the Bereans were that the Old Testament was opposed to a crucified Messiah; yet, as I too appeal to the New Testament, let me have a patient hearing and a calm judgment. Let my readers 'search the Scriptures whether these things are so,' and the result may be the conviction, that Protestant as well as Jewish education throws a veil over certain parts of the Word of God.

St. Chrysostom, however, makes an important reflection on the words of our blessed Lord, 'Search the Scriptures.' The Pharisees, he says, had been accustomed to read the Scriptures, not to *search* them. They had seen, therefore, only what was on the surface; but there was a rich treasure hidden beneath the surface, which they missed, because they did not dig for it. If the testimonies to Jesus Christ, who is the very end and scope of the Old Testament, do not lie on the surface, but have to be carefully and painfully sought out, no one need wonder if the testimonies to Ritualism are not obvious to every reader who is familiar with the letter of the New Testament. The real question is, Are they there? not, Are they there so as to force themselves on the notice of every one? They may require a hint, a clue to their discovery, just like the prophecies which spoke of Jesus Christ. May He open our minds that we may understand the Scriptures!

PART I.

THE PRINCIPLES OF CATHOLIC RITUAL

RECOGNISED IN THE NEW TESTAMENT.

CHAPTER I.

A GENERAL VIEW.

WE are met at the very outset of our investigation by a fact which, to certain minds, accustomed to the Protestant view of Scripture as the sole source of knowledge of things divine, may seem an insuperable obstacle in my path.

Any one who looks in the New Testament for an account of the worship proper to the Christian Church, will discover that there is no formal statement there of *any* system of worship peculiar to Christ's followers. He will find brief indications of some new rites, not gathered into a code, but scattered here and there in different writings; he will have glimpses of the assemblies of the first disciples of Jesus Christ for common worship, but no description given for the instruction of future generations, nor sufficient detail to provide a model for imitation.

This plain and acknowledged fact might be urged, indeed, against the Protestant view of Scripture just alluded to. It has been truly said. that 'if the New Testament were a profane book, the remains of a school of Greek philosophers, or the first accessible writings of a new Eastern sect, there is not a scholar among us who would not prove, from the ellipses, the allusions, and the suggestions (not to say the assertions) of the text, the existence of a much larger body of laws and customs than was there set down.'

That this is the true view of the New Testament will be shown in the second part of this Essay, so far as Ritual is concerned. In the present chapter, however, I have to consider how the matter appears to Protestants. They are accustomed to assume, not only that we have, in fact, at the present day, no authentic source of information regarding Christianity besides the New Testament, but that the New Testament was written with the intention of supplying future ages with all necessary knowledge of divine things. When this hypothesis is admitted, two conclusions will be drawn from the fragmentary and unsystematic notices regarding Ritual in the books of the New Testament. It will be said that few formal regulations are given, because there is really little to regulate. And then it will be argued, further, that if Ritual occupies but a small space in the inspired pages, and a large place in Catholic practice, Catholic practice is thereby condemned at once and as a whole, and requires no farther examination.

I shall consider these theories in order.

1. I suppose every one must have remarked the absence from the New Testament of any book like that of Leviticus in the Old Testament. Dr. Vaughan thinks that he sees in this a primary and invincible argument against Ritual. I will give his argument the benefit of his own statement.

'From what was done,' he says, 'in the case of the Hebrews, the conclusion is, that whenever the Divine Being imparts a revelation to a people needing such a Ritual as we find in the Book of Leviticus, He will Himself interfere and determine the matters of that Ritual, down even to the smallest provision to be included in it. The Divine Being changes not. Hence, whatever appears to Him to be good in given circumstances once, must appear to Him to be good in those circumstances always. Let it once be clear that it is a principle in His rules that wherever an elaborate ceremonial is desirable He will bestow it, as in the times of the Old Testament, and it must then follow, that where He has not bestowed it—as He certainly has not in the times of the New Testament—then, to attempt to do what He has not done, must be not only superfluous, but presumptuous, contrary to His mind. He gave the Book of Leviticus to the Hebrews because they needed it; and we may be sure He would have given us a similar book if we had needed it.'

With this last sentence I cordially agree. There is no code of Ritual in the New Testament because the Christian Church does not need it. But the reason she does not need it is not that assigned by Dr. Vaughan, that she has no Ritual to regulate; it is a very different one. It is that she has the Spirit of God, not given in the same way to the Jewish Church. Her law of Ritual is written, not with ink, but by the Spirit of the living God in the fleshy tables of the heart.

There is a fatal flaw running through Dr. Vaughan's argument. God is changeless, he says. This, of course, no one disputes. Therefore, he continues, under the same circumstances He will act in the same way. This might, perhaps, be questioned. A changeless God may speak 'in divers manners,' even under the same circumstances. But suppose we grant this also, what then? Therefore, he concludes, since God gave an elaborate Ritual to the Jews, wherever an elaborate ceremonial is desirable, He will Himself bestow it. But, with Dr. Vaughan's leave, this conclusion is not logical. It should stand thus:—Therefore, wherever, *under circumstances similar to those of the Jews*, an elaborate ceremonial *similar to theirs* is desirable, He will Himself give it.

If the Ritual of the Catholic Church is essentially different from that of the Jews; if the latter, from its very nature, could not have existed without revelation, whereas the former for its production requires only such gifts and graces as the Christian Church is allowed by all to possess, then Dr. Vaughan's argument falls to the ground. Now such is really the case.

Our opponent assumes that the *elaborateness* of the Jewish Ritual—that is, I suppose, the variety and splendour of its ceremonies—was the main reason why God Himself revealed it. But other and more urgent reasons can be assigned. First, then, the Jews were a prophetic people, and it was the will of God that their Ritual should be eminently prophetic or typical. But a prophetic Ritual can only come from Revelation. One of the great proofs of the Christian faith was to be in this— that its facts were prefigured in the ceremonies of a people who did not foresee them, and even rejected them when they were accomplished. If the Jews had embodied in symbols truths clearly revealed to them, and hopes which they cherished, this, perhaps, would not have required graces beyond what were given to them; but it required a divine revelation to create symbols, the meaning of which was reserved for future ages. Should an ignorant man write correctly in a language he could not himself read, we should be certain that another, more learned than he, had guided his hand. When I see the Jew performing a Ritual, of which he has not the key, but which I as a Christian find in its minutest circumstances typical of Christian facts and doctrines, I am convinced that the Jew did not invent that Ritual, but received it by revelation from God; and I have a new confirmation of my faith.

But such is not the Ritual of the Catholic Church. The truth is now fully revealed; and however numerous or elaborate are our ceremonies, they either embody truths known to the Church, or recall facts of her past history, or express thoughts and feelings of which she is conscious, or hopes which she has based on promise. Such a Ritual may demand many supernatural gifts for its formation, but it does not require an express and minute revelation like that of which Moses was the legislator.

Another difference between Catholic and Jewish Ritual is this, that much of the latter was imposed as a bondage. It was a hedge to separate the Jews from the idolaters who surrounded them; or it was a discipline to school them for better things. Such a Ritual requires to be imposed, and is not a spontaneous creation.

Again, the Jewish Church was national and transitory. It was possible, therefore, from the first constitution of the nation, to give to it a code fixed in the most important details, and which would serve for the particular purpose and limited period for which it was intended. But the Christian Church was to be Catholic, adapted to all times, all nations, all circumstances. The absence of a revealed code of Ritual in the case of such a Church is easily accounted for. We do not conceive how it possibly could have been given. If a modifying power was necessary to the Jews to shape the revealed Ritual to varying national circumstances,—as we see, for example, from the acts of David and Solomon,—a more than modifying, a creative power, was necessary for the Christian Church—supposing that she was to possess a Ritual at all—to suit it to her many phases of civilisation and world-wide variety of circumstances. Supposing, for example, that Jesus Christ wished His Church to possess splendour in Ritual, since it was also His will that she should pass through ages of persecution, He could not have required it from her in the Catacombs, but must have left her to create this feature at least in the days of her triumph.

I am of course not stating an argument in favour of Catholic Ritual, but replying to one that has been devised against it. This argument is a purely negative one, and negative arguments are often fallacious. The question to be decided is this— whether it can be the will of God that Christians should possess a minute and complex system of Ritual. Dr. Vaughan says this cannot be supposed, since, were such the will of God, the pages of the New Testament would contain a minute and detailed code, whereas no such code is there to be found, but on the contrary, notices of Christian rites, whatever these may be, are unfrequent and details very scanty. When he is asked for a proof that God can neither inspire nor permit a system of Ritual like that of Catholics without *codifying* His will, he replies that this is evident from the history of the Elder Dispensation. There, he says, God did certainly wish for such a system, and there He accordingly revealed a detailed code. I have replied that the two cases are in no way parallel. The admitted fact that God revealed to Moses a minute system of worship can be explained by causes which would in no case affect Christians; such as the peculiar character of Jewish Ritual, and the incapacity of the Jews to develop such a Ritual themselves. The admitted fact that Jesus Christ did not reveal a Christian Ritual with equal minuteness, since no such revelation is found recorded in the New Testament or attributed to Him by Tradition—this can also be accounted for without supposing the unlawfulness of Ritual worship among His followers. For ages such a worship has existed, and has been supposed by the worshippers to be the fulfilment of His will. They say that the gifts bestowed on the Christian Church precluded the necessity of a minutely revealed code; and that it was, moreover, rendered almost impossible by the persecutions through which the Church should pass, and by the universality of her existence among the various nations of the world and the fluctuations of succeeding ages—and this even supposing the express will of Jesus Christ that a minute and full system of Christian Ritual should one day exist. No wonder therefore that Jesus Christ did not do what was at once unnecessary and impossible.

But on the other hand, say the advocates of Catholic Ritual, Jesus Christ is known to have done what is in perfect harmony with Catholic views on this subject. If He exercised a different Providence from that of Sinai, it was because Catholic Ritual is very different from the Ritual of the Tabernacle. What that Providence was, and what are the characteristics of Catholic Ritual, it is the purpose of the following pages to explain. I will merely say now, by anticipation, that the Divine Founder of the Catholic Church either personally or by His Apostles established the essential and immutable rites of His religion. In the second place, He sanctioned in His own life the general principles of Catholic worship, such as symbolic actions, the employment in God's service of whatever is beautiful and costly, and the use of external means to make impressions on the soul through the senses. Of these two assertions I promise to give abundant proof from the New Testament. In the third place, Jesus Christ gave to His Church a spirit of worship, and conferred on her an authority, by which, on the basis of the Rites which He had instituted, and in harmony with the principle which He had sanctioned, she has developed, according to the circumstances in which she has been placed, that full system of Ritualistic Worship which she now possesses. Evidence from the New Testament will also be adduced of the nature and operation of the Spirit here claimed.

Those who see in the absence of a minute written code a proof against the lawfulness of Ritual, may be reminded that in the pages of the New Testament we find no minute code of Morals corresponding to what we find in the books of Exodus, Leviticus, and Deuteronomy. Will they explain this difference, after the example of Dr. Vaughan's syllogisms, by asserting that good works are less important to Christians than to Jews, or are intended to occupy a less-prominent place in their religious system? No. To the question why morality is not taught in the New Testament so formally and minutely as in the Old, all my readers would probably give the correct answer. They would say that in the Christian Church morality is to be more searching and minute than among the Jews, but it is to be of a higher character, and to be taught in a more perfect way. It will be taught by the spirit, rather than by the letter, for 'the letter killeth, but the spirit giveth life' (2 Cor. iii. 6).[1] The rules of Christian morality will be not so much a list of prohibitions as a series of life-giving maxims, such as those of the Sermon on the Mount. Life and power will be given to these maxims by Him who uttered them. His life will be the great Christian code of morals. And He will confer on His followers a spirit of charity which will make them treasure up His least word, study His life, participate in His spirit. Then in the course of ages will be produced that magnificent series of Christian Saints, that constellation of Religious Orders, that rich fruitfulness of good works of every kind, by which His Church will be recognised.

Now what has been said of morals is true also of Ritual, as will be shown in the course of this Essay. The life of Jesus Christ has been the great code of Ritual. The worship, the love, of Jesus Christ have recalled every word and act of His,

---

[1] Not of course the literal sense of Scripture as distinguished from some supposed higher conception of truth, of which it is the perishable husk (as Rationalists teach), but the mere external precept as distinguished from the interior grace to obey it.

or that regarded Him. The spirit with which He worshipped His Eternal Father, and the spirit with which ¡He was worshipped, have given birth to holy liturgies and holy rites. Thus in the course of ages, on the basis of rites instituted by the Divine Author of Christianity, in conformity with principles which He sanctioned, under the creative and fertilising influence of the Spirit promised and given by Him, has been formed that body of Christian and Catholic Ritual, which inspires admiration and awe to those who have made themselves familiarly acquainted with its beauty, variety, and sublimity, and which—whether it is accepted as divine or not—can be despised only by ignorance or stupidity.

2. The objection hitherto discussed was drawn from the absence of *systematic* teaching in the New Testament on matters of worship, and if it had any force would tell equally against dogma and morals as against ritual.

I pass on to another more specious difficulty, founded not on the method but on the amount of information given in the New Testament regarding the ceremonies of Christian worship. It may be alleged that, whatever these ceremonies may be, they are not prominent topics with the sacred writers, they occupy little space in their narratives and exhortations; they ought therefore to occupy a correspondingly small space in Christian life and Christian estimation. Look, the objector may say, at Catholics throughout the world—what a vast amount of their time and attention is bestowed on Sacraments, devotions, functions, and the externals of religion. Should we not read more about such things in the Bible, if they were intended by God to form such prominent features in Christian life?

In this objection there are errors of principle as well as an error of fact. It is a serious error in divine things to count words instead of weighing them. We must inquire what is said and not how much. Again, in historical documents, we cannot safely conclude anything from silence until we have weighed all the circumstances. We shall see in the second part of this Essay that there are circumstances that well explain the partial silence of the divine writers on matters of Ritual, without having recourse to the Protestant theory that there were few such matters to record.

The silence itself is also greatly exaggerated as will appear from the following chapters, in which we shall see that much, very much, is said in the New Testament, both directly and indirectly, concerning Ritual.

But for the moment I will try to soften my objector's prejudice by pointing out how the argument from supposed or real silence or partial silence concerns Protestant worship as well as that of Catholics. Let him consider first the importance of the Christian observance of the Sunday, and then the almost total silence of the Christian Scriptures regarding it.

No one probably will deny that, if what is called the Sabbath, the Sunday, or the Lord's Day, were abrogated, and all days reduced to perfect equality, a revolution would be accomplished in the Protestant religion of England and America, perhaps almost as great as that which transformed the national religion of England at the Reformation. It is indeed hard for us even to conceive what Christianity would be like without its recurring day of rest and worship. The experiment has never yet been tried on any great scale. Many Protestant writers of different schools have shown that the neglect of the Sabbath is the neglect of all practical religion. Would not then the abrogation of the Sabbath be the destruction of religion?[2] Great as is the importance of Sundays and holidays to Catholics, I venture to assert that the Catholic Church could forego their institution more easily than Protestants could dispense with that of the Sunday alone. Public worship among Catholics has never been confined to one day of each week as among Protestants. Taking the Protestant religion as a whole in the various countries where it prevails, and through the three centuries of its existence, it is notorious that the buildings set apart for

[2] I use here the word Sabbath in its proper signification of Day of Rest, irrespective of the day of the week on which it is kept. In Catholic ecclesiastical language Saturday is called *Dies Sabbati*, Sunday *Dies Dominica*. Yet the use of the word Sabbath as applied to Sunday is not unknown to Catholics. I have often heard in Ireland the expression 'to break the Sabbath on the Sunday,' a perfectly correct form of speech, meaning to labour or destroy the 'repose' of the Sunday.

public worship have generally been closed from Sunday to Sunday. Had there then been no recurring day on which to throw them open, what would have been by this time the public or private knowledge or practice of religion amongst Protestants?

But this being so, what is the sanction producible from the New Testament for this institution? Not one direct and clear passage, but at most a few obscure and disputed allusions. If this undeniable fact were well considered in all its bearings, Protestants would pause before they made against us a charge so easy to retort on themselves—that the character of our worship is unscriptural. A writer in a Presbyterian periodical says (and I quote the words as being a characteristic expression of the ordinary Protestant traveller): 'We once saw high mass performed in the grand old Cathedral of Cologne, and as a spectacle it was unique. And we once saw the same performance in that wonderful work of man, the Cathedral of Rheims. Ten years intervened between the two exhibitions, but one thought pervaded our minds and dominated all else on both occasions. How could all this ever have come out of the simple story of the Gospels, or the as simple story of the Acts of the Apostles?'

The perplexity of this gentleman, besides proving his ignorance of Christian history and the development of Christian ideas, proves that he had never reflected on the institutions of his own sect, and compared them candidly and philosophically with the Bible. Surely the whole of what I may call Protestant Sabbatical literature might warrant a similar question to that asked above. Let me choose one example out of multitudes. In Dr. Gill's *Body of Practical Divinity*, a learned work, and greatly esteemed, I am told, in Puritan schools, there are the following regulations regarding the observance of the Sunday: 'The whole of the day should be observed from morning to evening; the early part should not be indulged in sleep, nor any part spent in doing a man's own business, in casting up his accounts, and setting right his shop-books; nor in carnal pleasures and recreations, in games and sports; nor in walking in the fields, nor in taking needless journeys. But besides public worship, men should attend to reading the scriptures, prayer and meditation, and Christian conferences, and in such pious exercises should they spend the whole day.'³ The author of these minute prescriptions professes in the very title of his book that his doctrine is all 'deduced from the Sacred Scriptures.' He certainly did not derive them from the Gospels, in which the Sabbath is only mentioned in connection with our Lord's opposition to the Pharisaic tradition respecting it. Neither did he derive them from the Epistles, for 'no rules for the observance of the Sabbath are ever given by the Apostles; its violation is never denounced by them, Sabbath-breakers are never included in any list of offenders;'⁴ nor is Sabbath-keeping even once mentioned in the various abridgments of the decalogue given by our Lord or His Apostles, nor in any of their enumerations of virtues or good works (Matt. xix. 18, 19; Rom. xiii. 9; Gal. v. 19-23).

According to the Rev. F. Garden, 'when the early Fathers speak of the Lord's Day, they sometimes, perhaps, by comparing, connect it with the Sabbath; but we have never found a passage, previous to the conversion of Constantine, prohibitory of any work or occupation on the former, and any such, did it exist, would have been in a great measure nugatory.'⁵

As to ' the Lord's Day,' the name occurs indeed once in the New Testament (Rev. i. 10), but there is nothing in Scripture to prove that it was a Christian festival of any kind, or if so, to show whether it was of weekly, monthly, or annual occurrence. Much stress is often laid on certain allusions to the 'first day of the week' in connection with religious practices. But the writers just quoted admit that 'all these passages, even taken together, seem scarcely adequate to prove that the dedication of the first day of the week to pious purposes was a matter of apostolic institution, or even of apostolic practice,'⁶ much less that it was observed as a Sabbath. They add, indeed, that such passages acquire greater force and a distinct meaning from the history of the early Church. But this is of course to interpret

---

³ Gill's *Practical Divinity*, book iii. ch. 8.
⁴ Smith's *Dictionary of the Bible*, art. 'Sabbath.'   ⁵ *Ib.*
⁶ *Ib.* art. 'Lord's Day.'

and to supplement Scripture by tradition. If Protestants are willing to adopt this method with regard to the Sabbath, they must not quarrel with us if we adopt it systematically.

If, however, Protestants reject the help of tradition, and insist that every religious observance must be based on Scripture alone, they present a very pitiable spectacle in their defence of the modern Sunday, 'wringing the Scriptures, as old Bishop Andrewes says, 'for that which is not in them, and can therefore never come *liquide* from them.'

Milton, who has treated the Scripture testimony in great detail, and with much acuteness, has decided against the obligation of any Christian Sabbath, and remarking on the flimsiness of the Scriptural arguments alleged in its defence, warns his co-religionists that 'they ought to consider the dangerous tendency of such an example, and the consequences with which it is likely to be followed in the interpretation of Scripture.'[7] He allows, indeed, the Christian Sunday as a free ecclesiastical institution, but not as one of Scriptural obligation. His words deserve to be quoted, as showing the conclusion at which a learned and powerful reasoner arrived from the study of Scripture alone. 'Under the Gospel,' he says, 'no one day is appointed for divine worship in preference to another, except such as the Church may set apart of its own authority for the voluntary assembling of its members, wherein, relinquishing all worldly affairs, we may dedicate ourselves wholly to religious services, so far as is consistent with the duties of charity; and this may conveniently take place once every seven days, and particularly on the first day of the week; provided always that it be observed in compliance with the authority of the Church, and not in obedience to the edicts of the magistrate; and likewise that a snare be not laid for the conscience by the allegation of a divine commandment, borrowed from the decalogue.'

In arriving at this conclusion, Milton was influenced not so much by want of Scripture testimony in favour of the observ

---

[7] Milton, *The Christian Doctrine*, book ii. ch. 7. I quote Milton in preference to others who have held the same views, because of his concise and vigorous statement of them. It is strange that in Dr. Hessey's most elaborate account of Sabbatical controversies, no mention is made of Milton.

ance of a Christian Sabbath, but by the apparent evidence against it. Amongst other arguments he uses the following : ' Since the Sabbath was originally an ordinance of the Mosaic law, imposed on the Israelites alone, and that for the express purpose of distinguishing them from other nations, it follows that, if those who live under the gospel are emancipated from the ordinances of the law in general, least of all can they be considered as bound by that of the Sabbath, the distinction being abolished which was the special cause of its institution. It was for asserting this in precept, and enforcing it by example, that Christ incurred the heavy censure of the Pharisees: "this man is not of God, because he keepeth not the sabbath-day" (John ix. 16). So also St. Paul: " How turn ye again to the weak and beggarly elements, whereunto ye desire again to be in bondage? ye observe days and months and times and years. I am afraid of you, lest I have bestowed upon you labour in vain " (Gal. iv. 9-11). "Let no man therefore judge you in meat, or in drink, or in respect of an holy day, or of the new moon, or of the Sabbath days" (Col. ii. 16, 17). The law of the Sabbath being thus repealed, that no particular day of worship has been appointed in its place, is evident from the same Apostle : " One man esteemeth one day above another; another esteemeth every day alike : let every man be fully persuaded in his own mind" (Rom. xiv. 5). For since no particular *place* is designated under the gospel for the public worship of God, there seems no reason why *time*, the other circumstance of worship, should be more defined. If Paul had not intended to intimate the abolition of all Sabbaths whatever, and of all sanctification of one day above another, he would not have added in the following verse : "He that regardeth not the day, to the Lord he doth not regard it." For how does he *not regard the day to the Lord*, if there be any commandment still in force by which a particular day, whether the Sabbath or any other, is to be observed?'

With regard to the decalogue, Milton says, 'If, on the plea of a divine command, they impose upon us the observance of a particular day, how do they presume without the authority of a divine command to substitute another day in its place (viz. the first for the seventh)? To make any change in the commandment of God, whether we believe that commandment to be still in force or not, is equally dangerous and equally reprehensible; inasmuch as in so doing we are either annulling what is not yet repealed, or reënacting what is obsolete. It ought also to be shown what essential principle of morality is involved in the number seven; and why, when released from the obligation of the Sabbath, we should still be bound to respect a particular number possessing no inherent virtue or efficacy.'

I have quoted these passages in full, not because I agree with all that is contained in them, but because they put with much force the Scriptural difficulty which stands in the way of an observance, in many respects common to Catholics and to Protestants. So far as my purpose in making these remarks is concerned, it matters little whether the modern observance of certain fixed days is defended as a purely divine or purely ecclesiastical institution, or as being divine in substance and ecclesiastical in its determination to specific times (which is the general Catholic view); the important point is that the letter of Scripture seems against any such observance. That it is not so in reality is maintained by Catholics and by most Protestants. Yet I confess that first appearances are against us. Most certainly no one, without a previous knowledge of Christian history, would, from the letter of the New Testament, deduce any such observance as that of the Sundays and holidays, whether of Catholics or of Protestants, even if he can succeed in reconciling it therewith.

And indeed the most learned and moderate of Protestant writers on the subject of the Lord's Day seem quite satisfied to employ the Catholic method of defending it. They appeal to tradition as interpreting the allusions of Scripture. Thus, for example, Dr. Hawkins: 'We have absolutely no need of such an ample array of Scriptural proof, to convince us of the divine original of an ordinance, as we might have desired for our belief in a Revealed Doctrine. . . . We trace back the general religious observance of the Lord's Day to the very era of the promulgation of the Gospel. We find the universality of the practice recognised by the earliest extant writings, genuine or apocryphal—by Ignatius, Justin, &c. . . . Add, then, but a few recognitions in the Christian Scriptures themselves of the actual observance of the Lord's Day, even in the age of the Apostles, and with their sanction—nay, apparently, with the implied sanction of our Lord Himself and of the Holy Spirit—and we have all the proof which we really require of its Divine Authority.'[8]

This is, no doubt, an example of the mode of investigating truth which Milton denounced as of a dangerous tendency. It is in fact the true, reasonable, and Catholic method of interpreting Scripture by its results, or of interpreting what is obscure in Scripture by what is clear in tradition. Dr. Hessey, in his defence of the apostolico-divine origin of the Lord's Day, follows the same method, except that he begins with Scripture and confirms Scripture by tradition, instead of beginning with tradition and *adding* (like Dr. Hawkins) the allusions of Scripture. In reality the methods are the same, since Dr. Hessey would never have interpreted Scripture as he does had he been ignorant of tradition. He writes as follows: ' That the Lord's Day is indicated in the New Testament, and was observed by the Apostles and their immediate followers as distinct from the Sabbath, the obligation to observe which is denied, both expressly and by implication, in the New Testament; that being so acknowledged and observed by the Apostles and their immediate followers, it is of divine institution: . . . these propositions are *tolerably* clear. They will, I think, be proved to demonstration by notices to be found in writers of the next two centuries.'

After discussing these notices, Dr. Hessey supposes an objection made: 'That, considering the great importance which *we* are in the habit of attaching to the Lord's Day, they are hardly sufficient in number to warrant the belief that it was considered by the primitive Christians to be a Scriptural institution.' The answer that he gives to this objection is one in which I cordially agree; but I remark that it has a far wider bearing than the institution of the Lord's Day. He replies: ' It is, I think, impossible to estimate the comparative importance of an institution in the ancient Church by the number of

[8] Dr. Hawkins, *Bampton Lectures for* 1840, lect. v.

times in which it is mentioned. The Sabbath is seldom spoken of in the historical parts of the Old Testament, albeit it was "the sign" between God and the Israelites. It was always and everywhere implied.' I cannot agree with what the learned author next says, that the Lord's Day is implied wherever the Eucharist is mentioned, as if the Eucharist were only celebrated on the Lord's Day. In this he is interpreting antiquity by Protestant customs. There is more force in his next remark, that exhortations to the observance of Sunday suppose its neglect, and therefore might be very rare in times of great fervour. From this he concludes: 'So far, then, from considering the infrequency of exhortation to keep the Lord's Day to be an argument that it was not held by the primitive Christians to be a Scriptural institution, I conceive that it is an argument which tells just the other way. I should have been surprised to find more said about it.'[9]

Such, then, is the line of argument taken by eminent Protestant writers in defending one feature of Christian Ritual which they have retained—the weekly festival of our Lord's Resurrection. I have not made these quotations as a mere *argumentum ad hominem*, or in order to say that Protestants defend their religion just as we defend ours. I accept both the institution and its defence. I only regret that such writers are not more consistent in their method of interpreting Scripture. The Supremacy of St. Peter, the Sacraments of Penance and of Extreme Unction, which Dr. Hessey rejects, may be proved just as easily by these processes as 'Confirmation, Orders, and *Infant* Baptism,' which he admits on evidence of the same nature as he adduces for the institution of the Lord's Day.

All, then, who do not reject the observance of the Sunday as Judaic and antichristian (and very few have gone so far as this) ought to admit the following conclusions:

a. An observance may be of the utmost importance, of the most intimate and constant influence on the Christian life, and yet occupy very small space in the records of the New Testament. When the living observance is before our eyes, expres-

[9] Hessey's *Bampton Lectures for* 1860, lect. ii.

A General View. 37

sions, allusions, even words, become luminous, which, to those who do not know what we know, are without significance.

b. An observance may be eminently Christian, though something which bears an apparent resemblance to it is antichristian and condemned. The rejection of the Jewish Sabbath does not prove the unlawfulness of the Christian Sunday. So, also, much is said against Jewish Ritual in the New Testament, which it might be erroneous to adduce as valid against Catholic Ritual. In other words, a real, and not only a superficial, resemblance must be shown to exist between two things before they are alleged to fall under the same condemnation.

c. And lastly, all must be prepared for developments, of some kind at least, in Christian worship.

I do not assert as yet that the ceremonies which perplexed the English visitor at Rheims or Cologne are a legitimate development of the primitive celebration of the Holy Eucharist; but I say that it is puerile to reject them, simply because they are a development, or are strange to Protestant habits of worship.

The suspended business, the closed shutters, the multitudinous bells, the citizens with holiday attire and looks demure, of an English Sunday, are surely a great development of Apostolic practice, and would greatly startle an Apostolic Christian, could he suddenly appear in the streets of London or of Boston—to say nothing of the surplice or Geneva gown, and other appliances of Protestant worship. The only question, therefore, to be discussed is as to what observances are of divine or apostolic origin, and what developments are legitimate.

My purpose in the following chapters is not to attempt to derive a minute Code of Ritual from the New Testament, or to find in it a precedent for every ceremony known to Catholics, but rather to show how the distinctive features of Catholic Ritual are justified in Scripture, and its generating principles acknowledged as divine.

CHAPTER II.

SPIRIT AND TRUTH.

OUR Lord Jesus Christ has Himself declared that two of the principal characteristics of Christian worship are Spirit and Truth. Though these qualities belong rather to the interior than the exterior element of worship, yet the whole question of Ritual is intimately connected with them, and we cannot proceed a step in our inquiries until we have ascertained what relation Spirit and Truth bear to Ceremonial.

St. John alone among the Evangelists has recorded the conversation between the Samaritan woman and the Son of God. 'The woman saith to Him: Sir, I perceive that Thou art a prophet. Our fathers adored on this mountain, and You say that at Jerusalem is the place where men must adore. Jesus saith to her : Woman, believe Me that the hour cometh when you shall neither on this mountain nor in Jerusalem adore the Father. You adore that which you know not: we adore that which we know; for salvation is of the Jews. But the hour cometh, and now is, when the true adorers shall adore the Father in spirit and in truth. For the Father also seeketh such to adore Him. God is a Spirit, and they that adore Him must adore Him in spirit and in truth' (John iv. 19-24).

It is important to ascertain first what our Blessed Lord here says, and then what He does not say.

He says that hitherto the worship offered by the Jews in Jerusalem, and not the schismatical and heretical worship of the Samaritans, had been acceptable to God. He says that a new order of things is now commencing. The knowledge of God shall no longer be confined to one nation, nor His worship to one place. The worship, as well as the kingdom, of God shall be universal. He says that God seeks a higher class of worshippers than He has hitherto generally found; that the worship in which He delights must be akin to His own divine nature, which is spirit and truth.

Interpreters are not agreed as to the precise meaning of these two words, or as to their difference. The prevailing view seems to be that worship in 'spirit' is contrasted with the typical sacrifices of the Jews; worship in 'truth' with the erroneous and half-idolatrous worship of the Samaritans. To myself it appears most in accordance with the context and the scope of the discourse to take both words (if they really differ in meaning) to refer to the errors of the Samaritan woman whom our Lord is addressing. Which of the two places is the more sacred? she asks; which is God's chosen abode, Jerusalem or Garizim? Our Lord answers that hitherto the Jews have known what and how and where to worship, while the Samaritans have adored they knew not what. To this first error, which she had shared with her countrymen, Jesus Christ perhaps refers again when He says that God must be worshipped *in truth*, that is to say, with a true faith in His Nature and true knowledge of His Will. Her question had betrayed a second error. Which is the holy place? she asked; as if God's worship must be confined to some one place, as if He were not 'the God of the spirits of all flesh.' Perhaps too, in her ignorant mind, that holy place must needs be a mountain, as if to be nearer the sky was to be nearer God. To this our Lord answers that God is a Spirit, and therefore not confined to place, like a man or a heathen god. Hence, though for special reasons, regarding not Himself but His worshippers, He had chosen Jerusalem as the place of sacrifice, yet now the hour has come when altars may be erected in every place, and the worship will sanctify the place, and not the place gain acceptance for the worship. God then, being a Spirit, seeks worshippers who will worship Him in accordance with His nature, that is, in their own spirit. 'Do not think you must go up into a mountain to find God'—it is thus St. Augustin paraphrases our Lord's words—'God is a Spirit, seek Him in your own spirit, and make it fit to be His temple, and you will find Him.' But whether we assign to our Lord's words this or any other probable meaning, the result is substantially the same— that the essence of worship is in the soul and its acts, in true faith and hope and charity, sincerity, compunction, and the rest.

But we must remark also what our Lord does *not* say. He does not say that when the Temple at Jerusalem is no more, men shall worship without temples. It is curious that this doctrine, which, if our Lord was contrasting the externals of religion, would be the only inference which could be plausibly drawn from His words, is just the one conclusion that even Protestants do not draw. They will allow local buildings which our Lord *seems* to abolish, but not Ritual within them, of which our Lord says nothing. But if Jesus Christ does not forbid to build churches, but rather allows them to be built everywhere, He does not say that the future temples shall be inferior in beauty or riches to those of Jerusalem and Samaria. He does not deny that the future worship of the Church shall be exterior as well as interior. He does not say, He does not insinuate in any way, that the external element shall be in any degree less *elaborate* or less *splendid* than what has been offered up in the Temple.

If, indeed, worship in spirit and truth is irreconcilable with a minute or a splendid ceremonial; if even there is opposition between the two; then, of course, our Lord's words foretelling an increase of spiritual worship would also foretell an abolition or a diminution of the magnificence of external Ritual. But it must be remembered that, though this may seem an axiom to some Protestants, the vast majority of Christians of all ages deny it with convictions equally strong; and therefore it is a simple begging of the question to gather such a conclusion from our Lord's words.

Catholics see no antagonism whatever between piety and Ritual—no more than there is between believing with the heart unto justice, and confessing with the mouth unto salvation (Rom. x. 10). We see no opposition of any kind between fervour of *spirit* and magnificent rites, between *truth* of conception and minute and varied symbolism. The contrary opinion is not self-evident, and therefore cannot be legitimately deduced from our Lord's words, which do not explicitly contain it. Nor can it be imposed on them unless it be evident from other sources.

Writers of controversy seem often to be unaware that the interpretation they give to these words of Jesus Christ is not *necessarily* contained in them, and that for this reason, in controversy at least, they cannot assume, but ought to prove, their interpretation to be correct. Dr. Vaughan, for instance, affirms the Protestant view in the most dogmatic tone, as if no contrary opinion to his own had ever been entertained by a man capable of reading Scripture. 'The least,' he says, 'that can be inferrred from our Lord's words is, that no such Ritual system as the history of Judaism presents was to have any place in the Christian Church. If that Church is to know anything of ceremonies, it must be within such limits as to be next to nothing, compared with the ceremonies of the Church preceding it. Our Lord, it may be assured, did not mean to say less than this when uttering the words we have cited. For it is to be distinctly marked, that not only are the things existing to pass away, nothing resembling that order of things is to follow. The Local is to give place to the Universal, the Ritual to the Spiritual.'

Now our Lord says not one word, direct or indirect, about Ritual in the passage referred to. Yet it is taken for granted here that the words Ritual and Spiritual represent antagonistic ideas, just like Local and Universal. It is Dr. Vaughan, however, not Jesus Christ, who says this. It will be the object of this Essay to see whether anything in the life or teaching of our Blessed Lord implies such doctrines. All that I now ask is, that Protestant readers will suspend their judgment till they have weighed the evidence.

Let them also have the charity to believe that Catholics are no less zealous than themselves for the spirituality of God's worship; and that if we defend the use of Ritual, it is not as a hindrance, but as a help to interior piety. I am not yet entitled to assume that our views on this question are Scriptural o

Christian; but at least we have a view on the matter, and it may be well here to state it.

That the only worship pleasing to God is worship in spirit and in truth is acknowledged on all hands. That if the use of Ritual can be shown to be an obstacle to such worship, it must be rejected, is what we most readily concede. But that it is so in fact we strenuously deny. It is the belief of Catholics that, in order that man might be 'born not of the flesh but of God,' 'the Word was made flesh and dwelt among us.' Whence they conclude that through the senses man is spiritualised, as by the senses he had been enslaved.

Our theory may perhaps be stated as follows. In its ordinary state the soul is weighed down by the senses: the multitude of objects ever acting on the senses enthral the soul, and prevent it from soaring to things spiritual and divine. It requires a great effort to break this thraldom, and this effort is facilitated by the impressions made on the senses by the ceremonial of public worship. The senses are thus used against the senses, not to ensnare and captivate the soul, naturally free, but to set free the soul, naturally captive. The great pageant of things temporal, ever before the eyes, is, for a time, effaced by the imagery of things invisible; and the soul, escaping from its bondage, has a glimpse of the Eternal Spirit, and bows itself before Him in spiritual worship. And so, too, if the senses are used to release the *spirit* from its captivity to sense, the imagination is enlisted on the side of *truth*, to break the fascinating spell of error which acts quite as much by means of the imagination as of the reason. Reason may discover that things visible and transitory are but trifles. Yet visible and tangible trifles have an enchanting, a deluding power, a *lying* power over the soul, from which reason in vain strives to free itself. No doubt 'the just man lives by faith,' and it is faith which conquers the visible world by a lively realisation of things unseen and eternal. Yet faith not merely conquers the world; it reduces it to obedience, and makes a servant of what was before an enemy. Faith creates a ceremonial, a living embodiment of its own thoughts and feelings, which then helps faith in its turn in the contest against the lies and treachery of sense.

This is the worship of the kingdom, not *of* this world, yet *in* this world, which our Lord Jesus Christ has set up to fight against that world which He has condemned.

The Protestant opposition to ceremonial seems to be founded on the theory that the soul is uninfluenced by the senses until the moment when Ritual appeals to them. The action of Ritual on the soul would be consequently a downward one, like that of loading an angel with a human body. But a little reflection will show that this theory is erroneous. A soul enclosed in a human body is always under the influence of the senses. Their ordinary influence is a depressing one, because vulgar or sordid objects are mostly presented to the soul. The influence of Ritual, on the contrary, is an elevating one, awakening noble and spiritual associations.

Wordsworth exactly states the Catholic philosophy of Ceremonial in the following lines:

> '*Cast off your bonds*, awake, arise,
> And for no transient ecstasies!
> What else can mean the visual plea
> Of still or moving imagery?
> Alas, the sanctities combined
> By art to *unsensualise* the mind
> Decay or languish; or, as creeds
> And humours change, are spurn'd like weeds;
> The priests are from their altars thrust;
> Temples are levell'd with the dust;
> And solemn rites and awful forms
> Founder amid fanatic storms.'

The poet rightly considers that it is the purpose of Ritual by means of the senses to unsensualise the mind, entangled and debased as it is in ordinary moods by the constant perception of vulgar and trivial objects.

The gallant Major Hodson, the hero of Delhi, with that 'soldier's good sense,' as De Maistre calls it, which often reaches truth by a shorter and more certain road than book-learning, expresses the same Catholic view of the spiritual use of external objects, which he had gathered from his own experience in India. 'The more I think of it,' he writes,[1] 'the more strongly I feel the effects of mere external sights and

[1] From *Twelve Years of a Soldier's Life in India.*

sounds on the inner and better man. Our Gothic buildings, our religious-looking churches, have, I am sure, a more pacifying influence than is generally believed by those who are habituated to them, and have never felt the want of them. The wisdom and piety of our ancestors constructed such noble and stately temples—feeling, justly, that the human mind in its weakness requires to be called to the exercise of devotion by the senses as well as by reason and will. You may think this fanciful, but I am sure you would feel it more strongly than I do, were you to live for a time in a country where *everything but religion has its living and existent memorials and evidence.*'

Major Hodson, in these last words, has perhaps touched the very essential reason of Ritual. It is the belief of the Catholic Church that the principle embodied in the words of Jesus Christ, 'This do for a commemoration of Me,' is capable of a very wide application. She has built up by degrees a vast system of Ritual, embracing in its cycle of fasts and feasts the whole year, influencing in its varied forms the whole mind and heart, gathering to its service all things beautiful and stately, meeting men on all occasions, accompanying them from the cradle to the grave, entering into the world and confronting it, in order that it may not be said that, in Christendom at least, everything *but* religion has its memorials and evidence.

This may seem to some an unspiritual and unchristian theory, but as it is certainly no novel form of Christianity, nor one which has found little acceptance, it will be worth the attention of an earnest man to hear what proofs can be brought forward in its support.

I may here remark that the method I am about to pursue in order to discover our Lord's meaning is one that has generally been followed by sober interpreters of Scripture. Our divine Lord uttered the great maxims of His kingdom in short pregnant sentences, each of which was to be the germ of mighty things, and to be interpreted by results; but which ignorance or fanaticism can easily pervert.

'Swear not at all;' 'Resist not evil;' 'Lay not up treasures on earth;' 'Be not solicitous for to-morrow;' 'Do not think I came to send peace on earth;' 'Not that which goeth into the mouth defileth a man;' 'A rich man shall hardly enter into the kingdom of heaven;' 'Call none your father upon earth;' 'My kingdom is not of this world:' these and similar sayings of our Lord, when taken alone, and without regard to other words of the same divine Teacher, or other passages of the inspired writings, have been quoted to justify the most fanatical errors, and cast as objections against the most venerable and beneficent institutions of the Church and of civil society. In the same way, and with still less reason or sobriety, the sacred maxim about 'worship in spirit and in truth' has been interpreted without regard to the words and acts of Him who spoke it, and has been used to undermine the whole edifice of Christian Ritual.

And yet there is less excuse for error in the present case. Jesus Christ did say: 'He that hateth not father and mother is not worthy of Me.' But He did not say: 'He that hateth not Ritual cannot worship Me aright.' He said: 'Swear not at all.' He did not say: 'Use no ceremonial.' He did say: 'Resist not evil,' illustrating the divine maxim by examples which, if carried out literally and universally, would put an end to civil and criminal procedure, abolish lawyers and judges, benches of magistrates, and chambers of legislators. But He nowhere spoke in similar forcible language against rites and ceremonies. Why then, in matters of worship only, are our Lord's words pressed to conclusions, from which they are so carefully guarded, by all except fanatics, when other interests are at stake? I am far from implying that any sayings of the Son of God are not to be accepted simply and literally. But the literal meaning of certain forms of speech is not always the meaning *of the letter*. And besides this, in the present case, even the meaning of the letter justifies no conclusion against Ritual, for, as I have shown already, Jesus Christ, in the passage referred to, has praised spiritual worship, but has said nothing directly or indirectly regarding Ritual, except in so far as from other sources we may judge Ritual to be a help or a hindrance to spiritual worship. If Ritual is a help, then Jesus Christ has prophesied its increase in the Christian Church. If it is a hindrance, then He has foretold its decrease or its total abolition. We have yet to see what is the teaching of His own life on this question.

But as we are now delaying on first principles, and making a statement of the questions at issue, it is here the place to consider the full logical consequences of the Protestant theory of spirituality, as well as to explain the Catholic view of this matter.

The Protestant principles seem to be these: What has a body cannot be spiritual; or, spirituality must be sought in spite of the body, not by its help. As the Quakers have carried out these principles most logically, I take the following statement from one of their tracts:

> 'The Society of Friends believe that worship consists not in rites nor ceremonies, nor in an outward service. It is a heart-worship not to be performed by proxy one for another.
>
> 'Seeing that "God is a Spirit, and they that worship Him must worship Him in spirit and in truth," it is their practice to sit down together in silence, to seek individually, by heartfelt prayer, for the outpouring of the Holy Spirit, by whose aid alone true spiritual worship can be performed.
>
> 'The confession of the soul prostrate before God, the secret prayer of the afflicted, the earnest wrestling of spirit, the simple exercise of faith, the humble thanksgiving, the spiritual song and melody of the heart—these, though they may be unspoken, are among the sacrifices of true Christian worship, acceptable to God, through Jesus Christ.
>
> 'The Society of Friends regard vocal prayer and preaching as being also important parts of worship; but they believe that these exercises should not be begun and ended at stated times, nor by previous arrangement, but only under the guidance and by the immediate help of the Holy Spirit; consequently they do not make use of congregational singing, nor of stated forms of prayer, in their worship; nor do their ministers adopt the practice of preparing sermons beforehand.'

With the first three paragraphs of this tract I have no fault to find. Silent worship, meditation, or mental prayer is in common use with Catholics, though it is generally made kneeling, not sitting. But the last paragraph contains a fundamental error. It maintains that the Spirit of God is essentially eccentric. Though He can speak to man's soul in words which have a fixed meaning (for even Quakers must think by means of words), yet He cannot adapt Himself to prepared sentences! A collect, however exquisitely composed to express human wants or divine perfections, would hamper the Spirit of God!

He could not use it as an instrument or vehicle of spiritual prayer! Rhyme and rhythm are too narrow to express spiritual melody! The Divine Teacher could not illumniate by means of a sermon prepared beforehand with intellectual labour! Yet, by some strange anomaly, it would seem that Quakers do expect some blessing or enlightenment to follow from the use of printed tracts!

There are probably few Protestants who would accept the theory of spirituality as stated by this sect, yet it does not on that account cease to be the logical result of principles urged by Protestants in controversy with Catholics. For if the Holy Spirit can make use of a psalm for spiritual impressions, as most Protestants would admit, then why not also of a procession? Or if a Catholic function repels the Spirit of God, why not also a Protestant hymn-tune? In what respect are modulations of the voice more spiritual than genuflexions and prostrations of the body?

But I wish to point out an application of the Protestant principles mentioned above which deserves carefully to be weighed by those who venerate the Holy Scriptures.

The Society of Friends has told us in the tract just quoted, that to give greater scope for 'the immediate help of the Holy Spirit' they neither prepare liturgics nor even sermons beforehand. But if the Holy Spirit is hampered, or, as the early Puritans used to say, is 'muzzled' by set forms of prayer or exhortation, how is He not also hampered by the sentences of Holy Scripture? Why is not a material book as unfit an instrument for the Divine Teacher as Rites and Liturgies for the Spirit of prayer?

Thus, then, the very principle which Protestants have so constantly urged against Catholic Ritual is logically destructive of the Protestant Rule of Faith. This is not a fanciful conclusion originated by a Catholic controversialist, and having no confirmation in historical facts. Modern Rationalists, in their refusal to be bound by the letter of Holy Scripture, not only make use of the very same pleas that we have been accustomed to hear urged by Puritans against Ritual, but they loudly proclaim that they are only acting on old Protestant principles. As this view may be new to many of my readers, I will give some proof of what I advance.

Mr. Tayler, a clever writer of that school of modern critics, who have most completely forsaken the traditional belief both of Catholics and Protestants, and who most boldly question not merely the authority but even the authenticity of much of the Old and New Testaments, boasts that they do this in obedience to the fundamental tenets of the most anti-ritual of all Protestant sects. 'The early Quakers,' he says, 'had got hold of a great truth, when they maintained that the Spirit was above the Scripture; that the Scripture had, indeed, a high secondary value, but only in proportion as it was a true vehicle of the Spirit.' And he quotes the words of the Quaker Barclay : 'From the revelations of the Spirit of God to the saints have proceeded the Scriptures of truth ; but because they are only a declaration of the Fountain, and not the Fountain itself, therefore they are not to be esteemed the principal ground of all truth and knowledge, nor yet the adequate primary rule of Faith and Manners. They are a secondary rule, subordinate to the Spirit, from which they have all their excellency and certainty.'[2] Mr. Tayler, in another place, speaks still more to the purpose. 'A Scripture utterance of divine truth cannot be interpreted like a legal instrument, merely by a literal acceptance of the words which it contains. We must go through the words to the Spirit which fills them from the Highest Mind, and which can only be interpreted by a kindred spirit within our own. The old Protestant confessions, broader than the theology which grew out of them, appeal to the witness of the Spirit in the last instance as the consummating evidence of divine authority. Luther, with a rough boldness of speech, which would have made our modern scripturalists stand aghast, maintained that the Spirit of Christ was the only decisive test of the Apostolic origin.'[3]

I may give another instance of the tendency of Puritan principles to exalt the interior Spirit at the expense of the external Teacher. Milton was so absolute a scripturalist, that

---

[2] *The Character of the Fourth Gospel*, by Rev. J. J. Tayler, p. 176.
[3] *Ib.*, Preface.

though he would give perfect toleration to Arians, Lutherans, Socinians, in a word to any who professed to derive their errors from Scripture alone, yet he would allow no toleration whatever to Catholics, and this, as he often alleges, principally because they appealed to tradition as well as Scripture as the complete Rule of Faith. Yet Milton lays down principles regarding the interpretation of Scripture which are broad enough to sustain the whole edifice of modern Rationalism.

'It is difficult,' he writes, 'to conjecture the purpose of Providence, in committing the writings of the New Testament to such uncertain and variable guardianship, unless it were to teach us by this very circumstance that *the Spirit which is given to us is a more certain guide than Scripture*, whom, therefore, it is our duty to follow.'[4] It is well known that Milton's principles regarding spiritual worship made him a vehement opponent even of the modified Ritual of the Episcopal Protestants of England. With this language of the Puritan Milton we may compare that of Bishop Colenso, who has acquired a certain fame by popularising in the English language some of the criticisms of German Rationalism. 'It is perhaps God's will,' he writes, 'that we should be taught in this our day, among other precious lessons, *not to build up our faith upon a book*, though it be the Bible itself; but to realise more truly the blessedness of knowing that He Himself, the living God, our Father and Friend, *is nearer and closer to us than any book can be;* that the voice within the heart may be heard continually by the obedient child who listens for it; and *that* shall be our Teacher and Guide in the path of duty, which is the path of life, when all other helpers—even the words of the Best of Books—may fail us.'

The principle here laid down, in terms almost identical, by Luther and Barclay, Milton and Colenso—that the Spirit is a surer guide than Scripture—is repeated in every variety of form by modern writers. It comes in reality to this, that the Spirit that teaches themselves is surer than the Spirit that taught Matthew and Mark, Peter and Paul. But it sounds better to make it a contrast, not of men, but of methods. To

[4] *The Christian Doctrine*, ch. xxx.

say that 'the voice of the Father and Friend' speaks more clearly to Colenso than to Paul, or that Colenso listens more like 'an obedient child' to the voice speaking 'within his heart' than John, who laid his head on the breast of Jesus—this might seem arrogant. But by vague circumlocutions it may be made to pass as a bright and noble view of religion, to exalt spiritual insight over mere literalism, the living God over the dead book.

An exactly similar ambiguity is practised with regard to Ritual. Were any one to maintain that, in their adoration of God, Luther and Calvin were more 'spiritual' men than St. Bernard or St. Bonaventure, or that Protestants in general worship God more spiritually than Catholics,—such a proposition would sound ludicrous; whereas an air of plausibility can be thrown over the more abstract proposition that Ritual is the contradictory of Spiritual, and that there is more real religion where there is less ceremonial. It is always convenient for men bent on destruction to have a formula which seems constructive. Thus at the Reformation Catholic worship was abolished and Catholic churches were pillaged, with the cry of 'God is a Spirit, and requires spiritual worship.' At the present day the social order of Christendom is being pulled to pieces with the motto, 'A free Church in a free State;' and the Bible is being undermined with a pretence of free interpretation and deeper insight, as opposed to bondage to the letter.

My object here is not, however, to combat Rationalism, but to show that logically and historically it is the direct outcome of the principles on which Catholic modes of worship are opposed.

The Quaker's blunder in thinking that the action of the Spirit of God must needs be immediate, individual, and eccentric—that He cannot or will not make use of what has a material element or a fixed form—is the foundation of modern Rationalism. 'The Grace of God cannot be connected with sacramental rites,' cries the Puritan. 'The Truth of God refuses to be imprisoned in the dead phrases of Scripture,' echoes the Rationalist. 'What has the free love of God to do with legal works?' chimes in the Antinomian. Thus we have three branches from the same stem of false Spiritualism.

In opposition to them all, the Catholic Church holds that the Spirit of God is given to man to interpret and vivify the written words that He has inspired, to facilitate and sanctify the use of the outward rites that He has appointed, and to multiply and elevate the good works that He has commanded.

Worship in spirit and in truth has God for its ultimate Object, and God for its immediate Author; and though it is in no way necessarily dependent on the body, the body may be the useful servant of the soul, both in its conception and in its expression. This is the Catholic interpretation of our Lord's words; let us see how it is borne out by the history of His life.

CHAPTER III.

IMPRESSIVE RITUAL.

Section I. Divine Pageantry.

AMONG the characteristics of Catholic worship, that which attracts the attention and criticism of strangers most easily is magnificence or splendour.

It is perfectly true that, according to Catholic teaching, splendour has a legitimate place in the worship of God. We hold that it is lawful and good at times to make impressions on the soul through the senses. But no Catholic ever considered magnificence as an essential or even ordinary quality of ceremonial. Such a notion may exist among Protestants; but I am at a loss to account for it, except from the fact that few Protestants ever witness Catholic worship, unless when they have been attracted by the rumour of some extraordinary function; or read of it, unless in the newspaper report of a solemnity. Yet they talk of pomp and pageantry, and gorgeous rites, and imposing ceremonial, and sensational effects, as if these were the staple of our every-day worship. If they wish to account for the hold which the Church retains on the affections of a Catholic population, or her success in converting the heathen, the attractions of a gorgeous ceremonial are the ever-ready and adequate explanation. Now I have undertaken to justfy Catholic facts and principles, not the dreams of popular imagination; so it is necessary to state what really are Catholic principles in this matter.

First, then, magnificence is not of the essence of worship, whether private or public. We know well that true spiritual worship may exist without grand or imposing ceremonies, and often without rites of any kind; and that art and splendour may sometimes be unaccompanied by any interior piety.

We have no quarrel, therefore, with Dr. Cumming, when he asserts that 'forms and ceremonies, however graceful, beautiful, complicated, or ancient, do not *necessarily* create religious impressions of any sort, much less true and spiritual worship.' We perfectly agree with him that 'the taste may be regaled, the senses may be charmed'; but when the bright vision has faded, there may not be left one single transforming or living impression produced upon the heart.' How strange that so constant a preacher as Dr. Cumming did not reflect that all this may be said with equal truth about preaching, and that it is said by St. James when he speaks of the forgetful hearer, who contemplates Truth as a man may see his countenance in the mirror, and immediately forgets the object that he gazed upon! But it is as worthless an argument against ceremonial as it would be against preaching.

On the other hand, no Catholic ever thought of maintaining that splendour was necessary to true spiritual worship. We know that some of the truest worshippers that God ever found poured out the homage of their hearts to Him 'in deserts, in mountains, in dens, and in caves of the earth' (Heb. xi. 38). English, Scotch, and Irish Catholics would be the last of all men to deny this, since the persecution of their Protestant fellow-countrymen reduced them, till within the present century, to this very state; and they doubt not that the worship of their hunted forefathers was as acceptable to God as any they can now offer in their reconstructed sanctuaries.

It is admitted, then, on all hands, both that true spiritual worship can exist without the magnificence of external ceremonial, and that splendid rites can be performed without interior worship. The question of Ritualism is not whether these things can be separated, but whether they are naturally united. Does interior piety naturally seek to ally itself to external ceremonial? Does external ceremonial of its own nature foster interior piety?

Mr. Ruskin says that the Gothic cathedral, 'with every stone that is laid on its solemn walls, raises some human heart a step nearer heaven.' He expresses, in a particular instance, that which is the theory of the Catholic Church with regard to all the objects and rites she employs. Is that theory true? Is it Christian?

Dr. Cumming, on the other hand, asserts that, 'in proportion as we increase the amount of ceremonial in public worship, in the same proportion we injure and deaden spiritual religion.' Is this, rather, true Christian doctrine?

Such, in general terms, is the question at issue, and the appeal lies to the New Testament.

Protestants will not refuse the appeal. They think they have gained the victory if we attempt it. 'Our Lord's whole life on earth,' says one already quoted, 'was conducted in the very simplest and plainest manner. Should we not try to imitate His walk, if we are really anxious, for religion's sake, to act rightly?' 'Nearly all the pictures of the Lord's public life,' says Dr. Vaughan, 'place Him before us under lights which are moral and spiritual, rarely ever in connection with anything simply of a ritual nature. This, by the way, is anything but the Christ which the Jewish fancy or imagination would have given us. But this too is what our better intelligence might lead us to expect in One who was about to declare that all such visibilities had served their purpose, and were about to come to an end. Who can imagine Him as taking a part in such garish pageantries as are now presented to us by men who would be accounted eminently reverential and Christian in their doings?'

It would not be strange that Rationalists should speak in this tone, since they reject all that is supernatural in the Gospel, and think that the Evangelists coloured, according to their Jewish prejudices, the records even of those events, as to the substance of which they are trustworthy witnesses; but it is, indeed, surprising that those who accept the four Gospels in their integrity, just as they are accepted by the Catholic Church, should be able to read them over and over again, without remarking that, in spite of the humility and simplicity of our Blessed Lord's personal appearance, He is surrounded, from His birth to His ascension, by a ceremonial of God's own creation, so splendid that all the magnificence either of the Jewish Temple or of the most solemn Catholic 'functions' sinks into insignificance when compared with it.

There are two very different phases in the earthly life of the Son of God. The writers whom I have quoted seem to forget that that life has its glories as well as its humiliations. They have considered our Lord as worshipper, but they have neglected to contemplate Him as the Object of worship. They have seen that He worshipped in poverty, but they have not seen that He was worshipped in magnificence. They have sought to draw an absolute rule from the poverty of Jesus Christ, which was a passing dispensation for our sake, while they ought to have seen that the true rule for Christian worship should be drawn from His glories, which are eternal.

I will speak in the next chapter of the 'simplicity and poverty' on which so much stress has been laid; but, first, let me draw attention to the glorious phase of our Divine Master's earthly life, and see whether we cannot gather from it conclusions not only favourable to, but absolutely decisive of, the Ritualistic theory of worship. We shall have to pass in review the whole earthly career of the Son of God.

How, then, was He first introduced into the world? The shepherds, says St. Luke, were keeping their night-watches in the fields of Bethlehem, when an angel stood by them, and 'the brightness of God shone round about them, and they feared with a great fear;' and while the angel was comforting them with the joyful news of their Saviour's birth, 'suddenly there was with the angel a multitude of the heavenly army praising God, and saying, Glory to God in the highest.' St. Matthew tells us how a miraculous star led the Eastern sages to the crib of Bethlehem, and how, when the holy pilgrims found the Divine Child, 'they rejoiced with exceeding great joy, and falling down they adored Him, and opening their treasures, offered Him gifts, gold and frankincense and myrrh.' Now this is God's own Ritual of the Nativity; let us examine it. Is there no appeal here to the senses? Is there no splendour, no magnificence? Did 'the brightness of God' shine for the mind only, or for the eyes as well? Did the angelic voices sing for the conscience only, or for the ears also? Were the great fear of the shepherds and the great joy of the magians mere sensuous excitement? In a word, do we gather from this narrative that men with flesh and blood are to forget that they have senses, in order to worship 'in spirit and in truth'? On the contrary, we see that those angelic beings, who by nature are pure spirits, clothe themselves with visible form, and take human voices for no other purpose than to appeal to men's bodily senses, and so lift them up in a human way, to share angelic joy.

Nor are these miraculous appeals to sense confined to the birth of our Redeemer. They are the beginnings of a series which, though of course interrupted by His hidden life, glorifies His public ministry, His death, and resurrection.

St. Mark tells us that our Blessed Lord entered upon His public ministry by receiving baptism from St. John, and that, in addition to the ceremonies which the Baptist may have used, God accompanied this baptism by a Ritual of His own. 'Forthwith, coming up out of the water, he saw the heavens opened, and the Spirit as a dove, descending, and remaining on Him; and there came a voice from heaven, Thou art My beloved Son: in Thee I am well pleased.' How full of wonders are these few words! But let us confine our attention to the point at issue. On this occasion not only are the two senses of sight and hearing addressed, in order to inspire reverence for Jesus Christ, but this is done in the way most calculated to make a vivid and permanent impression. The reason given by Jesus Christ why God loves those who worship in spirit is that He is Himself a Spirit. Yet this ineffable Spirit not only causes the material sky to seem to open, as if that were His dwelling-place, but He speaks with a human voice, and deigns to appear under the shape and emblem of a Dove.

Again, in the Transfiguration on Mount Thabor, some of these same incidents were repeated, and other circumstances were introduced of a still more striking nature. The Transfiguration is a divine drama addressed to the imagination and feelings, for the purpose of confirming the faith, and hope, and adoration of the witnesses. Hence St. John says: 'We saw

His glory, the glory as it were of the Only-begotten of the Father' (John i. 14). And St. Peter: We were 'eye-witnesses of His majesty' when the voice came down from 'the excellent glory.' But this excellent glory was not merely spiritual; 'His face did shine as the sun, and His garments became white as snow,' says St. Matthew (xvii. 2). And St. Mark still more emphatically: 'His garments became shining, and exceeding white, as snow, so as no fuller upon earth can make white' (Mark ix. 2). And the cloud that overshadowed them was 'a bright cloud' (Matt. xvii. 5).

Bright clouds and white glistening robes would, in modern language, be contemptuously called *sensational;* and so indeed they were, and were intended by God to work powerfully on the senses, the imagination, and the feelings of the witnesses. 'They fell upon their face, and were very much afraid' (St. Matt.). 'And they were afraid,' says St. Luke, 'when they entered into the cloud' (Luke ix. 34).

May we not apply to these two scenes the remark our Blessed Lord made on another occasion (John xii. 30), when a voice spoke to Him from heaven in presence of the multitude: 'This voice came not because of Me, but for your sakes'? All this splendour was not necessary for Jesus Christ, but was given for the sake of His adorers.

Let us turn now to the history of our Blessed Lord's Passion. I will pass over, for the present, the triumphal entry into Jerusalem, and draw attention to the sensible signs that surrounded Mount Calvary with awe. It is enough to refer to the darkness that was over the earth 'from the sixth to the ninth hour' (Matt. xxvii. 45); to the 'loud voice' of our agonising Saviour, twice mentioned by the Evangelist (Matt. xxvii. 46, 50), and remarked on by the Apostle (Heb. v. 7); to the veil of the Temple rent from top to bottom; to the quaking of the earth, the splitting of the rocks, the opening of the tombs. Most certainly these signs were addressed to the senses, to the imagination, the feelings. They were God's own Ritual of the Passion; and they were exactly fitted to give rise to those strong emotions which are recorded as their effect. 'The centurion and they that were with him watching Jesus, having seen the earthquake, and the things that were done, were sore afraid, saying, Indeed this was the Son of God' (Matt. xxvii. 54). 'And all the multitude that were come together to that sight, and saw the things that were done, returned, *striking their breasts*' (Luke xxiii. 48).

A lecturer against Ritualism lately said in a published sermon: 'All the tendencies of Roman Catholic worship are to produce a sensuous religion, not a spiritual. The glittering processions, the rich array of vestments, the low soft music, the incense-clouds filling the church with fragrant fumes; all this is of the earth, earthy. If men analyse their thoughts after visiting those places, they will find that if these be of Christ, their thoughts are ever about the Man who is suffering, bleeding, dying—a sensuous thought—rather than about the grand idea of the Atonement.' Alas, well would it be if the crowds who, in England, go on Good Friday to hear a Protestant sermon on 'the grand *idea*' would return home 'striking their breasts' with compunction, like the crowds who in the Catholic churches have kissed the feet of the Crucifix, and who, while meditating on the grand *fact* of the Passion, have by no means lost sight —how could they?—of the Atonement thereby accomplished.

The circumstances of the Resurrection and Ascension of our Lord are of the same sensational character (if the word may be taken in a good sense) as those of the Nativity, Baptism, Transfiguration, and Passion. We read, again, of a 'great earthquake,' of an angel with a countenance as lightning, and raiment as snow, the fear of whom makes the guards become with terror as dead men (Matt. xxviii. 3, 4); of 'two angels in white, sitting' in the sepulchre, 'one at the head and one at the feet' (John xx. 12); of 'two men in shining apparel' (Luke xxiv. 4); of 'a young man sitting on the right side, clothed with a white robe' (Mark xvi. 5). So, too, at the Ascension we are told of the apparition of 'two men in white garments' (Acts i. 10).[1]

Some kind of answer might, perhaps, be attempted to the preceding arguments on the plea that the disciples of Jesus

---

[1] This *symbolic* character of vestments and their use in divine worship will be considered later on.

Christ were still carnal, and that the Holy Ghost had not yet come. But to do away entirely with this evasion let us examine whether the day of Pentecost introduced any change in the method by which God had hitherto sought out true worshippers. Jesus Christ is about to found a Church whose worship shall be in spirit and in truth. Let us see if there is any ceremonial in its dedication. When Solomon dedicated his Temple, 'fire came down from heaven, and the majesty of the Lord filled the house.' According to the Protestant theory, such a display well befitted a temple built for a carnal religion, but would be entirely unsuitable to usher into the world a spiritual worship. Was, then, the descent of the Spirit accompanied by purely spiritual phenomena? No; the day of Pentecost has a Ritual of its own, not inferior in splendour to those of the Nativity and Resurrection. It is enough to refer to the 'sound from heaven as of a mighty wind,' and the 'parted tongues as it were of fire' (Acts ii. 2, 3). Never were deeper impressions made on the soul through the senses than on that day, when pure spiritual worship was finally and fully established. On that day, too, St. Peter quoted the prophecy of Joel, in which the nature of the Church of Christ is sketched from Pentecost to the end of the world; and those must read Scripture very carelessly who fail to observe that immediately after God has said, 'It shall come to pass, in the last days, I will pour out My Spirit upon all flesh,' He adds, 'And I will show wonders in the heaven above, and signs in the earth beneath—*blood and fire and vapour of smoke*' (Acts ii. 17, 19). Sensational elements certainly!

That these wonders, these striking appeals to the senses, are not reserved merely for the terror of unbelievers at the last day, is proved by the events of Pentecost, and by a thousand histories recorded in the annals of the Church. Several examples occur in the Acts of the Apostles. On one occasion, when the Disciples prayed, 'the place was moved wherein they were assembled' (Acts iv. 31). On another, the shadow of St. Peter heals the sick (Acts v. 15). On another, the face of St. Stephen appears 'like that of an angel' (Acts vi. 15). On another, 'a light from heaven, above the brightness of the sun, shines round about Saul, and those in company with him' (Acts xxvi. 13). On another, a light shines in the prison, and the chains fall from the hands of St. Peter (Acts xii. 7). On another, a great earthquake shakes the foundation of the prison while Paul and Silas are praising God (Acts xvi. 26). I pass over, with a mere allusion, the signs which shall precede the second coming of our Lord Jesus Christ. He has Himself drawn out what I will again venture to call the Ritual of the Day of Judgment, in a picture that no one can forget. He has told us that, 'plain and simple' as was His first appearance, He will then come 'in the clouds of heaven, with much power and majesty' (Matt. xxiv. 30).

After this rapid summary of the history of the Son of God, I will simply recall the statement of Dr. Vaughan : 'Nearly all the pictures of our Lord's public life place Him before us under lights which are moral and spiritual, rarely ever in connection with anything simply of a Ritual nature. Who can imagine Him as taking a part in such garish pageantries as are now presented to us by men who would be accounted eminently reverential and Christian in their doings?' Were I an infidel, I should reply, 'Your Gospels, at all events, are filled with "garish pageantries!"' But being a believer, I answer in the name of the Catholic Church, 'Search the Scriptures, for you think in them to have life everlasting; and the same are they that give testimony of Me' (John v. 39). For, to apply, in a few words, all that we have been reading to the question of Christian worship, I may ask, is it reasonable to suppose that 'the last days'—the days of the knowledge and worship of Jesus Christ—should open with such emphatic and multiplied Ritualism as that which glorified our Lord's first appearance on earth, and should close with such ceremonies as those which shall usher in and accompany His second advent; and that, during the whole intermediate period, rites and ceremonial, art and splendour, should be considered as the attributes of 'a sensuous religion, not a spiritual'?

Without going beyond the pages of the New Testament, we have found that God Himself made use of appeals to the senses and imagination far more striking, more splendid, more gorgeous than any which have been at the command of the Catholic Church, in the grandest function that was ever celebrated beneath the dome of St. Peter's. What, indeed, are silken vestments, jewelled mitres, peals of the organ, blaze of tapers, clouds of incense, or any other means used to impress the worshipper in the richest cathedral of Christendom, compared with the bright clouds, glistening raiment, heavenly voices, dazzling splendours, splitting of rocks, great earthquakes, and mighty winds, which are some of the elements of God's own Ritual of the New Testament?

I can well understand that any one weighing this subject thoughtfully and dispassionately might object that, if our ceremonial is founded on such a model, it is too insignificant, too mean, too unworthy of the Majesty of Jesus Christ. But I do not understand how any one who believes in the Gospels can complain that our manner of worship sins by excess, by appealing too much to the senses and imagination instead of the pure reason.

To the former objection I would reply by admitting that Catholic worship is indeed, even under the most favourable circumstances, too insignificant; and I would call upon the objector to help us to offer worship less unworthy. But I would also remind him that the Catholic Church by no means seeks to emulate the pageantry of God.

When a review is held on the anniversary of a great victory, the terrible or splendid battle-scenes are not literally reproduced; but a certain military display is made *in harmony with* the event which is commemorated, and which may serve appropriately to recall it. This is all that the Catholic Church attempts or desires. Her memory is full of our Lord and of the Majesty of His Person, and the mysteries of His Life. Wishing to set before her children those mysteries, she employs not words only, but pictures and pictorial actions. The Catholic Ritual has only such relation to the supernatural scenes of the Gospel, as a sunrise or a sunset painted on canvas bears to the rays of light which tinge with beauty the mountains and the clouds. Say, if you will, that the picture is a mere daub, or but a poor attempt to represent the loveliness of nature; but do not find fault with the artist, because with the gross materials of his palette he seeks to recall and render permanent that transitory loveliness. Do not find fault with the Church because, with such appropriate means as she can command, she seeks to keep fresh the memory through all time of the heavenly splendours of her Lord.

Section II. Apostolic Worship.

Before I proceed farther in my subject, I must remove a difficulty,—the fundamental difficulty in the whole matter. It is Carlyle, I think, who says that an argument is not complete until we have not only refuted the error of our opponent, but also shown how he came by it.

How, then, in the very teeth, so to say, of all that I have related from the New Testament, did Protestants come by their theory of Simplicity?

I have already indicated the answer in the preceding chapter. They have taken a very partial view of our Blessed Lord's life; they have considered Him as a worshipper only, not as One worshipped; and they have forgotten that He was a worshipper under entirely exceptional or abnormal circumstances.

Why will not Protestants allow us to draw any conclusion from the nature of the worship our Divine Master offered in the Temple, or the ceremonies at which He then assisted? Because, they say, all this was transitory. Our Lord, and even His Apostles, lived in exceptional times. The old law was not yet fully abrogated. He was made under the law that He might set us free from the law. Even after it ceased to be obligatory and was dead, it was not at once deadly. Therefore Jesus Christ might attend the feasts and celebrate the Passover. Peter and John might go up into the Temple at the ninth hour of prayer (Acts iii. 1). Paul might shave his head in Cenchreæ because he had a vow (Acts xviii. 18), and make oblations and purifications in Jerusalem (Acts xxi. 26). But it by no means follows that Christians may now do any of these things; for the times have changed, and we take example from the normal, not from the exceptional, phases of the lives of our Lord and His Apostles.

This, I think, would be the Protestant answer, and I admit it in all points; and now I put an analogous question:—Why do not Catholics draw a precedent from the humility and poverty in which our Blessed Lord and the first Christians worshipped? I reply, Because their circumstances were transitory and exceptional. They were exceptional as regards the old worship, and they were no less exceptional as regards the worship that was to take its place. If the ancient form of worship was not yet completely abolished, neither was the new form of worship fully inaugurated. If, then, no valid argument can be drawn in favour of a splendid Ritual from the exceptional or transitory circumstances under which our Blessed Lord and His Apostles conformed to the services of the Temple, certainly no valid argument can be drawn against magnificence in external worship from those exceptional and transitory circumstances under which our Blessed Lord and His first disciples worshipped apart from the Temple—circumstances which made splendour naturally impossible.

The mere fact of external simplicity in primitive worship has no force as a lesson, until it is proved to have been the result of free choice, and not of necessity.

The only worship of which we read in the New Testament —apart from the supernatural events which I have related, and apart from the worship of the Jews—was offered up to God in streets and market-places, in private houses (Acts ii. 46), or in upper chambers (Acts xx. 8). The first Christians were poor and persecuted; art and riches were not at their disposal.

Now, when Catholics were hunted into back rooms or mountain caves, or when their poverty could only erect a thatched chapel with a mud floor (as was long the case in Ireland), their worship was as far from being 'gorgeous,' as that of St. Peter and St. John can be supposed to have been.

Would any one conclude that those poor Irish or English Catholics did not approve of a more elaborate and magnificent

Ritual? Would any one who should witness a grander ceremonial in the churches of Dublin or London reproach us with departing from the simplicity of our ancestors?

Well, just as poverty and persecution are the explanation of the meagre external worship of two centuries ago in these countries, so also are poverty and persecution a sufficient explanation of whatever may seem deficient in splendour in the worship mentioned in the New Testament. Protestants may not be willing to accept this explanation, yet they have no right to assume the truth of their own theory without proof. I remarked that it was a pure begging of the question to interpret our Blessed Lord's praise of spirituality as a condemnation of ceremonial. So now I maintain that it is begging the question a second time to interpret the necessary want of splendour of Apostolic worship as a studious choice of simplicity, and a condemnation of Ritual.

It cannot be said that I also am begging the question when I attribute this plainness to necessity; for before doing so I have given, as I conceive, abundant proof that the utmost splendour of worship, the most elaborate use of external means to cause spiritual impressions and emotions, are the very characteristics of the Christian dispensation; and that, far from finding a difficulty in associating the person of our Blessed Lord with pomp and magnificence, we are unable to recall the memory of the most touching scenes of His life apart from those associations. Thus, then, Catholics have the legitimate possession of their interpretation of those phases of our Lord's life which may seem in any way contrary to the principles of Ritualism. They have a right to attribute them to necessity rather than to choice, and the burden of proof lies on Protestants, if they wish to give another interpretation in harmony with their theories.

So, too, in interpreting the acknowledged poverty of Apostolic Ritual to have been the effect of necessity we are not without a good reason. When a man omits an action under circumstances which render it impossible, we may be doubtful whether he does so from choice or from compulsion. But if he is no sooner free than he does what he before omitted, we then have good reason to judge that he would have done it before had he not been prevented.

This is exactly the case of the Christian Church. All admit that there was little splendour in the Apostolic worship.[2] How is this to be accounted for? Was it wanting because of the necessities of the times, or was it deliberately rejected as unspiritual? To determine this question we may consider how the Church acted as soon as she was free to act according to her own desires and instincts. Whatever opinion may be formed of the worship of the Catacombs, it is certain that no sooner was the pressure of persecution removed from the early Church than in every country throughout the world she developed her worship with a splendour identical with that which Catholics approve and Protestants denounce. How was this? Protestants are obliged to explain it by another gratuitous assumption—by maintaining that in days of persecution the worship of the early Christians was less splendid by free choice, and that on the cessation of persecution they were universally unfaithful to the principles of true spiritual worship, for which they had endured so much, and adopted from Paganism the *sensuous* worship which for three centuries they had loathed. Is this reasonable? Is it not more natural to suppose that this development was the result of principles which they had held from the beginning, but till now had been unable fully to apply?

I cannot forbear quoting here an apposite reflection of the old Anglican Bishop Andrewes: 'Surely,' he says, 'the Israelites in Egypt had their service of God—it may be in a barn, or in some corner of a house. Yet when Moses moved a costly tabernacle, no man was found that once said: Our fathers served God well enough without one: why this waste? *ut quid perditio hæc?* After that, many Judges and Prophets and righteous men were well when they might worship before the Ark; yet when Solomon moved a stately temple, never was any found that would grudge and say: Why, the Ark is enough: I pray God we serve God no worse than they that knew

---

[2] I do not mean that there was little *symbolic* Ritual, but of this we are to speak later on.

nothing but a tent—*ut quid perditio hæc?* Only in the days of the Gospel, which of all other least should, there steps up Judas, and dareth to say that against Christ's Church that no man durst ever either against Moses' tent or Solomon's temple. .... God help us! when Judas must reform Mary Magdalen!'

But to return. It should be remembered that the apparent plainness of Apostolic worship is one of the Protestant's main arguments against Ritualism. This is the ground of those appeals to a 'common-sense' reading of the Gospels, to prove that Ritualism has no part in true Christian worship. I can easily believe that the Pharisees urged this very same ' common-sense' reading of the prophets to prove that Jesus Christ could not be the Messiah. The word 'common-sense' means in both cases 'superficial.' The Scriptures must be not only read, but *searched*, before they give up their true character.

The magnificent descriptions of the prophets were fulfilled in a Messiah whose life was humble and persecuted; the humble persecuted Church which He founded, and the beginnings of which we read in the Gospels and Acts of the Apostles, developed into a kingdom that has filled the earth, and in which that humble and persecuted Messiah is worshipped as the King of glory, with all that earth can offer Him most rich and glorious. There is no more contradiction in the one case than in the other; indeed, whatever apparent contradiction there is in either case is explained and removed by bringing the two together. There is a strange perplexing contrast at first sight between the glorious Christ of prophecy and the humble Christ of the Gospel; and there is a similar contrast between the humble Christ who worships in the Gospel and the glorious Christ who is worshipped in the Catholic Church. The first contrast scandalised the Jews, the second contrast scandalises Protestants. I have endeavoured in the preceding section to remove the scandal by showing that, to an attentive reader of the Gospels, the very same contrast is found there also. There is the Christ persecuted by Herod and the Christ worshipped by the Magi; the Christ of Thabor and the Christ of Calvary; and yet these are not two Christs, but one Christ; and to know that one Christ truly we must know Him in His glories as

well as in His abasements. We must know Him, not only
in His voluntary humiliation, but in the splendours of Old
Testament prophecy, the splendours of New Testament miracles,
and the splendours of Catholic Ritual.

There will be an opportunity to develop these observations
when I come to show how Catholic worship is the foreseen
reparation of our Divine Redeemer's abasements. For the
present I take leave of this subject, and pass on to another
difficulty, which, though it is not drawn from the New Testament, and, therefore, not properly within my limits, is too
important to be passed over without at least a few words of
explanation.

SECTION III. SUPPOSED DANGER OF ABUSE.

THERE are many whose heart and whose reason are disposed to admit the fitness and excellence of the use of art and
wealth to produce beauty, and even a certain degree of splendour, in the public worship of God, yet they shrink from the
danger of abuse.

They are so afraid that the senses, being charmed with
beautiful sights and harmonious sounds, may cause the soul of
the worshipper to rest in what is merely external, that they
think it safer to avoid whatever can be called magnificent or
splendid. Hence the charge of *excess* so often brought against
the pomp of some Catholic ceremonies. Hence the boast of
decency and sobriety so frequently made in favour of such a
modified Ritual as that of the Anglican Church.

Now, it would be uncandid to deny the possibility of the
abuse of ceremonial; and were I even disposed to do so, innumerable passages in Catholic writers warning Catholics
against this abuse would at once convict me of insincerity.
But admitting readily, as I do, the possibility and the actual
occurrence of the misuse of Ritual, I deny that the danger is
so urgent or so frequent as to demand more than ordinary
safeguards, or such as to justify the abandonment of Ritual
itself. Did God fear that the brilliancy of the Star would

beguile the Magi from the hidden glory of the Divine Babe? or that the darkness of Mount Calvary would obscure in the souls of the witnesses their sense of the crime committed? If not, why should we fear for the effect of Ritual on Christian hearts?

Yet, for the sake of sincere Protestants anxious for the purity of God's worship, I would make some observations which may perhaps lessen their fears. And first I remark, that the beauties and glories of Nature have been abused and turned from their true purpose, which is to teach us of God, a thousand times more frequently than the splendour of Ritual; and yet no one condemns the glorious spectacle of Nature as dangerous; no one counsels us to turn our eyes from it, or to use it *soberly*, lest it should ensnare our souls. No: for it is easily understood, that however frequent may have been this perversion, it is to the corruption of men's hearts alone, and not to the grandeur of God's works, that it must be attributed. 'For all men are vain,' says the author of the 'Book of Wisdom,' 'in whom there is not the knowledge of God; for by the greatness of the beauty and of the creature, the Creator of them may be seen, so as to be known thereby' (Wisdom xiii. 1-5). Why, then, should the possibility, rather than the frequency, of abuse, make men mistrust a Ritual that teaches much more directly and explicitly of God than the grandeur of the mountains or the fertility of the plains?

An accomplished traveller thus describes the impression made on him by the first sight of the Falls of Niagara: 'The spectator at first feels as if stricken with catalepsy. His blood ceases to flow, or rather, is sent back in overpowering pressure on the heart. He gasps, like a drowning man, to catch a mouthful of breath. All elements of soul and sense are absorbed in the magnitude and glory of one single object. The past and future are obliterated, and he stands mute and powerless, in the presence of that scene of awful splendour on which his gaze is riveted.... The objects presented by Niagara are undoubtedly among those which exercise a permanent influence on the imagination of the spectator. The day, the hour, the minute, when his eye first rested on the great Horse-shoe Fall, is an epoch in the life of any man. He has received an impression which time cannot diminish, and death only can efface. The result of that single moment will extend through a lifetime, enlarge the sphere of thought, and influence the whole tissue of his moral being.'[3]

On this passage I would remark that the author sees no necessity for caution, or sobriety, nor does he blame Nature as excessive. Why, then, should there be so much suspicion of the impressions produced by the ceremonies of the Catholic Church? These impressions are not of the overwhelming nature of those just described; yet they are as deep, while they are more intellectual and far more spiritual.

I cannot explain the feelings engendered in a pious Catholic by some great function of his Church better than by the words used by Coleridge to describe the effect upon his soul of one of the great spectacles of Nature. In his hymn, composed at the foot of Mont Blanc, he writes:

> 'O dread and silent Mount! I gazed upon thee,
> Till thou, still present to the bodily sense,
> Didst vanish from my thought; entranced in prayer
> I worshipp'd the Invisible alone.
>   Yet, like some sweet beguiling melody—
> So sweet, we know not we are listening to it—
> Thou, the mean while, wast blending with my thought,
> Yea, with my life and life's own secret joy;
> Till the dilating soul—enrapt, transfused,
> Into the mighty vision passing—there,
> As in her natural form, swell'd vast to heaven!'

Now I say without hesitation, that while out of a thousand gazers on Mont Blanc there will not be more than one or two who will lift their souls from that spectacle to the majesty of the invisible God,—of a thousand Catholics who enter the church during some unusual and splendid ceremony, such for example as that of the Forty Hours' Adoration, very few indeed, if any, will be so engrossed with what meets the eye, as *not* to rise from it to the contemplation of the Hidden Presence.

It required, perhaps, the intellect and the refined poetic feeling of a Coleridge to 'pass into the mighty vision' of the

[3] Hamilton, *Men and Manners in America*, p. 405.

mountain he was gazing on, to gaze with such intense feeling that the very object which excites his thought 'vanishes from his thought,' until he worships the Invisible alone. And yet, I know no words by which the effect of a really magnificent Catholic function, not on the gifted few, but on the great multitude, could be more correctly described, than those of Coleridge. The *Ritual* is blending with their thought,

> 'Yea, with their life and life's own secret joy,
> Till the dilating soul—enrapt, transfused,
> Into the mighty vision passing—there,
> As in her natural form, swells vast to heaven!'

If any doubt the truth of my words, he has but to test them by going to the nearest Catholic chapel the next time the Forty Hours' Prayer is announced, and there watching for one half-hour the conduct of the Catholic worshippers, whether they are men or women, whether they belong to the educated classes, or are the simplest of the unlettered poor.

In appealing as I do to observation, I virtually appeal to the testimony of travellers, and by this I should be prepared to stand, if only the facts they record be sifted from their too often prejudiced reflections. An example or two, taken from the first accessible volumes of travels in the shelves of a circulating library, will explain my meaning and confirm the truth of what I advance. A British officer, having witnessed, in Havanna, the Passion Procession of Good Friday, makes the following remarks: 'In spite of prejudice, I could not avoid being deeply struck by this solemn procession. The airs performed by the bands were slow and mournful, the voices of the singers were deep and musical, the dresses were rich to a degree of splendour, and the whole was gone through with much apparent devotion.' So far the witness speaks,—in the next words the Protestant is heard. 'No doubt, when regarded with the eye of reflection, the whole may seem something worse than ludicrous; but it is impossible to witness the scene and to reason on its propriety at the same time. As long as the pageant is before your eyes, you cannot help being powerfully impressed by it; nor is it till after it has disappeared that you

are inclined to ask yourself why you gave way to feelings of
that nature.'[4]

Had the gallant officer really solved the question as to why
he had been so powerfully impressed, he would have found
that his true human and religious feelings had been allowed
free play during the procession; and that it was only when the
good effect had given place to the ordinary prejudices of Protestantism that the 'eye of reflection,' jaundiced by those prejudices, had discovered in the pageant ' something worse than
ludicrous.' The reflection was certainly not philosophical,
which could make him think that what had touched even a
Protestant in a solemn manner could be ludicrous; nor was it
a Christian thought, that what had caused 'much apparent devotion' towards our Lord's Passion in the Catholic population,
could be '*worse* than ludicrous.'

Another English officer, Captain Cunynghame, after witnessing the Christmas festival at Manilla, thus writes:

'Doubtless many of their doctrines are erroneous, and the
pageants, of which their Church is both proud and fond, are
often absurd and ridiculous, and may be scoffed at by those
who from childhood have had instilled into them the essence
and spirit of pure religion; but in their performance they advantageously employ both mind and body, imperceptibly leading
the first to think of holy things by the exercise of the latter.
At all events, the superfluous funds of the more careless classes
are far better used in decorating a saint than in rioting and
drunkenness, which I am sorry to think is by no means un-
common in some of our own advanced and civilised communities.'[5]

We suppose the reader will hardly agree with this gentleman
that ceremonies which 'advantageously employ both mind and
body,' and which 'imperceptibly lead the mind to think of holy
things,' can be absurd; or that those who 'scoff' at them can
have had instilled into their minds from childhood 'the essence
and spirit of pure religion.' He may also be disposed to think
that the 'advanced and civilised communities,' which spend

[4] *Campaigns at Washington and New Orleans in* 1815.
[5] *An Aide-de-Camp's Recollections of Service in China.*

money in rioting instead of in religious processions, would do well to retrograde to the civilisation of Havanna and the Manillas. It is, however, a curious study how the traditional Protestant interpretation of 'in spirit and in truth' has warped minds otherwise intelligent and candid.

But I would add another observation regarding this supposed danger of abuse of Ritual. It is scarcely fair in Protestants to judge of Catholics by themselves. Our belief is not theirs. We believe in a Divine Presence in our churches and sacred ceremonies of which they know nothing. It matters not here whether that belief be true or false. It *is* our belief; and therefore influences our feelings in our worship in a manner of which Protestants have no experience.

This was remarked by the German Protestant Menzel. 'Everything depends,' he says, 'in the Protestant form of worship, upon the preacher for the time being. For the Catholic, all his churches are alike, and as he conducts his devotion without the priest, it makes but little difference what priest officiates. Hence there prevails, if I may say so, an undisturbed equanimity of devotion everywhere among Catholics.'[6]

An eloquent Catholic writer, from whom I have borrowed this quotation, adds some reflections which exactly harmonise with what I have already said. 'If there be in the world,' he writes, 'a class of men who, in a certain sense, are absolutely indifferent to ceremonial, although obliged to use it, and who, in celebrating the mysteries of their holy religion, are almost unconscious of its presence, the Catholic belongs to that class. Whether he assists at the Holy Sacrifice, which constitutes the chief act of his religion, or at any other of the divine offices which attract him with irresistible power to the house of prayer, his eye and heart are fixed, not on sensible objects, but on that Awful Presence, which at one time is veiled in the Tabernacle, at another manifested to the gaze of the faithful. Vestments, music, and incense—whatever meets the eye or ear— he hardly notes, for there is something there which speaks to the soul, and taxes all its powers. Let the accompanying ceremonial be meagre or imposing, it is with the mind of a

[6] *German Literature*, by Menzel, vol. i. page 147, ed. Felton.

Christian, not of an artist, that he marks its presence; all he asks is, that it shall not distract him; the rest, in the presence of those stupendous mysteries, is of little import. Like Mary and Salome, he is thinking of the body which he has come to adore, not of the "sweet spices" which he has brought to anoint it. He provides, indeed, out of reverent love, the "fine linen," the "myrrh and aloes," and whatever else his devotion may inspire or the Church appoint, for in this august action she leaves nothing to human caprice or invention; but all these accessories of his worship, from the least to the greatest,—the cloud of incense, the blazing lights, the swelling choir, and the jewelled robes,—have no worth and no significance but as offerings to Him who gives them all their value by deigning to accept them.'[7]

Yes; what the Catholic Church aims at in all her Ritual is that her children 'be not distracted' from the object of their worship. They would be liable to distraction if there was nothing which met their senses in harmony with Him on whom their minds are fixed. Therefore the Church tries to exclude those things which would remind the worshipper of his ordinary occupations, cares, and pleasures; and she surrounds him with whatever can recall the words, the actions, the sufferings, the humiliations, the glories, the Presence of Jesus Christ.

The worshipper would be 'distracted' if the appointed Ritual were carried out with irreverence, slovenliness, or want of taste on the part of the ministers of the sanctuary; and this is a danger which has often given occasion to the legislation of Synods, and excited the zeal of the Church's doctors and reformers. But the Church has not found that excessive splendour distracted the mind or heart from Jesus Christ; because no splendour can be excessive or incongruous where He is its object; and therefore the Church has not deemed it necessary to admonish or to legislate on a danger which was but imaginary.

Again, Protestants are liable to mistake the effect of Catholic Ritual on Catholics, because they judge of it by the

[7] *Christian Missions*, by T. W. M. Marshall, vol. ii. ch. iv.

effect it produces on themselves. It is to them so new, and therefore so strange, that, like all novelties, it produces an exaggerated effect. It distracts them, it makes worship impossible to them, because they do not understand it, cannot follow it, or take any part in it. To *them* it is not a help, but a perplexity and an obstacle. Is it fair to suppose that Catholics are affected in this way? To them all is familiar, simple, natural; what they have been accustomed to from their infancy, and trained both to understand and to use. No Protestant need take my word for this; for he has but to enter a Catholic church, and to contrast the quiet and devout demeanour of the Catholic congregation with the anxious, frightened, perplexed, or scornful looks and attitudes of the little knot of Protestant gazers, who will probably be gathered near the church-door.

And once more. Protestants have no right to judge of Ritual among Catholics from what is now going on among a certain section of Anglicans. They are contending for Ritual, and their efforts are resisted. Hence the subject has been brought into a prominence which it does not occupy with us. I do not say that an exaggerated importance has been attached to it; but during a time of controversy it is likely to be *relatively* exaggerated. With Catholics, the principles and practice of Ritual are part of the ancient tradition of the Church; and like everything settled and on which all are agreed, they scarcely excite the attention of Catholics at all. The Catholic priest is quietly instructed in his duty, and the Catholic layman, content with practice, bestows few thoughts upon the theory.

And besides all this, in the Catholic Church everything is regulated by authority. Public attention is not aroused by the eccentricities of individual clergymen. Congregations are not thrown into confusion by rites they have never before witnessed, and of which they neither know the origin nor the meaning.

We believe that Ritual is something supernatural, considered by God worthy of His own direct regulation in the old Dispensation, and of His no less real though indirect regulation in the Christian Church, through the Holy Spirit that dwells in her. Hence the Fathers of the Council of Trent pronounced an anathema against all who should say that the received and approved rites of the Catholic Church may be despised or omitted at the option of the priests, or may be changed by any pastor of the churches. 'A most important and incalculably beneficial sentence,' remarks Digby, 'which delivers Catholic piety from being at the mercy of weak, ignorant, though well-meaning men, who, in proportion to their weakness and ignorance, are generally vain of being reformers or modifiers of ancient things.'[8]

These considerations, it is hoped, will help to remove from the minds of Protestants those excessive apprehensions of abuse which prevent them from giving a calm attention to the lessons of the New Testament concerning Ritual.

But perhaps, also, these apprehensions would be mitigated by an impartial inquiry into the effects of the abandonment of Ritual in Protestant churches. Has the experience of the last three centuries gone to confirm the theory that spiritual worship is the ordinary result of a religion shorn of all splendour? It would not be fair to give a Catholic's answer to this question. It is not, however, a Catholic, but the Protestant Menzel who says, 'The characteristic badge of the Protestant world is religious indifference;' and who attributes this to the fact that 'people regard the preacher alone, because nothing else in the Protestant Church attracts attention.'[9]

It is not a picture of a very spiritual worship that Professor Wilson draws, when he notices how incense has been rejected by Protestants. The passage is slightly satirical, yet it is the good-natured satire of a friend. 'It is difficult for us,' he says, —by *us* meaning, I suppose, Presbyterians,—'to realise the immense difference between ancient and modern feeling and practice in reference to the use of perfumes; but we may imagine the emotions with which a Hebrew of the days of Aaron, or Solomon, or Herod, would worship in one of our Protestant

[8] *Mores Catholici*, book v. ch. ii.
[9] *German Literature*, vol. i. p. 147, ed. Felton.

churches. It would startle him to find that the ear had become the most religious of the senses; that the eye was scarcely appealed to, except to guide the ear; and that the nostril was not invited to take any part whatever in the service. He would be inclined to apply to the worshippers the words which one of his great poets applies to the gods of the heathen—"Noses have they, and they smell not;" till, looking round, he chanced to observe, that though the priest bore no censer, many of the female worshippers carried in their hands certain misshapen crystal vessels, which from time to time they offered to their nostrils, with the effect of rousing them to an animation such as the most eloquent passages of the preacher often failed to provoke. Yes, that is the only religious use the moderns make of perfumes; and I leave you to picture to yourselves the contrast between the Hebrew altar of incense sending its rolling clouds of fragrant smoke to heaven, and a modern church smelling-bottle or snuff-box passed from hand to hand along a row of sleepy worshippers on a drowsy summer afternoon.'[10]

The following contrast between Catholic and Protestant worship in New Orleans is from the pen of another Scotch gentleman, Mr. Hamilton, who says: "I am not a Catholic, but I cannot suffer prejudice of any sort to prevent my doing justice,' &c.

'Both Catholic and Protestant,' says this candid traveller, 'agree in the tenet that all men are equal in the sight of God, but the former alone gives practical exemplification of his creed. In a Catholic church the prince and the peasant, the slave and his master, kneel before the same altar, in temporary oblivion of all worldly distinctions. They come there but in one character—that of sinners; and no rank is felt or acknowledged but that connected with the offices of religion. *Within these sacred precincts the vanity of the rich man receives no incense;* the proud are not flattered, the humble are not abashed. The stamp of degradation is obliterated from the forehead of the slave when he beholds himself admitted to community of worship with the highest and noblest of the land.

'But in Protestant churches a different rule prevails. Peo-

[10] *Five Gateways of Knowledge*, p. 68.

ple of colour are either excluded altogether, or are mewed up in some remote corner, separated by barriers from the body of the church. It is impossible to forget their degraded condition even for a moment. It is brought home to their feelings in a thousand ways. No white Protestant would kneel at the same altar with a black one. He asserts his superiority everywhere, and the very hue of his religion is affected by the colour of his skin. Can it be wondered, therefore, that the slaves in Louisiana are all Catholics; that while the congregation of the Protestant church consists of a few ladies, arranged in well-cushioned pews, the whole floor of the extensive Catholic cathedral should be crowded with worshippers of all colours and classes ?'[11]

I will only add, in conclusion, that perhaps in facts like these might be found an answer to a question which a few years ago was much discussed in Protestant circles—why in England working men do not go to church? Have they not felt in England, like the negroes in America, that in Protestant churches, though no incense is offered to God, too much is offered by the congregation to the preacher, and by the preacher to the congregation? If this is not so universally, still there is a greater danger of this abuse than of the abuse of Ritual.

[11] *Men and Manners in America.* Catholics cannot with fairness be altogether held responsible in England for the separations and money-charges in some of their churches. These things have been forced on them by poverty, the result of spoliation, and are not the genuine result of Catholic principles, as may be seen by the very different order of things in Rome, and formerly in England. See *The History and Law of Pews,* by Alfred Heales.

CHAPTER IV.

SYMBOLIC RITUAL.

SECTION I. THE TEACHING OF OUR LORD.

IN order to treat properly the worship of the New Testament in its relation to Ritual, we must carefully distinguish the different aspects which Ritual may bear. Hitherto we have been considering only that feature of Catholic ceremonial which may be called Splendour, Grandeur, or Magnificence. But by far the greater number of the Church's rites have no pretension to this quality. The ordinary administration of the Sacraments, the ordinary prayers and benedictions of the Church, have nothing in them of the nature of splendour. There are parishes, and even whole countries, where the worshippers never saw a ceremony to which the epithets grand or imposing could with any propriety be given. It is really a ludicrous mistake on the part of many English writers to fancy that the senses and souls of Catholics are dazzled and subdued by a constant round of magnificent rites. Sir Emerson Tennent, in order to account for the attachment of the natives of Ceylon to the Catholic faith, says, 'Their imaginations were excited, and their tastes permanently captivated, by striking ceremonial and pompous pageantry.'

This is really a singular theory. Why, even a child would grow weary of a Christmas pantomime, if obliged to witness it every day for a month. Are there, then, savages of human kind in any part of the world whose imagination and tastes can be 'permanently captivated' by a mere monotonous display of pompous pageantry, which, when disconnected from doctrine and the feelings which spring from belief in doctrine, would not possess even the interest of theatrical display?

But facts are no less opposed to such theories than philosophy. I will quote here the commentary which the author of *Christian Missions* makes on the words just quoted. 'Does Sir Emerson Tennent,' he asks, 'suppose that Father Joseph Vaz, for example, when a fugitive in the swamps and jungles of Ceylon, converted 30,000 idolaters by "pompous pageantry"? Did St. Francis Xavier, whose ecclesiastical apparatus was limited to a hand-bell and a catechist, convert 700,000 souls by "gaudy ceremonial"? Did the venerable John de Britto gain his tens of thousands in the forests of Marava by the splendour of an imposing Ritual? Was it by the aid of such accessories that the martyred apostles of China and Corea, whose churches were huts and their vestments rags, won their triumphs? Was it "pageantry" which rescued 1,500,000 South American Indians from the worship of demons? Was it "Ritual" which caused the Holy Name to be adored on the banks of Lake Huron, by the borders of the Ohio and the Mississippi, and again, at a later date, in the plains of Oregon and the valleys of the Rocky Mountains? Is it by a "gaudy ceremonial" that the Franciscans are at this moment renewing their ancient victories in the far interior of Brazil, or the Lazarists in Syria, or the Jesuits in Columbia, or the Marists in the islands of the Pacific?'

I may add, has it been by means of a splendid Ritual that the Church has retained her hold on the affections of the Irish nation? Those Celtic souls are certainly not insensible to the impressions of the imagination; and yet for three hundred years have they worshipped the God of their forefathers in the bog or on the mountain-side, in the thatched hut or the slated 'house' with its mud floor; and generations after generations have passed away of confessors or martyrs to the Catholic faith, without having witnessed even the solemnity of a High Mass or seen the incense ascend at Vespers.

There is, however, another kind of Ritualism very different from what we have been considering. It makes use of the senses indeed, but not to impress them; they merely serve as instruments to convey ideas to the mind. To illustrate what I mean from Protestant worship, singing and instrumental music may be said to belong to the first kind of Ritualism, that which is æsthetic; kneeling to the latter. Now, it is certain that in her external worship the Church uses many actions not simply necessary, but which are purely symbolical, and that she gives mystic signification to a multitude of actions, movements, and objects used in her various rites. This too is a subject of accusation against her.

It is the nursery tale told to children that Catholics are slaves of a multitude of forms and ceremonies, and that they think to go to heaven by taking holy water, making genuflections, and counting Paters and Aves on their beads. And the old nursery tale is believed in after-life, so that it may be told boldly at any time and go unquestioned.

The notorious Lola Montez—whether she was really a champion of 'spiritual worship,' as understood in modern times, or more probably from hatred to priests, who had been the enemies of her scandals—in a lecture she delivered in America, speaks of the Catholic priesthood as 'a hierarchy of magicians, saving souls by machinery, opening and shutting the kingdom of heaven by a Sesame of incantations which it would have been the labour of a lifetime to make so much as intelligible to St. Peter or St. Paul.' Such language would not have been used had it not been known to be acceptable to the audience to whom it was spoken; and the language of this virago is, in every respect, as decent as that used, almost every day, from many pulpits, and deliberately printed in books against Catholics.

Dr. Vaughan seems not in vain to have invoked the shades of Wickliffe and of Knox. 'Baptism,' he says, 'in the hands of the Ritualist is a rite more fit to have come from the school of Simon Magus, a dealer in magic emblems, than from the school of Christ; and the scenic performances which the same authorities have connected with the Communion, remind us more of what we might have expected from an initiation into some heathen mystery, than the Supper for which the private room in Jerusalem was made ready some eighteen centuries ago.'

When I read passages like these from the pen of Protestant

ministers, I am reminded of a saying of the learned Anglican Johnson, in his *Treatise on the Unbloody Sacrifice*, that 'the candid Pliny gives us as *gentlemanlike* an account of the Eucharist, in his letter to Trajan the Emperor, as some that go for Christian divines in these latter ages.'

We have seen strong statements; let us examine whether they are based on equally strong proofs. I give the best I have been able to find in the various writers I have consulted. Of course, I confine myself to proofs or objections derived from Scripture.

Dr. Vaughan quotes largely from the denunciations of our Blessed Lord against the Pharisees for their external observances of human traditions, as the washing of cups and pots, brazen vessels and tables, together with their neglect of the commandments of God; but I confess to my utter inability to see by what process of reasoning Pharisaic observances and Ritualistic exactitude are identified.[1]

When the Jews clamour for the death of Jesus Christ, and yet are too scrupulous to enter into the judgment-hall, lest they should be defiled, I understand the force of the denunciation against such a mockery of religion. They, indeed, 'strain out the gnat and swallow the camel.' But when the Blessed Virgin Mary presses the '*Holy One*' to her bosom, and yet observes the law,—'She shall touch *no holy thing* until the days of her purification be fulfilled' (Lev. xii. 4),—is she too straining out a gnat and swallowing a camel? Or, is there no difference between the love which observes even the least thing pertaining to the honour of God, and the hypocrisy which, despising God and violating His laws, tries to create for itself a reputation for sanctity by exactitude in external trifles?—no difference between Zachary and Elizabeth, 'walking in all the commandments and justifications of the Lord without blame' (Luke i. 6), and the Pharisees, 'tithing mint and rue, and every herb, and passing over judgment and the charity of God'? (Luke xi. 42.)

Yet, even in the condemnation of the Pharisees, our Blessed Lord is careful to guard His words from abuse. He does not

---
[1] The accusation as regards *tradition* will be discussed in Part II.

blame them for observing little things, but for making that observance a pretext for the neglect of weightier matters: 'These things you ought to have done, and not to leave the other undone' (Luke xi. 42).

Let us not be deceived by superficial resemblances. There are different ways of contributing to God's external service. The men who sold in the Temple oxen, sheep, and doves pretended to be zealous for the sacrifices, though actuated only by avarice; and our Divine Redeemer, in His real zeal for the honour of His Father's house, drove them from it with a scourge of cords. There is a false zeal and a real zeal. So, too, there is a false Ritualism and a real Ritualism. I am not going to defend the zeal of the money-changers, but that of Jesus Christ; not the Ritualism of the Pharisees, but that of the Blessed Virgin and St. Zachary.

I cannot but think that this attempt of Dr. Vaughan to identify Ritualism and Pharisaism is eminently unfair. He says, that on no other ground can we understand why the Gospels should give us this everlasting Pharisee than that he is the type of Ritualists, and that Ritualism is a besetting sin of human nature. I willingly admit that the vices which our Blessed Lord denounced in the Pharisees are of all ages; I admit that there have been Catholics superstitiously resting in external ceremonies, substituting external strictness for solid virtue, and filled with disdainful pride. But I do not think that the spirit which makes men say, 'I thank God I am not as the rest of men,' is exclusively found among Catholics. Certainly the conduct of English Protestants in Continental churches, and the scorn that is written on their faces for the multitudes that pray around them, are generally interpreted to mean, 'I thank God that we English are not like the rest of the world, or as those wretched Papists who are beating their breasts yonder.' The tone of English Protestant controversy is such that the celebrated De Maistre remarked, 'One would think it was their belief that Christ died only for the English!' Were it necessary, I could illustrate the spirit of the Pharisee from more than one passage of Dr. Vaughan's own volume.

But, to leave these recriminations, let us admit that the

spirit of the Pharisee is detestable wherever it is found, either in a superstitious reliance on external practices, or in a supercilious disdain for those who adopt them. And since the true piety of the Publican is opposed in the Gospel to the boastful prayer of the Pharisee, let us inquire whether he shows that scorn of ritual observances which some now consider the very essence of 'worship in spirit and in truth.' On the contrary, our Blessed Redeemer has carefully noted no less than three different external ceremonies which accompanied his short but fervent prayer. He 'stood afar off' from the altar or the other worshippers; he 'would not so much as lift up his eyes to heaven;' he 'struck his breast.' He uses these three ritualistic and symbolic observances, for they are nothing less—respectful distance from what is holy, eyes cast down, striking of the breast—as means to excite or to express the humble sentiments of his heart. The legitimate conclusion, from our Lord's commendation of his conduct, as compared with that of the Pharisee, would certainly not be contrary to Ritualism, understood in the only sense in which the Catholic Church approves of it.

I have now considered the only argument of a positive nature which is alleged from the Gospels, so far as I can discover, against the use of ceremonial. Certain passages from the Acts of the Apostles and from the Epistles are brought as objections, the force of which I will examine presently.

I find, however, that our opponents rely principally on a negative argument. 'In no stage of our Lord's life,' says Dr. Vaughan, 'in none of His appearances to His disciples after death, is there the slightest indication that any rite beyond His simple ordinance of Baptism, and His simple service at the Last Supper, was designed to have a place among His followers.' 'The Saviour appointed two great sacraments,' says Dr. Cumming, 'Baptism and the Lord's Supper. If more had been requisite, He would have appointed more. But the very fact that He has appointed these two seems to teach by implication that more are unnecessary.'

What implication is really involved in certain silences and reticences of the New Testament, I will reserve for future consideration. I reply now to the above negative argument by an absolute denial of what is alleged. I will proceed reverently to gather up some of the ritualistic actions practised or taught by our Lord and His Apostles, as related in the Gospels. And let me remark, that if many of them are minute, it is for that very reason I record them. The grand and impressive ceremonial I have treated of already, and now pass over. I wish to see here whether our Lord sanctions minute and symbolic rites, as well as solemn and imposing ones.

In looking through the Gospel I find that the following acts are recorded of the Word made flesh: He *knelt* in prayer (Luke xxii. 41); He *fell flat* on the ground (Mark xiv. 35); He *raised His eyes* to heaven in giving thanks (Mark vi. 41); He lifted up and modulated His voice in obedience to harmony and rhythm (Mark xiv. 26); He employed in prayer formulas taken from the Psalms (Mark xv. 34; Luke xxiii. 46), and that too in the moment of intensest feeling, when, as His Apostle has remarked, ' *With a strong* cry and tears He offered up prayers and supplications' (Heb. v. 7); He approved in others those demonstrations of repentance which could not belong to Himself, as of the Publican, who casts down his eyes and strikes his breast (Luke xviii. 13), and of 'sackcloth and ashes,' as symbols of contrition (Luke x. 13).

Then, again, He receives the adoration and praises the faith of those who use ceremonies in their worship of Himself: of Peter, who 'falls down at His knees' (Luke v. 8); of the lepers, who 'fall on their face before Him' (Luke v. 12, xvii. 16); of the man born blind, who ' falls down to adore Him' (John ix. 38); of the woman who touches the hem of His garment, ' and falls down trembling before His feet' (Luke viii. 44, 47). Nor does He consider St. John Baptist superstitiously attached to external things, though he dresses in 'a garment of camel's hair with a leathern girdle,' just like a Catholic hermit, and expresses so great a reverence for the least thing that has come in contact with, or has relation to, his Divine Master, that he declares himself unworthy ' to loose the latchet of His sandals ' (Mark i. 7). And I may add, neither did the Apostle St. Paul consider it superstitious ' to lift up pure hands in prayer'

(1 Tim. ii. 8), nor for one under the influence of strong religious feeling to 'fall down on his face to adore God' (1 Cor. xiv. 25); nor did he consider it a matter of indifference whether men and women pray and prophesy in Christian assemblies with their heads covered or uncovered, and that for very mystical reasons (1 Cor. xi. 2-16).

Most of the instances above given are examples of the use of ceremonial in order to express interior feelings of piety already conceived. They prove that worship *in spirit* does not exclude worship with the body.

The examples that follow are proofs that ceremonial is equally well fitted to be a vehicle of *truth*. It expresses, sometimes more forcibly than words, the nature of what is done; and this is the basis and the justification of the rites used by the Catholic Church in the administration of the sacraments.

I remember but one example when our Lord works a miracle without word or sign—that of the change of water into wine at Cana (John ii. 7, 8). Either He uses a formula of words, as 'I will, be thou made clean,' or more often He gives emphasis to His word by action. Thus, when He says to the sea, 'Peace, be still,' He rises at the same time in an attitude of majesty (Mark iv. 39); He stretches out His hand to Peter on the sea, takes the dead maiden by the hand, imposes His hands on the crippled woman (Luke xiii. 13), or touches the leper and the feverish woman (Matt. viii. 3, 15).

These ceremonies are indeed very simple; but there are others more elaborate and mystical. I may instance the cure of the deaf-and-dumb man. Our Divine Redeemer takes him aside, puts His fingers in his ears, spits, and touches his tongue, looks up to heaven, groaning and pronouncing the word *Ephpheta*—*i.e.* Be opened (Mark vii. 33, 34); and again, the cure of two blind men is altogether mysterious. St. Mark tells us how Jesus Christ led a man outside the town, how He spat upon his eyes, laid His hands on him, and caused him gradually to see (Mark viii. 23); and St. John relates how, in another case, He spat on the ground, made clay with the spittle, spread the clay on the blind man's eyes, and bade him go and wash in a certain pool, the very name of which (Siloe, or Sent), as the Evangelist remarks, is not without a mystery (John ix. 6, 7).

Now, considering that the Catholic Church, in administering baptism, in order to express the spiritual deafness and dumbness from which the grace of Jesus Christ delivers men, employs these very same ceremonies, we may know what to think of Dr. Vaughan's assertion, that her Ritual of Baptism 'is more fit to have come from the school of Simon Magus than from the school of Christ.'

Dr. Vaughan's colleague in invective, Lola Montez, also calls the Church's sacramental Ritual a 'Sesame of incantations.' Had she remembered, that as, in the Arabian tale, the magic word SESAME is used to open the doors, so Jesus Christ in the Gospel used the word EPHPHETA to open the ears and loose the tongue of the deaf mute, she might more properly have worded her accusation in this way: 'The Catholic priesthood opens and shuts the kingdom of heaven by an EPHPHETA of incantations, which it would be the labour of a lifetime to make so much as intelligible (not to St. Peter and St. Paul, but) to those spiritual deaf mutes, who are such not merely by nature but by obstinacy, 'like the deaf asp that stoppeth her ears; which will not hear the voice of the charmers, nor of the wizard that charmeth wisely" (Ps. lvii.).'

But to return to the study of our Blessed Lord.

His manner of imparting spiritual graces and teaching lessons of virtue is no less ritualistic and symbolical than His method of working bodily miracles. He imposes His hands on the little children with prayer (Matt. xix. 15); He breathes on His disciples when giving them the Holy Ghost (John xx. 22); and lifts up His hands to bless them when He ascends into heaven (Luke xxiv. 50). At one time He writes on the ground when the Pharisees wish to stone the adulteress (John viii. 6); at another He curses and withers up the fruitless fig-tree (Mark xi. 21); and after the remarkable ceremonial of washing His disciples' feet before His Passion (John xiii. 4-15), He says, 'I have given you an example, that as I have done to you, so you do also;' which words have surely the same force to lead us to imitate His way of teaching as to practise the virtues which He practised.

But His disciples were not left to their own instincts in drawing this conclusion. We find several examples of ceremonies prescribed for their use, whether they teach, work miracles, confer spiritual graces, or worship God. They are told by their Divine Master to shake the dust from their feet against the cities which rejected them (Mark vi. 11); and they interpret and obey this injunction literally, as we read in the Acts (xiii. 51). They are told to anoint the sick with oil (Mark vi. 13), thereby prefiguring the unction afterwards promulgated by St. James (James v. 14); to baptise with water, and to celebrate the Holy Eucharist. (Compare Matt. xxviii. 19 with Acts viii. 36, and Matt. xxvi. 26 with 1 Cor. x. 16.) They also make use of the imposition of hands (1 Tim. iv. 14, v. 22; Acts xiii. 3, xxviii. 8) to cure, or convey grace or authority; they use relics to work miracles (Acts xix. 12) and exorcisms; and symbolic actions to convey truths, as when Agabus binds his own hands and feet to signify the captivity of St. Paul (Acts xxi. 11).

From all this it is abundantly evident that the religion that Jesus Christ taught by word and example is one replete with ceremonies;—to speak, to sing, to groan, to utter strong cries with the voice; to kneel or fall prostrate on the ground; to shed tears, to cast down the eyes to earth, to lift them to heaven; to strike the breast, to lift up the hands, to cover or uncover the head in prayer; to rise or sit; to wear unusual garments, to put on sackcloth, to sprinkle ashes on the head; to stretch out the hand, to impose hands; to write upon the ground, to breathe, to anoint with oil or with clay; to use spittle, to pour water; to shake the dust from the feet;—these, and such as these, are the rites of the New Testament. Are those prescribed to the Catholic priest in the Ritual of Paul V. either more numerous, more varied, or of a different character?

After this long enumeration of symbolic ceremonies used by our Blessed Lord and His Apostles, I scarcely know how to characterise the rule laid down by Dr. Cumming: 'Let the worship,' he says, 'be as pure, as perfect, as chaste and holy as can possibly be; but let it not be desecrated by alien symbols.' If he meant simply, let there be no symbols out of harmony with Christian doctrine and morality, this would be intelligible enough. But he does not mean this only. He asserts that symbols of every kind are repugnant to Christian worship. 'The Jewish religion,' he says, 'was a religion of symbols; but the Christian religion emerged from these, and the dead husks were buried for ever.' Of course, this proposition, in one sense, is a first principle among all Christians. No one can believe that Jesus Christ has come, and not understand that whatever prefigured Him has lost all meaning. No one can believe that the Christian religion is Catholic, without admitting that whatever was intended in the Jewish worship to be local and limited, must have been abolished. No one can believe that the Christian religion is one of freedom and love, and not perceive that whatever was imposed as a bondage has been removed. But that the principle of symbolism was peculiarly and exclusively Jewish is neither declared in Scripture, nor in conformity with common sense. Symbolism may either express the disposition, the thoughts and feelings of the soul,—and in this case it cannot be peculiar to Jews; or it may refer to some divine reality external to the worshipper,—and in this case it may belong either to the past, the present, or the future. Now, if the Christian religion deals with the past, the present, and the future, I am at a loss to understand why it should not refer to them by the language of symbols, as well as by that of speech. It would be equally reasonable to say, language was used by the prophets of old to foretell the coming of the Son of God, therefore, now that He has come, language can have no place in His religion.

But, perhaps, the Church has retained some of the old Jewish rites? No doubt she has; but Protestants also are fond of telling us how much of their service of Common Prayer is derived from the worship of the Temple and the Synagogue. We have certainly borrowed some few external rites, both from Mosaic and Pagan worship; because they were the natural symbols of sentiments that were good, and of doctrines that were true. We might as reasonably disbelieve the immortality of the soul, because heathens taught it, as object to symbols merely because heathens used them.

In a treatise on the reverence due to the altar, the Anglican Jeremy Taylor says: 'Will you give me leave to add the practice of the heathen? There's no hurt in it, for they, having not the law, yet by nature doing the things contained in the law, became a law unto themselves. I argue not from hence, because they do it, therefore we Christians must. But this: it is our duty by the law of Christendom and of all religions, and nature itself, as appears by the practice of heathen people; and let us not be more rude in our addresses to God than they that know Him not, lest our familiar knowing Him entrench too much upon contempt. It is no shame, believe it, for us who are entitled heirs of heaven by promise, to imitate so pious practices even of barbarous and heathen people.'

But Dr. Cumming is determined to leave us no resting-place. 'There ought,' he says, 'to be *nothing* symbolical in a Christian place of worship;' and then he proceeds to lay down a rule, which it would puzzle the whole Institute of British Architects to carry out. 'Make the building,' he says, 'as chaste, as beautiful, as perfect, as architectural taste can make it; but let there be nothing typical or symbolical in it.' Now, I really cannot call to mind, or even imagine, a religion in which such a principle is recognised or obeyed. Quakerism, which may occur to some, is certainly no exception. In a religion which is almost entirely subjective—rather a philosophy than a religion—the symbolism will be scanty, because there is little to represent, but it will not be the less real or intense. Quakerism has its pet virtue of simplicity; and the bare walls of the meeting-house, and the straight collars, plain bonnets, and drab-coloured clothes of its occupants, which are intended to symbolise this virtue, are in reality an excessive Ritualism, degenerated into Formalism. Is it not an instinctive Ritualism or Symbolism which Burns depicts in the Puritan home:

> 'The sire turns o'er wi' patriarchal grace,
> The big ha' Bible, ance his father's pride,—
> His bonnet reverently laid aside'?

What is this uncovering of the head but a symbol of interior respect? What is the bending of the knees but a symbol of humility? Indeed, scarcely a rite or ceremony can be named that is not symbolical. But the principle of symbolism, which all admit in practice, and most in theory, the Church applies consistently, systematically, and in detail; nor in this does she depart from the spirit or the teaching of the New Testament. It would be easy to point out how nearly every one of the ceremonies enumerated in the last chapter is symbolical; and a little reflection will be sufficient to convince the reader that those supernatural phenomena which run through the life of our Lord Jesus Christ are also symbolical, intended by exterior emblems to teach some truth, or, by exterior impressions, to arouse some analogous and appropriate feeling. On one symbolic feature alone of this divine pageantry will I dwell somewhat longer—that of Vestments.

SECTION II. SYMBOLISM OF VESTMENTS.

WE are all familiar with the quips and jeers which are cast at 'ecclesiastical millinery.' The subject of Church Vestments may of course be made to excite ridicule or disgust, either by the eccentricities of individuals or by its discussion being out of time and place. Though gentlemen do not consider their daily clothing or their court-dress a matter of indifference, they might yet be angry if the details, that regard the tailor or the master of ceremonies, were thrust perpetually or unseasonably upon their notice. So too Catholic laymen, jealous for the Church's traditions, and zealous for the glory of God's house, would nevertheless resent the continual discussion of the forms and colours of vestments, as if every Catholic was a member of the Congregation of Rites. If, then, it were thought that colours were occupying the attention due to truth, or that vestments only covered vanity or frivolity, I should not complain of the angry invective or sarcastic sneer.

Yet it would be as unchristian as it is unphilosophical to

teach that the use of colour and form in decorations or in vestments is to be discarded altogether. It is doubtful, indeed, whether any religious body has consistently rejected this auxiliary of worship. Whitewashed walls may be as symbolic as walls hung with rich and varied tapestries. The drab colour of the Quaker is as symbolic as the gold-embroidered chasuble of Catholics. The sects which manifest their habitual preference for black are influenced by symbolism no less than the Church whose alternations of hues they so strenuously reject. 'Some people,' says Beecher, 'think black is the colour of heaven, and that the more they can make their faces look like midnight, the more evidence they have of grace. But God, who made the sun and the flowers, never sent me to proclaim to you such a lie as that.'

Nevertheless there are those who, though they admit the fundamental principles of this form of symbolism, appear to think that Catholics have given to it a development which has no sanction in the New Testament.

The subject of Christian vestments has been learnedly treated by the Rev. W. Marriott in his *Vestiarium Christianum*. Catholic writers admit with him that it was long before the symbolism of ecclesiastical vestments, in form and colour, attained its present development. But Mr. Marriott asserts that 'the result of the Reformation has been that the customary ministering dress of the English clergy during the last three hundred years, has been in colour and general appearance all but exactly identical with that which we find assigned to the Apostles in the earliest monuments of Christendom, and which, upon similar evidence, we shall find reason to conclude was the dress of the Christian ministry in the primitive ages of the Church.' Even supposing this to be materially true, or near the truth, it is formally erroneous. For, on Mr. Marriott's own showing, Christian priests in those first ages wore, while ministering, habits the same in form and colour as their usual dress, though more splendid and perhaps of finer texture. But Anglican ministers wear, when ministering, vestments utterly different in form and colour from those of ordinary life. What would Mr. Marriott think of a Catholic priest who, to defend the use of

Latin in the Liturgy of to-day, should write a long and learned treatise to prove that it was the identical language used by the early Christians in Rome? Doubtless he would reply that the first Christians used their vulgar tongue, which we do not—that the resemblance is accidental, the difference substantial. The same simple answer disposes of the whole argument of his volume, as it is a defence of Anglicanism in its departure from Catholic usages, though not of its value as a repertory of interesting evidence.

I do not propose to enter into the details of modern vestments. My point of view is neither antiquarian, historical, nor artistic. The question for my solution is this: is there anything recorded in the New Testament that would seem to support the present usages of the Catholic Church? This has been often and angrily denied. That the denial may have the full benefit of a powerful advocate, it shall be here stated by a writer who, if he succeed not in convincing, will fail from the weakness of his cause, rather than from lack of earnestness in its support, or from want of intellectual vigour.

Milton then, whose poetical and æsthetic tendencies might have been expected to lead him to other views, writes thus passionately on the subject of vestments : 'They' (*i.e.* Catholics) 'hallowed the body, they fumed up, they sprinkled it, they bedecked it, not in robes of pure innocency, but of pure linen, with other deformed and fantastic dresses, in palls and mitres, gold and gewgaws fetched from Aaron's old wardrobe, or the flamin's vestry : then was the priest set to con his motions and his postures, his liturgies and his lurries, till the soul by this means of overbodying herself, given up justly to fleshly delights, bated her wing apace downward,' &c.[2] In another work against the Anglican prelates of his own day, he writes: 'Now for their demeanour within the church, how have they disfigured and defaced that more than angelic brightness, the unclouded serenity of Christian religion, with the dark overcasting of superstitious copes and flaminical vestures?.. Is our religion guilty of the first trespass, and hath need of clothing to cover her nakedness?.. Believe it, wondrous doctors, all cor-

Of Reformation in England, book i.

poreal resemblances of inward holiness and beauty are now past. "How beautiful," saith Isaiah, "are the feet of him that bringeth good tidings, that publisheth salvation!" Are the feet so beautiful, and is the very bringing of these tidings so decent of itself? What new decency can, then, be added to this by your spinstry? Ye think by these gaudy glisterings to stir up the devotion of the rude multitude; ye think so, because ye forsake the heavenly teaching of St. Paul for the hellish sophistry of papism.'[3]

Good words, Master Milton; methinks such heat neither beseemeth the philosopher nor the poet. The heavenly teaching of St. Paul is not so forgotten by 'papists,' as you, in your proud conceit of Bible-lore, imagine. Keen eyes and holy hearts had conned God's Holy Word long ere Calvin or Beza began to rail. Men like the Baptist, clothed in the modest garb of penance, have lifted up fearless voices, in every age of the Catholic Church, against abuses, and not least against the luxury and pomp of dress. They lacked not purity of heart to detect, nor courage to denounce, had 'hellish sophistry' lain hid beneath the golden cope of the prelate or shone from the jewelled tiara of the pontiff. Whenever these things were made subservient to personal vanity or haughty pomp, warnings as bold and severe as ever were uttered by inspired prophet, have been spoken by simple monks or apostolic bishops, and have been recorded in books familiar to us still. But holy men of old knew well how to distinguish between the 'purple and fine linen' which ministered to the every-day ostentation and luxury of Dives (Luke xvi. 19), and the 'fine linen and purple' which adorned the 'valiant woman,' when 'her husband was honourable in the gates, when he sat among the senators of the land' (Prov. xxxi. 22, 23). Both the learned and the simple of the Catholic Church know that 'pure linen' is not 'pure innocency;' but they know that the latter is well symbolised by the former. The learned at least have read in the Apocalypse how the bride adorned herself for the marriage of the Lamb: 'it is granted to her, that she should clothe herself with fine linen, glittering and white; for the fine linen are

[3] *The Reason of Church Government urged against Prelacy*, book ii. ch. ii.

the justifications of saints' (Apoc. xix. 7, 8); and they consider a symbol displayed to the eye no more a 'hellish sophism' than a symbol depicted to the imagination. The simple too have not forgotten what they have so often heard in the Gospel, of angels in shining and bright apparel, and of the Master of the angels in the snow-white glory of His Transfiguration; and when the Church tells them of these events in her yearly festivals, they are not so dull but that their eyes detect the harmony between what they see in the sanctuary and what they have listened to from the pulpit. It requires other sophistry than that which is current in the Catholic Church for men to read of the visions of angels in white robes at our Lord's tomb, and then to conclude that 'all corporeal resemblances of inward holiness and beauty are now past.' The Catholic philosopher who has dwelt with loving and adoring heart on every incident of the Resurrection, and marked, with the attentive and inspired Evangelists, how the angels sat, not anyhow or anywhere, but in one case 'on the right side,' in another 'one at the head and one at the feet,' will be little moved by those who rave at priests being 'set to con their motions and their postures.'

But dress has its origin in sin! How then employ this memorial of our degradation as a symbol of holiness? And has not the variety of languages its origin in sin? and have not the ornaments of human speech been abused to sinful ends? Yet Milton would have been the last to think that learning, eloquence, and poetry cannot be consecrated to the service of religion.

They understand but little our Lord's Redemption who fail to see that the very signs and punishments of our fall have, by divine grace, become means of merit or emblems of triumph. He who was stript of His clothes on Calvary, to expiate by the shame of nakedness the ignominy of Adam and Eve and the vanities and shamelessness of their descendants, and was crowned with thorns, the produce of a cursed soil, was seen afterwards by St. John in heaven: 'On His head were many diadems, and He was clothed with a garment sprinkled with blood, .. and the armies of heaven followed Him, clothed in fine linen, white and clean' (Apoc. xix. 12-14). What new decency, Milton here would ask, were he consistent with himself, what new decency, O wondrous seer, do you think to add to Jesus Christ and His redeemed, by these visions of spinstry? See you not what handle you will lend to the sophistries of priests and prelates in future ages, who will pretend that if red garments symbolise the Passion, then red garments may well be used on the festivals of the Passion that they will institute; and if white symbolises the purity of the redeemed, then will albs and rochets, surplices and cottas, be frequent in the sanctuaries, and white chasubles and copes adorn the feasts of confessors and virgins?

Seriously, will a dispassionate man maintain that clothing is too cursed in its origin to be consecrated to the service of God, when he reads that aprons taken from the body of St. Paul cured diseases and drove out evil spirits? (Acts xix. 12.) Will he maintain that the form and colour of vestments have no symbolic teaching—useful not only to the rude multitude, but to the learned and the spiritual also—when he reads all that is related in the New Testament of divine visions, whether seen by the mental eye alone, as by St. John at Patmos, or witnessed by him and others with bodily eyes on the Mount of Transfiguration or around the Sepulchre?

But, since Milton appeals against our 'hellish sophisms' to the 'heavenly teaching of St. Paul,' I will here transcribe a passage from that Apostle's First Epistle to the Corinthians, which is so minute and mystical on an *apparently* trifling point of Ritual, that if it were found in Durandus, instead of in a letter of the great Apostle, it would certainly be mocked at as a piece of Popish folly. As the whole passage is rather obscure, I will give it in the excellent translation of Mr. Conybeare rather than in either the Catholic or Protestant version.

'I praise you, brethren,' begins the Apostle, 'that (as you say) you are always mindful of my teaching, and keep unchanged the rules which I delivered to you. But I would have you know that Christ is the Head of every man, and the man is the head of the woman, as God is the Head of Christ. If a man should pray or prophesy in the congregation with a veil over his head, he would bring shame upon his head (by wearing the token of subjection). But if a woman prays or prophesies with her head unveiled, she brings shame upon her head as much as she that is shaven. I say, if she cast off her veil, let her shave her head at once; but if it is shameful to a woman to be shorn or shaven, let her keep a veil upon her head. For a man ought not to veil his head, since he is the likeness of God, and the manifestation of God's glory. For the woman's part is to manifest her husband's glory. For the man was not made from the woman, but the woman from the man. Nor was the man created for the sake of the woman, but the woman for the sake of the man. Therefore the woman ought to wear a sign of subjection upon her head, because of the angels. . . . . Judge of this matter by your own feeling. Is it seemly for a woman to offer prayers to God unveiled? Or does not even nature itself teach you that long hair is a disgrace to a man, but a glory to a woman? for her hair has been given to her for a veil. But if any one thinks to be contentious in defence of such a custom, let him know that it is disallowed by me, and by all the Churches of God' (1 Cor. xiv.).

It is not necessary for us to enter into questions as to the force of the precepts here given, or to inquire whether it was the Apostle who had abolished the custom of the tallith or veil which the Jews put over their heads when they entered their synagogue. What concerns the matter of symbolism is this—that for these external practices the Apostle assigns deep doctrinal reasons. He will have the doctrine to be expressed by symbols. And with regard to these and similar practices he had already given rules. Ritual had been part of his authoritative teaching. He does not treat the matter as one of simple indifference, in which each man may abound in his own sense. Though he appeals to reason when he says, 'Judge by your own feeling,' yet to any man who should say that he feels differently, he replies, 'Neither I nor the Churches of God admit of your custom.' Mr. Conybeare gives to the expression, 'Let the woman be veiled, *because of the angels*,' an interpretation which, if it is admitted, adds another reason for ritualistic discipline. 'The angels,' he says, 'are sent as ministering ser-

Symbolic Ritual. 97

vants to attend upon Christians, and are especially present when the Church assemble for public worship, and they would be offended by any violation of decency or order.'

Was it fair in Dr. Vaughan merely to say, 'You may read epistle after epistle of St. Paul, and not find one word touching upon anything of a Ritual nature'—a thing which might be said of nearly every Papal Encyclical—and then, without even a reference to the above passage, to conclude that St. Paul was a decided anti-ritualist?

SECTION III. SYMBOLIC LANGUAGE.

THIS will be the proper place to consider whether a legitimate argument in favour of symbolic ceremonial may not be drawn from the figurative style used in Holy Scripture, both by the prophets when speaking of the times of the New Testament, by our Blessed Lord in His parables, and especially by St. John in the Apocalypse. I find this distinctly denied by Dr. Vaughan. 'It is true,' he says, 'the language of the New Testament is often pictorial and symbolic; but the picture and the symbol are in the teaching, that they may *not* be in the worship. They have so done their work to the mind, as to have become superfluous to the senses.' I must confess that the philosophy of this assertion is not very apparent; it not only contradicts the general instinct of mankind, but it is directly opposed to the testimony of Holy Scripture. Try by it such passages as the following : ' There came from Judea a certain prophet named Agabus. He, when he was come to us, took Paul's girdle, and binding his own feet and hands, he said, Thus saith the Holy Ghost: The man whose girdle this is, the Jews shall bind in this manner in Jerusalem,' &c. (Acts xxi. 11). On this occasion, neither did the prophet Agabus nor, I think I may safely add, the Holy Ghost, deem the symbolic action superfluous to add emphasis to the divine announcement. Or again : ' He breathed on them, and He said to them, Receive ye the Holy Ghost; whose sins you shall

H

forgive, they are forgiven them,' &c. (John xx. 22). Is not the breathing here symbolical, representing the procession of the Holy Ghost, His communication to the Apostles, and probably —as our Blessed Lord on this occasion gives to them the powers of a new life—alluding also to the saying in the Book of Genesis: 'The Lord God formed man of the slime of the earth, and breathed into his face the breath of life, and man became a living soul'? (Gen. ii. 7.) Was the breathing, then, superfluous? I might adduce multitudes of similar instances.

It is customary for Protestants to reply, when such examples as these are alleged, that this was the Oriental mode of teaching. But besides that this is not appealing to the New Testament, but snatching at a reason for not conforming to the Bible, I will give an answer in words, which are not the less applicable to Ritualism because the Protestant author probably never dreamt of such application. Unconscious testimonies to principles are often the most valuable. The writer says: 'It was not without a wise forecast of the world's necessities, and a knowledge of human nature, that God ordained that the Bible should be constructed in the *East*. Our unimpassioned, taciturn, and often cloudy temperament needs an infusion of the piety which grew up in those lands of the sun. Such an infusion of the Oriental life-blood into the stock of our Christian experience would bring us into closer sympathy with the holy and refined types of Scripture, which are redolent with beauty and sensibility.'

The amiable authoress of the *Calm Hour*, from whom I have borrowed this quotation, adds most truly, and even still more to my purpose: 'The most grand and beautiful objects in creation have their parallel in the vast range of revelation. Did we examine more minutely the various characters of the symbols used in Scripture, they would help to impress the realities more deeply on our memories. Our knowledge of God is in its infancy, and we are infants. Let us take a lesson from the way in which we train *our* infants. We set before them *pictures* of history, of persons, and events, which we wish them to retain in their memory.'

Perhaps the illustration may offend the pride of some, who

have not been wont to meditate on the divine sentence, 'Unless you become as little children, you shall not enter the kingdom of heaven.' And they might quote against me the words of St. Paul, who reproached the Hebrews: 'You are become such as have need of milk, and not of strong meat; for every one that is a partaker of milk is unskilful in the word of justice, for he is a little child. But strong meat is for the perfect' (Heb. v. 13). But without staying here to reconcile the words of the servant with those of the Master, and without doing more than suggest that there is no clearer proof of spiritual infancy in the bad sense than the thought that we are already among the perfect, it may soothe the minds of such objectors to know that Milton, when his mind was not warped by Puritan bitterness, considered symbolic teaching as not simply a condescension to human weakness, but as founded in the very nature of things. It is thus he makes the Archangel Gabriel address our first father:

> 'And what surmounts the reach
> Of human sense, I shall delineate so,
> By likening spiritual to corporal forms,
> As may express them best: though what if earth
> Be but the shadow of heaven, and things therein
> Each to other like, more than on earth is thought?'[4]

Symbolism, then, is a law of human nature fully recognised in every part of the Scriptures; and since the example of our Blessed Lord, no less clearly than common sense, tells us that symbolism may be presented to the senses as well as to the imagination, it need not seem a very strained or far-fetched argument which a Catholic might construct on these principles in favour of the Ritualism of his Church. I read, for instance, in the prophet Isaias, the promise made to the Christian Church: 'The glory of Libanus shall come to thee, the fir-tree and the box-tree and the pine-tree together, to beautify the place of My sanctuary, and I will glorify the place of My feet' (Isa. lx. 13). I need not to be told that God's sanctuary is here the congregation of the faithful, and that the precious woods are but the symbols of the gifts and graces of the Holy Ghost. All this I know full well. But I reflect that, if a magnificent temple, seen

[4] *Paradise Lost*, book v. line 570 *sqq.*

by the prophet in imagination, can typify the people among whom God dwells, the objective reality from which the image was drawn will be no less perfect a type. If gold and silver and precious stones and wood are fit emblems when spoken of, they are no less fit when seen. They could not be symbolical in language if they were not symbolical in their own nature and in reality. I am at a loss to understand why it should be right for a spiritual person to recall material objects to the memory, and unlawful to present them to the senses.

I read the vision of St. John in the Apocalypse: 'Another angel came and stood before the altar, having a golden censer; and there was given to him much incense, that he should offer of the prayers of all the saints upon the golden altar which is before the throne of God. And the smoke of the incense of the prayers of the saints ascended up before God from the hand of the angel' (Apoc. viii. 3, 4). Now, is it intelligible that a golden censer should be lawfully spoken of and conceived in imagination, while to manufacture and use it would be a crime, or at least an absurdity?—that a Protestant, who sees and smells the fragrant cloud of incense only in fancy, should be a spiritual worshipper, and the Catholic, who perceives them with the organs of sense, should be looked down on as grovelling and carnal?

Still Dr. Vaughan ridicules the idea that the Apocalypse can furnish an argument in favour of Ritual. 'Every man of intelligence must feel,' he says, 'that an attempt to bring the symbolism of the Apocalypse into the service of the Christian Church must be a hazardous experiment.'

What is the meaning of sayings like this? Was St. Augustine not a man of intelligence? or St. Chrysostom? or St. Thomas? or Bossuet? or Dante? Have not millions of men of intelligence made this experiment, and seen no hazard in it? Why not give a reason without claiming a monopoly of intelligence? I fear the reason that Dr. Vaughan gives does not quite bear out this claim. 'If this course is taken at all,' he asks, 'where is it to stop? If, because an angel is said to cause the smoke of incense to ascend before the Almighty in heaven, Christian priests should cause it to ascend from the

Church on earth, why should not the priest imitate the next thing said to be done by the angel, viz., fill the censer with fire, and cast it forth to summon up "voices and thunderings, and lightnings and earthquakes"? Many other strange things the angels are said to do in the services of that world; are they all precedents to be followed by Christ's ministers in this world? If not, who is to separate between the symbolism to be taken, and the symbolism to be left?'

Who is to separate? I might answer: The Catholic Church, guided by the Holy Ghost. But without taking ground so high as this, I reply: Good sense and good taste will separate. How does an artist discriminate between the poetical descriptions or divine visions he will try to represent on canvas, and those which he may not attempt? By the rules of art, doubtless. He knows that the capabilities of painting are not those of language; that though his art has certain great advantages,

'Possessing more than vocal power,
Persuasive more than poet's tongue,'

as Campbell sings, yet it has not the range which belongs to language. The latter admits a more subtle play of fancy, glancing lightly from earth to heaven. It admits of change and movement, which cannot be expressed on canvas. The artist, therefore, will not attempt to reproduce everything which he admires in poetry. Yet it would be a strange thing to assert that, because he cannot copy everything, he must not venture on anything. A similar answer may be given to Dr. Vaughan's questions concerning the Apocalypse. Where must the Ritualist stop? Who is to separate between the symbolism to be taken and the symbolism to be left? Who? Why, the traditions and rules of the art of Ritual, based on common sense, good taste, and the very nature of things.

Though in some respects the symbolism of art or of action has advantages over the symbolism of language, it has, nevertheless, a much narrower field. A Catholic youth would know that many of the allegories of the Apocalypse are unfit subjects for Ritual, and that many images taken from the forest and the field, from the strife of the elements or the occupations of men, cannot be transferred to the sanctuary of a church. Yet it is not absurd or unreasonable to maintain that, when the allegory has been derived, not from nature, but from the sanctuary, the representation of the allegory may be a very fit subject for Ritual. Dr. Vaughan speaks as if Catholic worship was an attempt to represent on earth what St. John had seen in heaven; whereas St. John transfers to his description of heaven what he had first seen on earth. The golden censers, the clouds of incense, the lamps and candlesticks, the altar, the thrones and crowns, the white robes, the precious stones, the harps and singing, the prostrations and adorations, are not realities of heaven which we try to copy on earth; they are realities, symbolic realities, belonging to earthly worship, which St. John considered fit emblems of heavenly mysteries in themselves ineffable. It matters not in the least whether, in the time of St. John, any of these things was used in Christian worship, or whether he and those for whom he wrote had only seen them in the Temple of Jerusalem. If St. John sees in them the most adequate emblems of Christian mysteries, of heavenly and eternal truths, then they belong more truly to the Church than to the Temple, and they are as fitly represented to Christian eyes as they are read of to Christian ears.

Indeed, the symbolism of the Bible is not intended merely to illustrate truth by means of images taken from what we have seen in past time, or what we have read of; it is intended also, in very many cases, that the truth and the image, having been once associated in our minds, the sight of the image may serve to recall the truth. This is, perhaps, one reason why our Blessed Lord chose so many of His types from what is most familiar in human life. This view of our Lord's teaching has been beautifully developed by Mr. Beecher.

'What wonderful provision,' he says, 'God has made for us, spreading out the Bible into types of nature! What if every part of your house should begin to repeat the truths which have been committed to its symbolism? The lowest stone would say, in silence of night, "Other foundation can no man lay." The corner-stone would catch the word, "Christ is the corner-stone." The door would add, "I am the door." The taper burning by your bedside would stream up a moment to tell you, "Christ is the light of the world." If you gaze upon your children, they reflect from their sweetly-sleeping faces the words of Christ, "Except ye become like little children." If, waking, you look towards your parents' couch, from that sacred place God calls Himself your father and your mother. Disturbed by the crying of your children, who are affrighted in a dream, you rise to soothe them, and hear God saying, "So will I wipe away all tears from your eyes in heaven." Returning to your bed, you look from the window. Every star hails you, but chiefest "the bright and morning Star." By and by, flaming from the east, the flood of morning bathes your dwelling, and calls you forth to the cares of the day, and then you remember that God is the Sun, and that heaven is bright with His presence. Drawn by hunger, you approach the table. The loaf whispers, as you break it, "Broken for you," and the wheat of the loaf sighs, "Bruised and ground for you." The water that quenches your thirst says, "I am the water of life." If you wash your hands, you cannot but remember the teachings of spiritual purity. If you wash your feet, that hath been done sacredly by Christ, as a memorial. The very roof of your dwelling hath its utterance, and bids you look for the day when God's house shall receive its top stone.'

The Church has entered into the spirit of this Providence of God. She does not think herself bound slavishly to embody in her worship all the emblems of Holy Writ. Yet she has loved to do so when no reason of religion or of taste opposed; and a thousand objects, casually seen, bring back to the memory and heart of the Catholic, familiar with her rites, the divine lessons of prophets and apostles, and especially of the Great Master, by whom those objects were employed as types. In the course of ages, many a figure besides those used by inspired writers has been added by holy men to the Church's Ritual. Fools, who rush in where angels fear to tread, may deride those holy rites, and blaspheme what most they are ignorant of; but those whose minds and hearts have been attuned to heavenly things are lost in admiration. 'How beautiful is everything!' exclaims Digby; 'how serene! as if the harmonious wisdom of the Church had actually moulded the external form of matter to its own perfection. Catholicism has produced all the lovely forms which order can assume within the narrow limits of space and time.'

Yes, the Church's rule is, let everything be symbolical, so that the Christian may drink in lessons by every sense. Nor is it wise to object that but few know or think of what is contained in all these symbols. The same may be said of the symbolism of nature; yet God has made provision for the few prudent, as well as for the thoughtless multitude. But I will consider the objections in another section.

SECTION IV. MULTITUDE AND OBSCURITY.

THE preface to the Anglican Prayer-Book says that the Reformers put away some of the old Catholic rites, 'because the great excess and multitude of them hath so increased in these latter days that the burden of them was intolerable; that many of them were so dark that they did more confound and darken than declare and set forth Christ's benefits unto us. And besides this, Christ's Gospel is not a ceremonial law (as much of Moses' law was), but it is a religion to serve God, not in bondage of the figure or shadow, but in the freedom of the spirit.' Two charges, then, are made against the ceremonies of Catholic Christendom: that they are too numerous and too obscure:—a bondage and a puzzle. It is, of course, impossible to answer charges like these completely, without examining these various ceremonies in detail, which is foreign to my scope. It will be enough for me to refer to some of the principles of the New Testament. This, I think, will be a sufficient vindication.

1. And, first, as to their multiplicity.

One can easily understand that a thing may be good in moderation and burdensome by excess. *Ne quid nimis* is a very old proverb. Does this proverb contain the condemnation of the practice of the Catholic Church regarding Ritual?

Symbolic Ritual.   105

It is the common Protestant tradition that it does. When the poet Crabbe, who is generally careful in the selection of his epithets, wants one distinctive of a Catholic, he speaks of

> 'The burthen'd Papist,
> He who new robes for every service takes.'

The 'text' that has been generally selected from the Protestant arsenal to demolish Catholic Ritual is taken from the speech of St. Peter before the council of Jerusalem. 'Why tempt you God,' says the Apostle to the Judaisers, 'to put a yoke upon the neck of His disciples, which neither our fathers nor we were able to bear?' (Acts xv. 10.) It is asserted, by those who cast these words in our teeth, that the numerous ceremonies of the Catholic Church are identical in principle and in effect with the ceremonial law of the Jews, and that they proved such an intolerable burden, that 'our fathers' of the Reformation threw it off, and that the free necks of Protestants now refuse to submit again to the yoke. It was not, however, calm criticism that suggested this application of St. Peter's words.

The Apostle certainly was not speaking of the splendour of the ancient Temple, nor of the ceremonies used by Jewish priests in the immediate worship of God. Regarding those there was no controversy. The question agitated before the council was one of discipline rather than of worship. The yoke that it was attempted to lay on the necks of the disciples was the obligation of circumcision, and the observance of all the multiplied and inconvenient prescriptions and restrictions of the Mosaic law. It was not their mere difficulty that made these so heavy a yoke; but it was that their fulfilment was attended by no equivalent spiritual gain. These observances did not help in themselves to piety or sanctity; these restrictions were not useful safeguards against sin. The Judaisers would not understand that this yoke, having been imposed to distinguish and separate those whom God had intrusted with His revelation from the surrounding idolatrous nations, could only serve as an impediment, now that the Church was to be Catholic and the heathen invited to the faith. Under similar circumstances Catholics would exclaim as loudly as Protestants against observances or restrictions that would needlessly and fruitlessly hamper their civil and social intercourse, or impede their missionary success.

This is not the place to discuss the disciplinary laws of the Catholic Church, or it would be easy to show that they have nothing in common with the abolished prescriptions of Judaism. If these are anywhere to be found among Christians, it will be in the Puritan legislation of Scotland and of New England regarding the 'Sabbath.' But we are concerned only with ceremonial in the strict sense. And I assert, that the ceremonial of Jewish worship was neither a yoke to the fathers of whom St. Peter spoke, nor to St. Peter himself; and that the ceremonial of Catholic worship, far from being a yoke, was the solace and delight of our Catholic fathers, as it is of ourselves.

St. Peter neither did nor could speak of the worship of the Temple, with its splendour or its symbolic rites, as a yoke that his fathers could not bear. He would have contradicted every fact of Jewish history, and almost every page of Scripture. If Jewish worship had been a yoke, could the prophet Isaias have promised: 'You shall have a song, as in the night of the sanctified solemnity, and joy of heart, as when one goeth with a pipe, to come into the mountain of the Lord, to the mighty One of Israel'? (Isa. xxx. 29); or could David have exclaimed: 'How lovely are Thy tabernacles, O Lord of hosts! My soul longeth and fainteth for the courts of the Lord'? (Ps. lxxxiii.) Who that reads of the joy with which David celebrated, in triumphal procession and with all the pomp of Ritualism, the bringing of the Ark to Zion, will maintain that St. Peter called such ceremonies a yoke that his fathers could not bear? Or who that reads of the joy of St. Peter himself, when he cried out upon the Mount of Transfiguration, 'Rabbi, it is good for us to be here,' will believe for a moment that St. Peter looked upon splendour as a hindrance and a burden to devotion?

Or again, is it not evident beyond all contradiction, that when our Divine Redeemer, with so much emphasis, washed

His disciples' feet, or when, with minute and mystic ceremonies, He opened the ears and loosened the tongue of the deaf-mute, this ceremonial neither burdened His own Divine Heart, nor was a clog to the devotion of His disciples? Yet, if we look in Scripture for a parallel to the rites of the Catholic Church, we shall find it in such portions of the life of our Blessed Lord, or in such circumstances of the Old Testament, as I have just referred to; not in the disciplinary and ceremonial laws which St. Peter condemned.

We do indeed read of one to whom Ritualism was a yoke. The haughty Michol derided the religious pomp of her husband. In a spirit identical with that of some of our modern revilers, she looked on David's dancing before the Ark as 'antics,' and called him boldly a 'buffoon' (2 Kings vi.). But God was so far from being pleased with her thoughts and language, that it is written of her: 'Therefore Michol, the daughter of Saul, had no child to the day of her death.' Those who have inherited Michol's spirit seem also to have inherited her punishment. They have neither had the gift of fruitfulness to convert the heathen, nor power to attract the multitudes of their own land.[5]

It is evident, then, that it is not enough to prove that Ritualism is burdensome to certain minds; the inquiry must be, whether it is an impediment to the spirit of prayer, to the Spirit of God, or whether it is only obnoxious to pride and sloth, and all that is called in Scripture 'flesh and blood.' Modern writers are accustomed to despise the ancients for their *à priori* reasonings. It is the boast of modern science that it progresses by induction. Yet this method of reasoning is seldom applied by Protestants to their controversies against the Catholic Church. There is the experience now of many centuries and of many countries, that might be consulted in order to test the truth of theories. Let men of good-will search out this question for themselves from the annals of Catholic nations. They will find those annals to prove that great exactness in the detail of God's worship has no tendency to burden the soul or impede its flight to God; on the con-

---

[5] 'Bonus ludus quo Michol irascitur et Deus delectatur' (St. Bernard, Ep. 87).

trary, that the holy priests, whose piety at Mass has melted the soul into tears of tenderness or raised it into ecstatic raptures, have been remarkable for their minute observance of the very slightest rubrics; and that only those ministers of God who are unworthy of the name,—those whose faith has grown dull, whose lives are sensual and worldly,—those only find the ceremonial of the Church an intolerable yoke that they are anxious to throw off.

2. The second objection brought by the Anglican Reformers was that much of the symbolism of the Catholic Church is so obscure that it requires quite a technical education to find out its meaning.

Let me take note of this objection before I reply to it; for it contains a peremptory refutation of another objection more common, though less specious. It is commonly asserted that the worship of the Catholic Church is theatrical. If by this it was merely meant that it has a scenic or representative character, I would willingly admit the word. But when it is meant that the Church uses a display intended to attract and captivate the idle and curious gaze, the word is singularly inappropriate. The truth is, that the idle and curious gazers are always offended by her ceremonies, because they cannot comprehend them, and they have little charm for the mere eyes and ears. So many ceremonies have a spiritual and hidden meaning, so many prayers contain deep and mystic allusions, which can only be perceived and understood by those who are instructed and attentive. The ceremonies of Holy Week, for example, possess little attraction to the curious Protestant or the worldly Catholic; but they are full of inexhaustible charm to the devout worshipper, who has taken pains to ascertain their meaning and meditate attentively on the events they recall and the allusions they contain.

Yet, if some of the Church's rites are obscure, it is not after the fashion of certain 'initiations,' the obscurity of which is their only value; nor are they like Egyptian hieroglyphics, whose secret was known only to the sacerdotal race; nor are they rites like those, the pattern of which was shown to Moses on the Mount, intended to conceal rather than explain truths, for the utterance of which the time was not yet come. They are like the parables of Jesus Christ, by the very texture of the veil provoking a holy curiosity to look beneath it; they are the mirror in which we see now enigmatically what as yet we cannot gaze on face to face.

It is quite true that the stranger to our faith, who comes amongst us to pry, perchance to mock, will go away filled with scorn, for our ceremonies are a cloud of darkness to the Egyptians, while they are a light by night to the Israelites. But it is in great measure to the emblematic and profound nature of the Church's rites that is due the singular fact that, while to witness them but once is tedious to the incredulous or the worldly, their constant recurrence never wearies the devout. Each year, as the same festivals revolve, those who have eyes to see and ears to hear discover new depths, new beauties, new harmonies, new lights, new joys and consolations. Is it not right it should be so? Is there to be no reward for the diligence, the attention, and the perseverance of the devout? Or are we to be blamed because some rites are calculated to impress the senses, and so to enlighten the minds of the ignorant and arouse the careless from their torpor, and then censured anew because there are rites which suit only the learned and the spiritual? Must not the Church care for all her children? Taught by the same Holy Spirit who inspired the Scriptures, she has composed her Ritual on the same plan. 'In Holy Scripture,' says St. Augustine, 'there are many things plain, by which God feeds the soul even of the simple. There are other things obscure. The very obscurity of these provokes curiosity and prevents satiety: there is a pleasant labour in seeking the hidden truth, and when it is discovered it is enjoyed in proportion to the labour of its acquisition. And thus a novelty is given even to what was old, by the newness of the form that envelops it. Quid est hoc, rogamus vos, fratres, unde dulciora quo obscuriora? Conficit nobis potionem ad amorem suum quibusdam miris modis.'[6]

And on what plan but this was God's own Ritual composed? Look again to Calvary. The darkness, the earthquake, the

[6] St. August., Enar. in Ps. 138.

loud voice, were signs which even the simplest could understand; and they struck their breasts with compunction for the crime, and they felt there was a mystery, though they knew not well its nature. But there were other words and signs the people could not read. Why was the veil of the Temple rent? Why were the graves opened? Why was no bone broken? Why did blood and water flow from the pierced side? What was the meaning of the agonising cry, 'My God, My God, why hast Thou forsaken Me?' Why were those words quoted from a psalm? What relation had that psalm to Him who used it? Why did He speak these words in the Hebrew tongue? These are questions which the people could not have answered. Perhaps Mary alone, of all the witnesses, knew the full meaning of all the circumstances of the Passion. But they are mysteries which invite us to reflection; and he who seeks gains more profit from his search than if all things had been laid bare to him at first.

SECTION V. ON THE USE OF DEAD LANGUAGES.

IN treating of the charge of obscurity made against Catholic Ritual, I ought perhaps to notice the use of dead languages, and the objections so often derived against it from St. Paul's regulations concerning the gift of tongues (1 Cor. xiv.). There are few passages of Scripture more difficult to understand thoroughly; yet when the history and the theory of Catholic usage are known it will be apparent that it falls under no apostolic censure.

I. *Discipline past and present.*

Several languages are in actual use in Catholic Liturgy; in the East, principally Greek and Chaldaic; Latin universally in the West. No intrinsic sacredness is attributed to a language.

Most, if not all, of these languages have ceased to be vernacular in the countries where they are used; but they were living languages when first employed.

It cannot be argued from this that what many authors say about the advantage of a dead language in concealing sacred mysteries from the profane and ignorant, according to our Lord's words, 'Cast not your pearls before swine,' is an innovation on primitive discipline; since, while the vernacular was used, the *Discipline of the Secret* prevailed, by which only the well-initiated were admitted to the celebration of the Holy Sacrifice.

It is acknowledged that this is a matter of discipline which may vary with circumstances. Thus Pope John VIII. (A.D. 880), at the prayer of St. Methodius, granted the use of the vernacular in Holy Mass to the newly-converted Sclavonians. One reason for this concession was, that it was difficult to find priests of that nation who possessed a sufficient acquaintance with Latin. Hence, two centuries later, when circumstances were changed, St. Gregory VII. recalled the permission.

When the question of language was brought before the Council of Trent, it was decided that it was not expedient to grant permission to celebrate everywhere in the vernacular tongue.

That there is no contradiction whatever between these decrees, but only a variation of discipline in accordance with circumstances, may be seen by comparing them.

John VIII. wrote to Count Swentopulch, Prince of the Moravians, as follows: 'The authority of Scripture teaches us to praise God, not only in the three tongues' (in Hebrew, Greek, and Latin), 'but in every language: "O praise the Lord, all ye nations; praise Him, all ye peoples" (Ps.). The Apostles, filled with the Holy Ghost, published in every tongue the wonders of God; and St. Paul, that heavenly trumpet, teaches us this, when he says "that every tongue should confess that the Lord Jesus Christ is in the glory of God the Father" (Phil. ii.). The same Apostle speaks fully and clearly on the subject in the first Epistle to the Corinthians, where he teaches us to edify the Church by the use of different languages. Assuredly there is nothing contrary to the principles of our holy faith to sing Mass in the Sclavonian tongue, to read the Gospel in it, and the lessons of the Old and New Testaments, if well translated and explained, or to sing the other parts of the Divine Office.'

This was written in the ninth century. I subjoin the decree of the Council of Trent in the sixteenth :

'Although the Mass contains great instruction for the faithful people, nevertheless it has not seemed expedient to the Fathers that it should be everywhere (*passim*) celebrated in the vulgar tongue. Wherefore the ancient usage of each Church, and the rite approved of by the Holy Roman Church, the mother and mistress of all Churches, being in each place retained; that the sheep of Christ may not suffer hunger, nor the little ones ask for bread and there be none to break it unto them, the Holy Synod charges pastors and all who have the cure of souls, that they frequently, during the celebration of Mass, expound, either by themselves or others, some portion of those things which are read at Mass, and that, amongst the rest, they explain some mystery of this most holy Sacrifice, especially on the Lord's days and festivals' (session 22, ch. viii.).

That my reader may understand the reasons on which this discipline of the Church is based, and may be able to judge whether or not it is in harmony with the doctrine of St. Paul, it will be necessary that he should first have a true conception of the Catholic theory of worship, and next that he should take an historical and philosophical view of the nature and variations of human speech.

II. *Catholic theory of worship and of prayer*.

The main difficulty experienced by Protestants in witnessing Catholic worship arises from their not understanding the difference between a common *act* and a common *prayer*. The acts of the Church, such as processions, expositions of the Blessed Sacrament, the administration of Sacraments, and above all the holy Sacrifice of the Mass, are indeed always accompanied by prayer, and generally by prayers of priest and people, though not necessarily by united or common prayer. In any case, the act must be distinguished from the prayers.

A Protestant may easily understand what is meant by this distinction by aid of a few illustrations :

Suppose a ship, filled with a mixed crew of French, Spanish, and Portuguese, is being wrecked on the coast of England. A crowd is assembled on the cliff, watching with intense earnestness the efforts being made by the captain and crew on the one hand, and by lifeboats from the coast on the other, to save the lives of the passengers. A great *act* is being performed, in which all are taking part, some as immediate actors, others as eager assistants. We may suppose this act carried out in the midst of united prayers. English, French, Spanish, Portuguese, each in their own tongues, and many without spoken words at all, are sending up petitions to Almighty God for the safety of the passengers. It is a common act at which they assist; it is accompanied by the prayers of all; but they are not *common* prayers, in the sense of all joining either vocally or mentally in the same form of words.

When the priest Zacharias had gone into the temple of the Lord to offer incense, and 'all the multitude of the people was praying without' (Luke i. 9), there was a common act performed by priest and people—by the priest as actor, by the people as assistants—and the act was accompanied by united prayers. But it mattered not to the people what language was spoken by the priest or what sacred formulas were used. Their intentions were joined with his. Their individual and varied petitions were one great Amen said to his sacerdotal invocations; and all ascended together in a sweet-smelling cloud of incense to heaven.

Or to come still nearer to the reality of Catholic worship, let the reader represent to himself the great act of Calvary. Our Lord Jesus Christ is Priest and Victim. He accompanies His oblation of Himself with mysterious and most sacred prayer. Two of His seven words are from the Psalms; and it has therefore been conjectured that He continued to recite secretly the psalm, after giving us the clue to it, by pronouncing aloud the words, 'Eloi, Eloi, lamma sabacthani?'—'My God, My God, why hast Thou forsaken Me?' Or again, 'Father, into Thy hands I commend My spirit.' There were many assistants at that act, and among those who assisted piously—the Blessed Mother of Jesus, the Apostle St. John, the holy women, the centurion, the multitude 'who returned striking their breasts'—there was a certain unity in variety, not a uniform prayer, yet a great act of harmonious worship.

There are, then, prayers used in Catholic churches in which the whole congregation joins, such as the singing of hymns, the recitation of the Rosary, performing the Stations of the Way of the Cross, and especially the chanting of Vespers or Complin. Such prayers are either recited in the vernacular, or, when Latin is used, they require some little education in those who take a direct and vocal part in them. But the great act of Catholic worship is the Holy Mass, or the unbloody Sacrifice of the Body and Blood of Jesus Christ. 'One alone stands forth and makes the awful offering; the rest kneel around, and join their intentions and devotions with his; but even were there not a solitary worshipper present, the sacrifice both for the living and dead would be efficacious and complete. To join in this act of sacrifice, and to participate in its effects, it is not necessary to follow the priest or to use the words he uses. Every Catholic knows what the priest is doing, though he may not know or understand what he is saying, and is consequently able to follow with his devotions every portion of the Holy Sacrifice. Hence a wonderful union of sacrificial, of congregational, and of individual devotion. The prayers of the priest are not substituted for those of the people. No one desires to force his brother against his will. It is the most marvellous union of liberty and law which this earth can show. The beggar with his beads, the child with her pictures, the gentleman with his Missal, the maiden meditating on each mystery of the Passion, or adoring her God in silent love too deep for words, and the grateful communicant, have but one intent, one meaning, and one heart, as they have one action, one object, before their mental vision. They bow themselves to the dust as sinners; they pray to be heard for Christ's sake; they joyfully accept His words as the words of God; they offer the bread and wine; they unite themselves with the celebrant in the Sacrifice of the Body and Blood of Christ, which he as their priest offers for them; they communicate spiritually; they give thanks for the ineffable gift which God has given them. Their words differ, their thoughts vary; but their hearts are united and their will is one. Therefore is their offering pure and acceptable in the sight of Him who knows their secret souls, and who accepts a man, not for the multitude or the fewness of his sayings, for his book or for his beads, but for the intention with which he has, according to his sphere and capacities, fulfilled His sacred will, through the merits of the Adorable Victim who is offered for him.'[7]

It will be seen from this that, supposing the existence of cogent reasons for the use of a dead language, there would be no such difficulties in its employment in the Holy Sacrifice and Divine Office of the Catholic Church as there would be in what Protestants understand by public and congregational service.

III. *Reasons for using dead languages.*

I have therefore now to state how dead languages came to be used in Catholic Liturgy, and why they are retained.

The Church, then, is Catholic, both in time and place. Unity and universality are her attributes. Now in nothing, perhaps, is there more variety and mutability than in language. The Church therefore, from the outset, had to deal with a very perplexing problem: how to reduce the varieties of human speech in religious matters to a minimum.

Divine Providence seems to have prepared the way for her to solve this problem in the West. She found Latin the dominant language of Europe. It was a majestic tongue suited to her needs. It was the language of civilisation. Before the Church had been four centuries in existence, this language, besides the treasures of heathen literature, contained some of the most glorious achievements of Christian thought. Almost the same may be said of Greek in the East. The Church was therefore led by the Divine Spirit who assists her to cherish these two languages. She thus gained three great advantages. First, she secured the immense treasures contained in Greek and Roman literature, both heathen and Christian; secondly, she formed a bond of union between many nations; and thirdly, as these languages ceased to be vernacular they became fixed, and she thus acquired a language which would share and

---

[7] The above quotation is abridged from No. 61 of the *Clifton Tracts*. In this valuable collection there are several tracts which explain simply, truthfully, and fully the theory and practice of Catholic devotion and ceremonial. They are published by Messrs. Burns & Oates.

express her own immutability amidst the incessant changes of human affairs.

But the knowledge and use of Latin among priests and people was mainly due to its being continued in the sacred offices and rites of her Liturgy.

It is almost impossible to over-estimate the advantages which have accrued to the Church from this discipline. To mention only some:

1. By the knowledge of one or at most two languages, Latin and Greek, we have immediate access to the accumulated treasures of eighteen centuries of Christianity. The use of Latin throughout Western Christendom makes accessible to us, not only ancient liturgies, but canon and civil law, and the writings of all the great men of every country and every age, which, had they been written in the spoken dialects, would be now as hidden from the majority of men as Anglo-Saxon, Norse, or Sanscrit literature.

2. We have a medium of communication between all parts of the Church, in correspondence, in travelling, in the assembling of general councils, &c.

3. The Sacred Liturgy is secured from the errors which would certainly creep in with frequent changes. If it is remembered that the Ritual and Liturgy are among the principal channels of tradition, and the most practical teachers of divine things, it will be seen that this benefit alone is of vast importance.

4. The very labour and expense of constant translations and re-translations of the liturgical books into the hundreds of dialects of the human race, changing age after age, are formidable considerations. Protestants may indeed point to the achievements of Bible societies. But they must remember that cheap printing is a modern invention; nor have all nations the disposal of British wealth.

5. Even were it possible to give each nation and tribe and dialect a vernacular ritual at the present day, many would be losers by it. Not only ecclesiastics, but educated laymen, and to some extent the uneducated also, feel themselves at home wherever they travel; and can take part, wherever they may be,

in the divine offices which use has made familiar to them. All this would be prevented by a multiplicity of liturgies.

Protestants, whose religions are national, and have but one, two, or at most three centuries of existence, and have never known the want of a printing-press, are slow to perceive the necessity or advantages of a dead and universal language. But enough has been said on this point for those who seek the truth.

IV. *Catholic discipline compared with the doctrine of St. Paul.*

I must now beg my reader to go carefully through the whole of the fourteenth chapter of the first Epistle to the Corinthians. It will not be necessary, so far as the present controversy is concerned, to enter into the difficult question of the nature or purpose of the gift of tongues. One thing is evident, that in the above passage the gift of tongues is not a supernatural means of communication between two persons who otherwise would not understand each other, but rather the very contrary. Of two persons who speak the same language one receives the gift of tongues, by which he becomes unintelligible to his companion without the aid of an interpreter.

Now, if it is sought to establish any parallel between the state of things in Corinth and that among Catholics, to the prejudice of the latter, then Protestants who blame the use of Latin amongst Catholics as a human abuse must contend that strange tongues in Corinth were a human abuse also. But, far from this, they were a Divine operation, a great gift of God. It was God Himself who taught men to utter these strange languages, 'not in the work of teaching, but in that of praise and adoration, and who made them speak mysteries, pray, bless, and give thanks in unintelligible accents.'[8]

If any conclusion can be drawn from this fact as regards ourselves, it would rather be that He who inspired such prayers formerly for wise reasons may also have directed the Catholic Church for wise reasons to employ a dead language in her public Liturgy.

But still, it will be said, St. Paul blames something. No doubt. But it is not the use of tongues, for he says, 'forbid

---

[8] See article on 'Tongues' in Smith's *Dictionary of the Bible*.

not to speak with tongues' (v. 39). What he blames is the disorderly and indiscreet exercise of their gift; and if we inquire what these disorders were, we shall find that they have no parallel in Catholic discipline.

1. First, then, he seems to complain that 'every one had his psalm, his doctrine, his revelation, his tongue, his interpretation' (v. 26); that every one wished to display his own gift, without considering how far it would edify the assembly; that thus, either there was a long succession of persons uttering rapturous prayers unintelligible to the rest, or that several spoke at once, so that ignorant or unbelieving persons coming in would think them an assembly of madmen (v. 23). Most certainly no parallel to this could be found in any Catholic assembly, though perhaps it would be easily found among some Protestant sects.

2. The Apostle wishes that 'everything be done decently and according to order' (v. 40). He decides therefore, not indeed to prohibit the use of tongues, but that only two, or at most three, should speak, and that there should be an interpreter (v. 27). Now, in the Catholic Church there is no confusion; all is regulated, *and the interpreter is there.*

Let me explain. I have shown already that it was by considerations of general good, *i.e.* of decency and order, that the use of a dead tongue was retained in the Church.

It must be remembered that the prayers of the Church are not the extemporaneous effusion of an individual (as was the case in Corinth), requiring an interpreter to stand up immediately, in order to render them intelligible to the bystanders. Our prayers have been in use for many centuries throughout the world. They are uttered in a language which, though not the vulgar tongue of modern nations, is the best-known language of the world. It thus happens that the Liturgy is easily and widely interpreted. Use has made it, to a certain extent, familiar even to the unlearned. Manuals of translation are in the hands of those who can read. The priests are charged by the Council of Trent to explain the prayers and mysteries of the Mass to the people from time to time. Most assuredly this does not make everything familiar or intelligible to all.

But neither would the use of the vernacular make intelligible what is essentially difficult and mysterious. Such obscurities have a divine purpose.

3. The degree of 'understanding,' therefore, which men attain in prayer (see v. 15) will, of course, vary with their capacities, gifts, opportunities, and diligence in the use of them. Certainly, the use of a dead language, as it obtains in the Catholic Church, does not prevent men from this more excellent kind of prayer. And again, nothing could be more admirably contrived than the whole system of Catholic worship, to enable him 'who holds the place of the unlearned to say, Amen' (v. 16). How he could do this to the long extemporaneous prayer of a Protestant minister, much of which he could not follow or understand, I will not decide. But he knows that every word that the Catholic priest utters is the composition of God Himself, or of saints and doctors, and has the approval of the holy Church. He can give therefore the most hearty assent to all her prayers, blessings, and thanksgiving.

4. I would observe, lastly, that St. Paul considers that these matters of public worship must be regulated by lawful authority, and will not allow men who think themselves to be spiritual to rebel against his decision (v. 37).

Catholics know with certainty that the judgment of their Church cannot contradict that of the Apostle. As I have now shown that Protestants have attempted in vain to set one against the other, I am entitled to ask them to consider seriously whether they run no risk in allowing their private and discordant judgments to condemn the unanimous voice of Christendom.

CHAPTER V.

EFFICIENT RITUAL NOT MAGICAL.

THE Catholic Church teaches, not merely that holy impressions may be conveyed to the soul through the senses, and that holy sentiments find by means of the senses convenient expression; but also that, by a positive institution of Jesus Christ, certain rites have been selected as instruments to convey to the soul graces with which they have no natural proportion. The former class of ceremonies the Church may institute at will, or the worshipper adopts them at his own choice; but it is evident that the latter cannot be of human institution.

Bossuet, in his Exposition of the Catholic Faith, thus writes: 'The Sacraments of the new covenant are not merely sacred signs which represent grace, nor seals which confirm it, but instruments of the Holy Ghost serving to apply that grace to our souls, and conferring it upon us in virtue of the words that are pronounced, and of the action that is exteriorly performed, provided we ourselves, by our bad disposition, put no obstacle in the way.

'We acknowledge seven sacred ceremonies or signs, established by Jesus Christ, as the ordinary means of sanctifying and perfecting the new man. Their divine institution appears in the Holy Scripture, either by the express words of Jesus Christ who established them, or by the grace which, according to the same Scripture, is annexed to them, and which necessarily points out an ordinance of God.

'When God annexes such a grace to outward signs, *which of their own nature bear no sort of proportion to so wonderful an effect*, He clearly shows us, that besides all we can possibly do within ourselves, by our good disposition, towards our sanctification, there must still be a special operation of the Holy Ghost, and a particular application of the merits of our Saviour, which are exhibited to us by the Sacraments; so that this doctrine cannot be rejected, without doing an injury to the merits of Jesus Christ, and to the working of divine power in our regeneration.'

It is curious that the very consideration by which Bossuet thought to recommend the Sacraments to the Puritans of his day—that *they bear no natural proportion to their effects*—is the main ground of opposition urged by the Rationalistic Protestants of our own days.

One of the critics of the first edition of this Essay wrote as follows: 'We quite agree with the author that the New Testament does not discountenance symbolism and even splendour in worship; . . . but Ritualism, as the expression or illustration of the supernatural character and efficacy of certain rites which are believed to be of divine institution and essential to salvation, is quite a different thing. . . With Ritualism, regarded as mere symbolism, the æsthetics of worship, we can heartily agree. There is a marked reaction in our own churches against the tame, cold, uncongregational service in which our fathers delighted—if so warm a word can be applied to something so frigid as the old Dissenting worship—and we now give free expression to the natural love of the beautiful in the Church, as well as in the home. . . . But if Ritualism is regarded as the expression of sacramental doctrines, if it is connected with priestly pretensions, against which we rebel with all our mind, and soul, and strength—then we repudiate and abhor the whole system as an imposture and mere mechanical jugglery.'

If by 'priestly pretensions' this author means the Catholic belief that Jesus Christ is the Great High Priest, who by His death has reconciled us with God and God with us, and that He has conferred on certain men a share in His priesthood, and given to them powers in relation to sacrifice and sacraments, for the good of their fellow-men, which He has not given to all alike—then he 'rebels with all his strength' against a most certain and most merciful Providence of God.

I have already said in the Introduction that I do not intend to dwell at any great length on this view of the subject, in spite of its importance, because the institution of the Sacraments has been treated frequently and exhaustively in books of easy access. I will, however, propose some few considerations, rather on the general principles involved in Sacraments than on the specific details of their nature and their number. For the same reason I shall omit the great subject of Christian Sacrifice.

1. The language of the New Testament seems studiously chosen to connect together exterior acts with interior and divine operations. I give a few specimens in the Protestant version : 'Except a man be born of water and of the Spirit, he cannot enter into the kingdom of God' (John iii. 5) ; 'Repent, and be baptised . . . for the remission of sins, and ye shall receive the gift of the Holy Ghost' (Acts iii. 38) ; 'Arise, and be baptised, and wash away thy sins, calling on the name of the Lord' (Acts xxii. 16) ; 'According to His mercy He saved us, by the washing of regeneration and renewing of the Holy Ghost' (Pet. iii. 5) ; 'He breathed on them, and saith unto them : Receive ye the Holy Ghost' (John xx. 22) ; 'Whosesoever sins ye remit, they are remitted unto them' (John xx. 23) ; 'They laid their hands upon them, and they received the Holy Ghost' (Acts viii. 17) ; and the like.

Now it cannot seriously be doubted that by all these forms of speech the relation of cause and effect is apparently expressed ; and that this would never have been called in question, were it not for the disproportion between such external acts as washing, breathing, anointing, imposing hands, and such interior results as the remission of sins, regeneration, and gift of the Holy Ghost. But this disproportion is removed, and therefore with it all cause for explaining away the natural force of words, when the external acts are regarded as of divine institution, and therefore as instruments employed by God. Strange indeed that any one should believe in the Incarnation, and therefore that the whole life of the Son of God on earth was one great Sacrament, so to say, and should still find difficulty in allowing the sacramental principle a place in the Christian religion !

2. But the objector contends that such a principle must be unchristian, for it implies 'a system of mechanical jugglery,' it is a 'system of magical influences borrowed from paganism.'

Let the reader who is moved by this objection read carefully the eighth chapter of the Acts of the Apostles. We have there the history of one of these pagan magicians, Simon by name. He had long 'bewitched the people of Samaria with his sorceries.' What is sorcery or magic? It is the production of wonderful effects by inadequate external means of an unholy nature. An occult power works, or is supposed to work, with the external sign. Simon, at the sight of Philip the deacon's miracles, so far superior to his own sorceries or jugglery, believes and is baptised. He remains, however, still in heart a magician; and his wonder is excited, not by the depth and holiness of Philip's teaching, or the sanctity of his life, but 'by the miracles and signs which were done.' Then come St. Peter and St. John the Apostles to complete St. Philip's work. Simon watches them with still greater curiosity, and he discovers that in their case the extraordinary spiritual effects follow a certain law, and are attached to definite forms. 'He saw that *through* laying-on of the Apostles' hands the Holy Ghost was given.' It seems also that he learnt that the Apostles could communicate their powers, whereas Philip the Deacon could not do so; for he made an offer to the Apostles which he had not made to Philip. 'He offered them money, saying: Give me also this power, that on whomsoever I lay hands he may receive the Holy Ghost.'

What, then, induced Simon to make this offer? It was this, that, just as certain persons at the present day detect a superficial resemblance between the Sacraments of the Catholic Church and magical incantations; so also Simon detected a superficial resemblance between the operations of the Apostles, and his own former practices or attempts. Dazzled by the miraculous gifts which accompanied the presence of the Holy Ghost, and careless of the nature of that Divine Spirit, he looked on the imposing of hands as *a superior sort of magic.* He notices that the power to produce such results is not attached to the external act only, but to the act as performed by certain persons. Though baptised, he has it not, and he covets it.

Now let us examine the Apostle's answer. St. Peter is very indignant. Like the writer whom I have been quoting, he 'rebels with all his mind and soul and strength' against something. But he is moved to indignation by a very different cause. He does not say to Simon, 'You know nothing of the Christian religion if you think that grace can be annexed to the laying-on of hands. This would be a mere repetition of your own mechanical juggleries and magical rites.' He does not say, 'You are utterly wrong in thinking that the power of imposing hands with spiritual effects is restricted to certain persons. These are "priestly pretensions" which we repudiate.' No. St. Peter says, 'Thy money perish with thee, because thou hast thought that the gift of God may be purchased with money.' Simon's error and wickedness consisted in fancying that the divine sacraments and the power of administering them could be matters of sale and purchase, to be exercised for the profit or ambition of the administrator rather than for the benefit of the receiver.

This sin of Simon has given a name to a species of sacrilege recognised both by Protestants and Catholics; yet among Protestants the sin of Simon *the magician* could scarcely be reproduced as among Catholics. The temptation would be wanting. The sacramental powers which Simon coveted are not recognised.

3. It may be useful, therefore, to point out one of these supposed parallels in a matter not foreign to our present subject. The Catholic use of relics has often been compared to the pagan use of talismans. The study of this comparison may help to elucidate the points of likeness and of divergence between sacraments and magical formulas.

Again I have recourse to the Acts of the Apostles, that book so full of instruction on the principles of Christianity and of God's dealings with man. The nineteenth chapter gives the history of St. Paul's stay at Ephesus, the great centre not only of all the commerce, but of all the religions, of Europe and of Asia. The goddess Diana, there worshipped in her magnificent temple, was not the chaste and savage huntress venerated under that name in Greece, but a hideous idol, representing the goddess of impurity, or the forces of nature personified. In fact, the great object of worship throughout the East was the Universe: *i e.* matter independent of spirit, without intelligence, yet all-powerful.[1]

The superstitious pagans imagined that there were some occult arts, by the knowledge of which they could master the secret powers of the universe, and make them minister to their lusts. Mysterious symbols, called 'Ephesian letters,' were engraved on the crown, the girdle, and the feet of the goddess. These letters, when pronounced, were regarded as a charm, and were directed to be used, especially by those who were in the power of evil spirits. When written, they were carried about as amulets. The study of these symbols was an elaborate science, and books both numerous and costly were compiled by its professors.[2] We can form some estimate of the fearful extent to which superstition and magic prevailed in Ephesus, from the single fact recorded in the Acts of the Apostles, that when the converted heathens burnt their books of magic, the cost was estimated at fifty thousand pieces of silver (Acts xix. 19), or two thousand pounds of English money.

Now, I would ask any candid Protestant to answer this question: If he had read, in a book of Catholic missions, that some savage tribe, addicted to charms and witchcraft, had been taught by the missionaries to put trust in blessed beads, medals, scapulars, or relics, would he not at once exclaim, that the priests, instead of eradicating superstition, encouraged it; that they left the instinct in full force, and only gave it another object to feed upon? This, I think, is what would be said of the conduct of Catholic missionaries; but what explanation would such an accuser be able to give of the conduct of St. Paul? He finds the people of Ephesus addicted to the grossest superstition. They believe in the occult forces of nature; they seek to obtain cures, and to deliver themselves from malicious spirits by means of amulets and charms. Does the Apostle

[1] Count Franz de Champagny, *Les Cæsars*, tom. ii. liv. ii. ch. 2.
[2] Conybeare and Howson, *Life and Epistles of St. Paul*, ch. xiv.

teach them that no material object can be of use in seeking help from God? that the worship of God, in spirit and in truth, requires that they should banish from their minds the idea that mysterious virtue can reside in anything visible or tangible? Certainly this was not St. Paul's teaching at Ephesus. He bids his disciples destroy their shrines, their charms and amulets, and burn their books of magic. But he tells them that there is a Name more powerful than 'Ephesian letters'—the mighty name of Jesus; and he tells them that that Name is virtually invoked whenever recourse is had, with true faith, to what has been consecrated to His service. So, instead of amulets and charms, the Ephesians use the 'handkerchiefs and aprons' of St. Paul; and the God who seeks for worshippers who will adore Him in spirit and in truth (John iv. 23) approves of their conduct, and grants to them the very benefits they had vainly sought from their heathen practices—the cure of diseases, and the deliverance from evil spirits (Acts xix. 11, 12).

If, then, I am told that the use of relics instead of charms is but the substitution of one object of superstition for another, I reply, that the invocation of the name of Jesus for that of Diana, was but the substitution of one object of worship for another. Yet the difference is not slight, but total and absolute; and so also with the substitution of the relics of saints for the talismans of heathen worship. It is the whole difference of the worship of God from the worship of the devil.

When wicked people seek extraordinary benefits from some hidden and mysterious power without change of their unholy lives, that mysterious power they invoke can be no other than the evil spirit. But when they believe in an Almighty God, Creator of all things, the Sovereign Master of His creatures; when they seek to propitiate His mercy by a holy life, and ask what may conduce to their salvation; when they invoke His power and mercy by the use of what is consecrated to His service, or belongs to His faithful servants; then, though what they use is a material thing, yet their use of it is altogether spiritual, and free from the slightest taint of superstition.

One would have thought that it would be impossible to read this history without seeing the absolute identity between the Catholic veneration of relics and that of these Apostolic Christians. Yet I find Milton thus writing on the subject of relics :

'A pretty scantling of Constantine's knowledge may be taken .. by the excessive devotion, that I may not say superstition, both of him and his mother Helena, to find out the cross on which Christ suffered, that had long lain under the rubbish of old ruins. . . . Part of the cross, in which he thought such virtue to reside as would prove a kind of palladium to save the city wherever it remained, he caused to be laid up in a pillar of porphyry by his statue. How he or his teachers could trifle thus with half an eye open upon St. Paul's principles, I know not how to imagine.'[3] Yet in what did the devotion of St. Helen and of Constantine differ from that of the Ephesian Christians? And who knew the principles of St. Paul better than they? 'He had not spared to declare unto them all the counsel of God. He had kept back nothing that was profitable to them' (Acts xx. 27, 20). And their love for his doctrine and devotion to his person were testified by the recourse they had to the objects he had used.

The Christians of Ephesus venerated St. Paul, not in blind stupidity, as they had venerated Diana, but as the servant of the One, Invisible, and Sovereign God. They believed his body to be holy because it was the temple of the Holy Ghost, and the instrument of heroic virtue. They believed his garments to be holy, because they belonged to that sacred body, and therefore to that faithful soul, and therefore to the God whom Paul served. It is even probable that there is a mystery in the selection of the miraculous garments. St. Paul would not use his apostolic right of being supported by his disciples. He laboured with his own hands at the trade of tent-maker, which he had learned in his youth. The 'handkerchiefs' were probably used in wiping the sweat of labour from his brow; and the 'aprons' in the occupation of his trade; and God, to glorify the humility of His servant, and to prevent these recent converts from despising a master who worked with his hands, and to teach them the holiness of labour, per-

[3] Milton, *Of Reform in England*.

formed 'more than common miracles, by these symbols and instruments of apostolic charity.'

This circumstance has been noticed by more than one Protestant commentator. It is strange that they did not perceive how the same principles would explain why the Catholic Church venerates the Cross of Jesus Christ, and why God has been pleased, through its means, to work so many miracles, as monuments of every age attest. If Christians venerated the handkerchief that imbibed the sweat of St. Paul's toil, how much more would they venerate the Cross that imbibed the Precious Blood of their Redemption?

The things above related are no doubt contrary to the Protestant theory of spirituality in worship and negation of sacramental influences; yet as instinct is often stronger than theory, it would be easy to gather a multitude of illustrations of the Catholic and apostolic principle from Protestant literature and history.

I restrict myself to one or two examples. I have quoted the words of Milton carping at Constantine for his veneration of the true Cross. Time brings its revenges. Among the sonnets of Leigh Hunt, another great scoffer at Catholic faith and practice, is one bearing this title:

ON A LOCK OF MILTON'S HAIR.

'It lies before me there, and my own breath
Stirs its thin outer threads, as though beside
The living head I stood in honour'd pride,
Talking of lovely things that conquer death.
Perhaps he press'd it once, or underneath
Ran his fine fingers, when he leant, blank-eyed,
And saw, in fancy, Adam and his bride
With their rich locks, or his own Delphic wreath,' &c.

Had Mr. Hunt or Milton seen a Catholic bending tenderly over a relic of the Son of God or of a patron saint, no doubt the first instinct would have been to deride the devotion, and the second to question the authenticity of the relic.

Another of our opponents, often quoted in the course of this work, is the Rev. Dr. Cumming, minister of a Scotch church in London. Of course he must throw his handful of dirt at the Catholic Church on the subject of relics. We read, therefore, as follows: 'The Romish Church must see Christ as with the senses. We are satisfied to see Him by faith. She is not satisfied unless she can touch the hem of His garment. We are content to believe in the unseen. She will only accept that which she can handle. Hence she must have the wood of the true Cross—the very robe that He wore, the holy coat —a visible altar,' &c.[4]

But the doctor seems to forget these boasted principles of Protestant spirituality when, farther on in the same book, he quotes with approbation a saying of Dr. Chalmers, that, after the Resurrection, 'instead of being transported to a state of dimness and mystery, so remote from human experience as to be beyond all comprehension, we shall for ever dwell in a place replenished with those sensible delights and sensible glories which, we doubt not, will be most profusely scattered over a new heaven and a new earth. But though a paradise of sense, it will not be a paradise of sensuality. It is not the entire substitution of spirit for matter, but it will be the entire substitution of holiness for sin. It is this which differences the Christian from the Mahometan paradise; not that sense and substance and splendid imagery are absent, but that all that is evil in principle or voluptuous in impurity will be utterly excluded from it.' Thus far Dr. Chalmers. After quoting this passage and developing at some length his own thoughts on the matter, Dr Cumming continues: 'In the absence of disproof, it seems to me far more beautiful—not less scriptural—that Calvary, Gethsemane, and Olivet should remain visible for ever, *as the shrines of grand recollections;* that the air which Jesus breathed should be purified, not annihilated,' &c.[5]

It would seem, then, that Dr. Cumming hoped to attain in heaven to those pious instincts which he blamed Catholics so severely for possessing already. They are so 'far more beautiful, and not less scriptural'!

So much, then, on this silly and blasphemous charge of magic. There are men who, in spiritual matters, seem to lose all discernment, and who confound together things the most

[4] *Voices of the Day*, p. 81.   [5] *Ibid*. pp. 139, 159.

contradictory, because of some mere external and accidental resemblance. Thus Lord Macaulay classes together the austerities of St. Francis Xavier and the diabolical penances of the Brahmins. Such men would see no difference between St. John Baptist, living in the desert with his garment of camel's hair and leathern girdle, and the demoniac, called Legion, who wore no clothes, and dwelt in sepulchres and in the desert. Such were the men who mocked at the Apostles as 'full of new wine' when they were overflowing with the gifts of the Holy Ghost.

CHAPTER VI.

THE REAL PRESENCE AS REGARDS RITUAL.

SECTION I. PROTESTANT VIEW OF THE REAL PRESENCE.

LORD MACAULAY, after praising Ranke for writing his history of the Popes 'in an admirable spirit, equally remote from levity and bigotry, serious and earnest, yet tolerant and impartial,' attempts an account of the Catholic Church, no doubt in the same 'admirable spirit.' He tells us that, for several reasons, 'he has ceased to wonder at any vagaries of superstition,' even among men of the highest intellects and acquirements; that 'in religion there is no constant progress;' that 'we have no security for the future against any theological error.' He brings his illustrations to a climax in these words: 'When we reflect that Sir Thomas More was ready to die for the doctrine of transubstantiation, we cannot but feel some doubt whether the doctrine of transubstantiation may not triumph over all opposition. More was a man of eminent talents. He had all the information on the subject that we have, or that, while the world lasts, any human being will have. . . . We are therefore unable to understand why what Sir Thomas More believed respecting transubstantiation may not be believed to the end of time by men equal in abilities and in honesty to Sir Thomas More. But Sir Thomas More is one of the choice specimens of human wisdom and virtue; and the doctrine of transubstantiation is a kind of proof charge. A faith which stands that test will stand any test.' In other words, according to Macaulay, the undoubted fact that the wisest and best of men have been ready to shed their blood for the truth of the Real Presence can only be explained by despairing altogether of the human race, and by admitting that in religion at least we are given over by God to error and uncertainty without remedy.

Yet Macaulay must have felt that his brilliant sentences were self-contradictory. For while he maintains that there is no preservative in talent, in science, in virtue, against any error, he himself feels certain that the belief in the Real Presence is an error, 'an absurdity,' so gross an absurdity as to be 'a kind of proof charge' against those who hold it, and to be a 'vagary of superstition.' What, then, has preserved him and his fellow Protestants from the delusion of those who share Sir Thomas More's faith? Not the grace of God. He lays no claim to it. Not superior science or virtue. He says expressly that no science or virtue can preserve men from any error in religion. Logically, therefore, a Macaulay was as likely to be mistaken, in thinking the Real Presence an absurdity, as a Sir Thomas More in thinking it a divinely revealed Truth. But though Macaulay could declare the human race doomed to endless and hopeless error in believing, he could not suspect the possibility of being in error himself in disbelieving.

Some years later, in writing his *History of England*, he attempted another solution of the phenomenon that so much perplexed him—that wise men have believed, and do and will believe, in the Real Presence. Formerly he had accounted for it by himself despairing of the powers of reason; now he explains it by asserting that it arises from this very despair, when united at least with a wish to believe something, a wish with which Macaulay certainly never betrays any sympathy. 'It is not strange,' he writes, 'that wise men, weary of investigation and longing to believe something, and yet seeing objections to everything, should submit themselves absolutely to teachers who, with firm and undoubting faith, lay claim to a supernatural commission. Thus we frequently see inquisitive and restless spirits take refuge from their own scepticism in the bosom of a Church which pretends to infallibility, and after questioning the existence of a Deity, *bring themselves to worship a wafer*.'[1] Here again Macaulay has no hesitation in selecting

[1] *History of England*, vol. iv. p. 28.

the Catholic faith and worship of the Blessed Sacrament as the lowest conceivable form of superstition. He thinks that men of intellect can hold it only in a passive, despairing, sceptical kind of manner, as a drowning man clutches a straw.

To any Catholic taught by experience, and I may say to any earnest and thoughtful Protestant, nothing can be more flimsy and unsatisfactory than these two theories. The former is self-contradictory; the latter contradicts the former, and is itself contradicted by facts. The men of great intellect who have been most celebrated for their zealous and devoted attachment to the doctrine of the Real Presence, whether they have been brought up in that faith or become converts to it, have been in no way characterised by a spirit of credulity or a spirit of scepticism. Any one who will candidly consult history will find that belief in the Real Presence, far from being a recoil from temptations to Atheism, springs from and results in a most vivid faith in the existence and providence of a *living* God. But in this matter both historians and divines seem to prefer theories and sneers to historical investigation.

English Catholics of the present day are somewhat in the predicament of St. Paul when discoursing before Festus and Agrippa. Festus, the cultivated Pagan, hearing of the mysteries of religion, and judging of them by his gross worldly sense, cries out, 'Paul, thou art mad.' 'I am not mad, most excellent Festus,' replies the Saint; 'but I speak words of truth and soberness;' and he appeals to the Jewish king, who ought to have taken a greater interest in questions of religion, and to have acquired more accurate information. 'The king knoweth of these things, to whom also I speak with confidence; . . . for neither was any of these things done in a corner' (Acts xxvi. 24-26). But Agrippa has no relish for this appeal, and only answers with a sneer.

If the apparition of Jesus Christ to St. Paul, and its effect upon his life, were ascertainable and measurable facts, much more so are the belief of Catholics in the Real Presence, and its effects on private and public life, and on the history of nations. These are not things done in a corner. If the mere politician or literary man can only hear of them with an exclamation of pity, we might expect a more candid and philosophical judgment from men whose life has been devoted to the study of religion. Unfortunately the time has not yet come when Englishmen will study as dispassionately the religion of their Catholic forefathers and of millions of their fellow-countrymen as they do the religions that they find in their most distant and insignificant possessions. Dr. Vaughan, for instance, would probably have been ashamed to betray gross ignorance of the doctrines and practices of Brahmins, Budhists, Mahometans, or Thugs; yet he seems almost to boast that he knows nothing of the religion of Catholics. 'It must be conceded,' he says, 'that Protestants generally do not profess to comprehend such language as is sometimes used by Catholics on the subject of the Real Presence. What is more, we are quite sure that the persons who use these strange forms of speech have not themselves learnt to attach any clear or steady ideas to them.'

A man must be utterly ignorant both of Catholic theology, Catholic books, and Catholic religious life, to venture on such an assertion. If he knew anything of the history of the Church, or had ever mixed with Catholics, he would know that the Real Presence, far from being some vague mystic dream of a few, is a doctrine most clearly defined, most popularly understood, of the most practical consequence. It is the very centre of the whole devotional, disciplinary, and ascetic system of Catholics. Probably there is no idea among those that can be called religious more 'clear and steady' in the minds of every class than this.[2]

That Dr. Vaughan's ideas on the subject are far from being clear, as he indeed confesses, is evident from his next words: 'Protestants,' he says, 'believe that our Lord, who may be said to be especially present in the Communion service, is as really present everywhere, and that union with Him, comprehending in a sense oneness with Him and growth in Him, is available to the devout in all places and at all times. Why the persons

[2] See the treatise of Monseigneur Gerbet called *Le Dogme générateur de la Piété Catholique*—The Fountain-Head of Catholic Piety. The author of the present Essay has, since the appearance of the first edition, illustrated from history what he here treats in theory. See *History of the Holy Eucharist in Great Britain*, in two vols. (Kegan Paul, Trench, & Co.)

who would restrict the presence of the Saviour, in the manner described, to a particular service, should be necessarily more pious than those who feel that He is accessible to them everywhere, is not explained. How the pretensions of priests may be served by such a doctrine, we can understand; but how Christian piety should be served by it is not so intelligible. But there are minds so mystical in their tendencies, and to which deep excitement of some sort is so indispensable, that almost any illusion which shall produce the coveted elevation is sure to be accepted and valued. In the Church of Rome there have always been religionists of this intense order.'

Dr. Vaughan ought to know that Catholics hold, certainly not less than Protestants, that union with Jesus Christ is 'available to the devout in all places and at all times.' He ought to know that no Catholic ever thought of restricting the presence of the Saviour to a particular service. What purpose can it possibly serve thus to misstate a doctrine? How can any one hope to confute principles that he is not willing or able to understand? 'Catholics, at least,' says Cardinal Newman, 'have a lively illustration and evidence of the absurdity of Protestant private judgment, as exercised on the Apostolic writings, in the visible fact of its absurdity as exercised on themselves. They, as their forefathers, the first Christians, are a living body; they too preach, dispute, catechise, converse with innumerable tongues, saying the same thing, as our adversaries confess, all over the earth. Well, then, you would think the obvious way was, if they would know what we really teach, to come and ask us, to talk with us, *to try to enter into our views*, and to attend to our teaching. Not at all; they do not dream of doing so: they take their 'texts,' they have got their cut-and-dried specimens from our divines, which the Protestant tradition hands down from generation to generation. . . . As they have their chips and fragments of St. Paul and St. John, so they have their chips and fragments of Suarez and Bellarmine, and out of the former they make to themselves their own Christian religion, and out of the latter our Antichristian superstition.'[3]

[3] *Lecture on the Present Position of Catholics.*

However, all are not such, unwilling to know the truth. There are some who, before they judge, would like to hear our explanations. It is for such I write, and I hope to make it *intelligible*, at least to them, how Christian piety is served by the doctrine of the Real Presence. Let it, however, be understood that it is quite beyond my present scope to treat of the Holy Eucharist either as a sacrifice or a sacrament, or to enter upon any theological proofs of the Real Presence. I have only to explain the place this Mystery holds in Catholic belief, and how it affects the character of our worship.

SECTION II. AN ARGUMENT FROM ANALOGY.

MARVELS often lose their strangeness by being multiplied. When exceptions grow into a series, we feel that they happen according to some higher though unknown law, and they give support and credibility to one another. Thus, when the angel announced to Mary her virginal maternity, he made known simultaneously that Elizabeth had conceived in her old age, and that it was now the sixth month with her who had been called barren; and this to show that no word shall be impossible with God. It was not intended that Mary should test the truth of one prodigy before believing the other; neither did she do so: she accepted both by faith. But it was easier for faith to grasp two miracles in harmony than one in isolation. If, then, the doctrine of the Real Presence stood in perfect isolation in the midst of all God's dealings with man, it might still be true, but it would task men's faith severely. It has, indeed, no parallel, any more than the virginal conception of Mary. But it has many harmonious and analogous facts, both in the New Testament and in the history of the Elder Dispensation.

Transubstantiation has two terms—bread and wine, and the Body and Blood of Jesus Christ. Those who believe in the multiplication of the loaves of bread related in the Gospel, and in the change of water into wine at Cana, ought not to be startled if bread and wine become the subject of a marvellous operation of divine power in the Holy Eucharist. Those who believe in the Body of Jesus Christ walking on the surface of the sea, transfigured on Thabor, passing through the sealed tomb and the closed doors, ought to find little *strangeness* in its Presence beneath the species of bread and wine. Those who accept as authentic history the long series of marvels related in the books of the Old Testament ought to be so prepared to accept the marvels of the Catholic Church that the absence of such marvels would be a far greater perplexity to them than their presence. I ask my reader's attention to one class of these marvels, by which the truth of the Real Presence and its influence on worship are now illustrated, and by which men's minds were prepared for this incomparable gift of God.

Scanty as are the records of man's abode in Paradise, yet from the Book of Genesis we learn that before the fall, while man was in a state of innocence and happiness, he was honoured by the visits of his Creator, and by sensible manifestations of God's presence. The mind of Adam was unclouded by sin and passion; everything he saw reminded him of the power, the wisdom, the goodness of God. He knew that God was everywhere, and at all times present. There was in his heart no aversion, no turning away from God, no forgetfulness of the Divine Presence; and yet even then God did not consider that clear knowledge which Adam possessed to be sufficient. The mere knowledge that God is present, the faith, even the lively faith and reflection on this truth, can never touch the heart of man so powerfully as some sensible sign, some token addressed to sight or hearing, by which God says to His creatures, 'See, I am here, and I am thinking of you.'[4]

The reason is perhaps that, however certainly we may be assured that God is near to us, and thinking of us, yet we see in this no special proof of God's love or care for us. God cannot be absent; He cannot cease to think of us. But what is the nature of His thoughts? Are they thoughts of peace or thoughts of affliction? (Jerem. xxix. 11.) The mere fact of God's omnipresence does not answer that question. But when God calls to man by a voice, or appears to him in a sign, then

[4] *Emmanuel*, by Abbé Martinet.

man exclaims, 'God is thinking of me, God is caring for me, God is loving me;' and his heart begins to beat, and he exclaims, 'Who am I, that God should be mindful of me, or that the Almighty and All-holy should love me?'

We are not told the precise nature of God's manifestations of Himself to Adam. We read that 'they heard the voice of the Lord God walking in Paradise in the afternoon air' (Gen. iii. 8). It has been thought by some that the Presence of God was announced to them by a sudden and mysterious rustling in the tops of the trees, and that, whether God appeared to them under a human form or not, they heard Him speak to them with human voice, as a friend speaks with a friend.

But man remained not long the friend of God. Sin made him His enemy, and destroyed this loving intercourse; and when our first parents, after their fall, heard the usual token of God's visit, their guilty consciences smote them, and, instead of hastening as formerly to welcome Him, they were afraid, and tried to hide themselves from the face of God amongst the thick trees. Alas, man, fleeing away from God, hiding from God, telling God in fear or in hatred to keep away from him, to begone to heaven, to leave him alone with his guilty conscience and his sinful pleasures on earth! That is the history of the human race, except so far as the mercy and grace of God have cleared away that guilt, and won back that reluctant heart to purity and love. And the mercy of God has thus pursued after man. If man has ever fled from God, God has ever sought for man. We should have been treated justly and according to our merits if, when by sin we rendered ourselves unworthy of intercourse with God, and even fled in terror from His approach, He had withdrawn from us that special Presence. And, indeed, for many ages the apparitions of God were few and rare; and sometimes even when He appeared and spoke, it was as to Cain, with words of anger and of judgment. Yet still the human race knew that God had not entirely deserted it. Men knew that though no vision and no voice was granted to themselves, yet there were some few favoured souls, patriarchs or prophets, to whom God appeared, with whom He conversed, and by whom He sent messages to them of warning, of love, and of mercy. Of Henoch, who lived before the flood, we are told that 'he walked with God,' and was seen no more, because 'God took him;' and we understand that to this holy man somewhat of the privilege of Paradise was given, that he enjoyed the familiar intercourse and conversation with his God, probably under some sensible form, that had been granted to Adam before his fall.

But it would take too long to relate how God showed Himself in visible form to Noe, to Abraham, Isaac, and Jacob, to Moses, and to Josue, to Elias, to Daniel, and so many of the prophets. These things are related in the sacred history in detail, and they prove that, besides His universal Presence with every man at all times, God has in every age bestowed, in the time and manner He thought fit, a more special Presence on certain of His favoured servants.

For many years God had appeared only at uncertain intervals to some few saintly men. There was no permanent sensible Presence of God upon earth. There was no one place of which it could be said that God's glory dwelt there more than in others. But as what is called in Scripture the 'fulness of times' drew nearer, this great gift was bestowed more liberally.

God chose for Himself a peculiar people, and His perpetual visible Presence was to be at once their bond of unity, their strength, their consolation, and their glory.

It will be sufficient for me merely to refer here to the mighty apparition of Mount Sinai. It was the inauguration of the perpetual sensible Presence of God among men. Moses by God's command made the Ark with its 'propitiatory' (or mercy-seat) of purest gold, covered by the wings of the two cherubim. 'Thence,' said the Almighty, 'will I give orders, and will speak to thee over the propitiatory and from the midst of the two cherubim' (Exod. xxv. 22). 'After all things were perfected,' adds the sacred historian, 'the cloud covered the tabernacle of the testimony, and the glory of the Lord filled it. Neither could Moses go into the tabernacle of the covenant, the cloud covering all things, and the majesty of the Lord shining' (Exod. xl. 33). From that day God was said to sit between the cherubim; and for ages after, the history of the Jews is in great measure the history of the Ark. When they remembered this Divine Presence, when they were grateful for it, when they put their trust in it, when they worshipped it, and surrounded it with holiness of life, then, indeed, they were blessed by God, they were protected by Him against their enemies, and thus dwelt as it were under His wings in the abundance of peace.

But, when they either forgot this Presence of God in the midst of them, or when they put a superstitious trust in it, thinking that it would deliver them like a charm, in spite of their sinful lives, they then experienced God's anger. It was indeed to this Divine Presence that all holy men and women looked and prayed. It was this that made David, the royal prophet, exclaim, when obliged to live a fugitive in the mountains, at a distance from the Ark of God, 'How lovely are Thy tabernacles, O Lord of Hosts! my soul longeth and fainteth for the courts of the Lord. Blessed are they that dwell in Thy courts above thousands. I have chosen to be an abject in the house of my God, rather than to dwell in the tabernacles of sinners' (Ps. lxxxiii.).

How many beautiful histories are related in the Old Testament of the devotion of God's people to His Presence in the Ark, whether preserved in the Tabernacle or the Temple! It localised without circumscribing their thoughts of God. It was the source of no error. It did not make them think of God as the heathens thought of their idols; though Moses could well say to them, 'There is not any other nation so great, that hath gods so nigh them, as our God is present to all our petitions' (Deut. iv. 7). At the dedication of the Temple, Solomon prays, 'Is it then to be thought that God should indeed dwell upon earth? For if heaven and the heaven of heavens cannot contain Thee, how much less this house which I have built?' (3 Kings viii. 27.) But though this particular Presence of God produced no error regarding His divine nature, it impressed on the Jews in a wonderful manner the sense of God's providence over them, and His peculiar love for them, and it inspired them with a filial confidence in their necessities.

The Real Presence as regards Ritual.

Wordsworth, in his *Excursion*, has beautifully noted this providence of God:

> 'Jehovah, shapeless Power above all powers,
> Single and one, the omnipresent God,
> By vocal utterance, or blaze of light,
> Or cloud of darkness, localised in heaven;
> On earth, enshrined within the wandering ark,
> Or out of Sion thundering, from His throne
> Between the cherubim; on the cherish'd race
> Shower'd miracles, and ceased not to dispense
> Judgments, that fill'd the land from age to age
> With hope and love, and gratitude and fear,
> And with amazement smote, thereby to assert
> His scorn'd or unacknowledged sovereignty.'

I will choose, from among many, one illustration of these truths, and of the manner of devotion of the Jews to the Presence of God.

When Ezechias received the insulting letter of Rabsaces, 'he went up to the house of the Lord, and spread it before the Lord, and he prayed in His sight, saying, O Lord God of Israel, who sittest upon the cherubim, Thou alone art the God of all the kings of the earth: Thou madest heaven and earth: incline Thy ear, and hear: open, O Lord, Thy eyes, and see: and hear all the words of Sennacherib' (4 Kings xix. 14-16).

Certainly Ezechias believed in the omnipresence of God, 'who made heaven and earth.' Why, then, did he not pray in his own palace? Why, if he must *show* God the letter, did he go and spread it before the Ark? All this may not be intelligible to Dr. Vaughan. He might perhaps include King Ezechias among those minds of 'mystical tendencies, to which deep excitement is indispensable.' No doubt he was a 'religionist of that intense order such as are often found in the Church of Rome.' Yes, it would be easy to find a parallel to this Biblical scene in the devotion of Catholics. Let my reader enter any day into a Catholic chapel, at an hour when no public service is being carried on, and I doubt not he will see some poor man making his 'visit' to the Blessed Sacrament, with a faith and confidence, and external devotion, just like that of Ezechias, though he may never have heard of the name of the

Jewish king, or of the Ark of the Covenant, before which he prayed. But I must continue the history of God's Presence.

The Ark of the Covenant has long since disappeared, and the magnificent Temple was destroyed by the pagan emperor, who declared that in this he was urged on by a power he could not resist, and that he was the instrument of the anger of God. The Jewish historian Josephus informs us that shortly before the destruction of the Temple, those who ministered at the altar heard mysterious voices from behind the veil, saying, 'Let us depart!' as if God was removing from the Jews His sensible Presence for ever. But, before the Temple was destroyed, a far different Presence of God had come down on earth. 'The Word had been made flesh, and dwelt among us.' This was the Presence announced of old by the prophets. It was the foreknowledge of this Presence which made Isaias break forth into the words, 'You shall say in that day, Praise ye the Lord and call upon His name: make known His works among the people: rejoice and praise, O thou habitation of Sion, for great is He that is in the midst of thee, the Holy One of Israel' (Isaias xii. 4-6).

Let us notice some of the points of difference between the manifestation of God in the humanity of Jesus Christ and any of those apparitions that had gone before.

First, then, God's Presence is now a Real one. The voice that Adam heard in Paradise was not really the voice of God; the flames of the burning bush, before which Moses hid his face, were not really the everlasting substance of God; the light that shone on the mercy-seat was not really the inaccessible light in which God dwells. These things were signs and tokens of God's Presence, but they were not God Himself. Whereas he that saw Jesus Christ saw God Himself. He did not, indeed, see the divine nature, but he saw the human nature, which God had made His own. The voice which spoke as never man spoke, and whose command the wind and the sea obeyed, was the voice of God; the eyes whose glance converted St. Peter were the eyes of God; the feet over which Magdalene wept were the feet of God; the heart on which St. John rested his head at the supper-table was the heart of God.

Yet, on the other hand, if God's Presence was now Real, it was more hidden and mysterious. Hitherto the apparitions of God had been objects of sight rather than of faith. They could be seen alike by sinner as by saint, by the man of faith as by the infidel; or, rather, he who saw them could not be an infidel, for the miracle convinced him even against his will. But it was not so with the Word made flesh. Many who saw Him believed that they gazed on a mere man; some even saw Him and despised Him, and called Him an impostor; and they scourged Him and crucified Him in their incredulity, and they knew not, as the Apostle says, that they were crucifying the Lord of Glory. It was not by His external appearance, but by His mighty works, by His divine wisdom, by His spotless life, by His loving heart, that Jesus Christ was known to be God, living in the midst of us. Externally He was like other men, and before He began to manifest Himself it was necessary that the finger of St. John Baptist should point Him out: 'Behold the Lamb of God.' St. John Baptist could say to the crowd, 'There hath stood One among you whom you knew not.' God had come down on earth, and He had stood in the midst of a crowd of His own creatures, and He had been lost in the crowd, and been crushed, and jostled, and pushed hither and thither in the crowd; so hidden and mysterious is now the Presence of God.

Consider, again, how much more gentle and loving is this manifestation of God's Presence. When the lightnings flashed through the thick clouds of smoke which rose from Mount Sinai as from a great furnace; when the thunder-peal rolled around its summit; when the loud trumpet-note pierced the ears and made the hearts of the Jews tremble with fear, they prayed that God might no longer speak to them thus immediately, lest they should die, but that He would make known to them His will by the human lips of Moses. Then were the eyes of Moses opened, and he saw a great mystery which should be in days to come. He understood that the God who now appeared in such terrific majesty would one day lay aside all His terrors and appear as a man on the earth. And Moses replied to the people's prayer, 'You wish that I should speak to you. Well, God will raise up a Prophet like to me, and to Him you shall give heed' (Deut. xviii.). Like to Moses, not in majesty, power, or holiness, but in human form, in humility, and weakness.

And when the day of which Moses had spoken at length came, how changed was the scene! Instead of the dense clouds of smoke that rested on Mount Sinai, was the overshadowing of the Spirit of God on the bosom of the Blessed Virgin; instead of the flashes of lightning, were the loving glances interchanged between Mary and her Babe; instead of the piercing trumpet, were the plaintive cries of the Divine Child; instead of the peals of thunder making the people's hearts die within them for very dread, were the angelic songs on the hills of Bethlehem, saying, 'Fear not, we bring you tidings of great joy.'

Emmanuel had come. At His first appearance He sought hospitality, and was refused even at the inn. Then He became the guest of Mary and of Joseph. When He left their roof, sometimes He had not a place to lay His head, and sometimes He went to be the guest of the publican or the pharisee. Alas, He came unto His own, and His own received Him not. But when they were preparing His death He was preparing the divine memorial by which it should be shown forth until His second advent; and He gave His Body and His Blood, and He said, 'Do this;' and He promised, 'I am with you all days to the consummation of the world.'

We have seen that a special Presence of God on earth is a great mercy of God, exactly suited to our nature and our wants. We have seen that the frequency and permanence of this Presence was God's original plan of dealing with His sinless creatures in Paradise. We have seen that this plan was broken by the irruption of sin, but that it was gradually restored in the course of ages, becoming more and more perfect as our redemption drew nearer. We have brought down this history to the Incarnation, when the Presence took a more real though in some sense more hidden form. We have come to the times of which Isaias said, 'Rejoice and praise, O habitation of Sion, for great is He that is in the midst of thee, the Holy One of

The Real Presence as regards Ritual. 145

Israel.' Is this history now complete? Has it come to an end? Is there to be any longer a special and sensible Presence of God upon the earth, or is it henceforth to cease? To these questions the Protestant answer would be, These apparitions, these special manifestations of God, came to an end with the Incarnation. On that day on which Jesus Christ ascended into heaven from Mount Olivet, and when the cloud hid Him from the longing gaze of His Apostles, vanished from the earth the last sensible token of God's Presence amongst men. The days of apparitions are gone by. Henceforth the world is more spiritual, and needs no sensible signs; and so in the Christian Church, for the last eighteen hundred years, there has been no place, as among the Jews, where the glory of God has dwelt.

Far different from this is the Catholic faith. We believe that the fulness of times brought with it the fulness of God's sensible Presence amongst men. We believe that all that went before the Incarnation was but a figure and a prelude of what followed, of what now is and will be to the end. We believe that ere Jesus Christ took away from the eyes of men the sight of His sacred humanity, He took means to perpetuate to the end of time His Presence, in a certain sensible manner, on the earth. We believe that in the Holy Eucharist, He still dwells in the midst of us—that there especially He is Emmanuel, God with us. We believe that His Presence in the Blessed Sacrament is as real as when He lay in the manger, walked in Jerusalem, or hung on the Cross—that His Presence is permanent, and will never cease till the end of time; above all, that it is no longer confined to one place, but that it girdles the whole earth. This is our faith, and this is why we rejoice and praise, because He that is great is in the midst of us, the Holy One of Israel. 'Thus saith the Lord of Hosts: I am returned to Sion, and I will dwell in the midst of Jerusalem, and Jerusalem shall be called the city of Truth, and the mountain of the Lord of hosts, the sanctified Mountain' (Zach. viii. 3).

We are told by Protestant writers that the Jews 'manifestly expected the return of the Shechinah in the days of the Messiah.'[5] Their expectation was most reasonable. It was founded on the conviction that the localised Presence of God was a great boon to man, and that the fulness of all God's gifts was reserved for the latter days. But, alas, they are like the Samaritan woman, in the presence of the Messiah whom they are expecting, yet disputing against Him. 'O, that they did but know the Gift of God!' (John iv. 10.)

To understand the fulfilment of ancient types we must remark that two things that were necessarily separate in the Old Law are united in the Christian Church. In the Jewish Tabernacle there was a Presence, and there was also Sacrifice. Between these two there were many intimate relations, but the Presence and the Sacrifice could not coalesce. Worship was offered *by means of* sacrifices, but it was offered *to* the Presence. But both Presence and Sacrifices pointed to Jesus Christ, in whom they were to meet. He was to be God-man —on account of His Godhead the Object of our supreme adoration, and through His Humanity Priest and Victim to God. He is the Splendour of His Father's Glory; yet through the defacement of that Splendour He cleanses us from sin (Heb. i. 3). He is the eternal God whose years fail not, yet by His Incarnation He was able and willing to taste death for us (Heb. i. 12, ii. 9). When He comes into the world in the humiliations of His infancy, the decree goes forth: 'Let all the angels of God adore Him;' yet in the agony of His passion He prays with cries and tears, and an angel is sent to strengthen Him (Heb. i. 6, v. 7). He has entered within the veil, a High Priest for ever after the order of Melchisedech; yet in fulfilment of His type He brought forth bread and wine, and changing them into His Body and Blood, said: 'Do this for a commemoration of Me' (Heb. vi. 20; Luke xxii. 19). There needs no more a succession of bleeding victims, which by their very multitude testify to their impotence. A Victim offered once for all on Calvary has wrought for us a perfect Redemption. The same Victim, offered in an unbloody manner a million times, testifies to the exhaustless nature of that Redemption which He is ever applying to the world.

[5] Smith's *Dictionary of the Bible*, art. 'Shechinah.'

The Real Presence as regards Ritual. 147

The last of the Old Testament prophets had said, 'From the rising of the sun even to the going down, My Name is great among the Gentiles, and in every place there is sacrifice, and there is offered to My Name a clean oblation' (Mal. i. 11). And He who gave the New Testament renewed this promise when He said, ' The hour cometh, and now is, when the true adorers shall adore the Father in spirit and in truth ' (John iv. 23); and He made the Testament which fulfils both when He said, ' This do for a commemoration of Me.'

SECTION III. OBJECTIONS AND THEIR RESULTS.

Two objections, which, however, contradict each other, are continually cast against the Catholic belief in the Real Presence, and often by the very same lips. It is said that it is unspiritual, and that it is too spiritual.

There are some who pretend that those sensible tokens of God's Presence that were granted to men in old times were condescensions to their weakness, to their carnal and unspiritual state, and that therefore they are not granted to Christians who are to live by faith.

The answer to this objection is easy. The visible Presence of God was *not* granted to man because he was carnal and sensual. It was granted to him in Paradise, when his soul was pure, his mind undimmed by sin, his sensual nature in entire subjection to his soul. It was granted to him because it fitted his double nature of soul and body.

> ' Upon the breast of new-created earth
> Man walk'd ; and when and wheresoe'er he moved,
> Alone or mated, solitude was not.
> He heard upon the wind th' articulate voice
> Of God ; and angels to his sight appear'd,
> Crowning the glorious hills of paradise,
> Or through the groves gliding like morning mist
> Enkindled by the sun. He sat and talk'd
> With wing'd messengers, who daily brought
> To his small island in th' ethereal deep
> Tidings of joy and love. From these pure heights
> Fell human kind, to banishment condemn'd.' [6]

---

[6] Wordsworth, *Excursion*, book iv.

When man fell into sin, he almost forfeited the great gift of God's sensible Presence. It was but gradually restored to him. As the fulness of times, the time of redemption, drew nearer, it became more perfect and more permanent, and was consummated only in the person of Him who came to redeem us from sensuality, and make us spiritual. To assert that the absence of any sensible token of God's Presence is a more spiritual and perfect state is to attack the whole doctrine of the Incarnation.

Another objection made is, that this Presence is too spiritual, that there is not enough for the senses. The language of many a Protestant is somewhat in this fashion. 'The patriarchs and prophets,' they say, 'had tokens given them which clearly showed them the Presence of God. Catholics assert that God is present among them; yet we look at the Eucharist, and we see nothing to denote His Presence; we have no proof whatever that God is in the midst of them.'

To this I answer, that the just man lives by faith. We do indeed believe that a sensible sign, an object that meets the senses to remind them of the Presence of God, is a great gift; but, at the same time, we know that it is God's will that we should live by faith, and not by sight. In the Eucharist we have something for the senses, something that tells us that God is present in a certain place in a special manner—not from necessity, but from love, and for our sake; yet, at the same time, this object that meets our senses and touches our hearts has no meaning or power except over those who live by faith.[7] It is well worth a Protestant's calm consideration that the very mystery which is the object of the most elaborate and splendid Catholic ceremonial is called by Catholics preëminently *Mysterium Fidei*, 'The Mystery of Faith.'

It happens with regard to the Blessed Sacrament, as it happened to our Lord Jesus Christ when He was living on the earth. He stood in the midst of men, and they did not know that He was near them. So too men are often in the presence

---

[7] 'Visus, gustus, tactus in Te fallitur
Sed auditu solo tuto creditur
Credo quidquid dixit Dei Filius
Nil hoc verbo Veritatis verius.' ST. THOMAS.

The Real Presence as regards Ritual. 149

of the Blessed Sacrament, and they do not know that God is near them, in the greatest prodigy of His power and love. Again, Jesus was pointed out to men; yet many, even when told that He was the Son of God, disbelieved it, and they despised Him, and struck Him, and spat on Him, and put Him to death. So, too, it is preached that Jesus is in the Blessed Sacrament, and many when they hear it disbelieve and scoff; and often they have gone so far as to outrage the Blessed Sacrament and trample it under their feet. They will one day find that they were trampling under foot the Lord of Glory and the God of Love quite as truly as the Jews crucified Him; with this difference, however, that then He suffered, now He is beyond the reach of man's malice; He can suffer no longer, however much men may outrage the veils of bread and wine behind which He lies concealed.

How admirable is this mystery! What a manifestation does it contain of the attributes of God! When Moses and Aaron, Nadab and Abiu, and seventy of the ancients of Israel, went up into Mount Sinai, 'They saw the God of Israel, and under His feet as it were a work of sapphire stone, and as the heaven when clear. Neither did He lay His hand upon those of the children of Israel, that retired afar off, *and they saw God, and did eat and drink*' (Exod. xxiv. 9-11). That men could return to ordinary life, could eat and drink, after seeing this manifestation of God's Presence, is recorded as a prodigy. What is it, then, not merely to see the tokens of God Incarnate, but for God Incarnate through those species to become our food and our drink? Yet this is so. His own lips have spoken it: 'This is My Body;' 'This is My Blood;' 'As the living Father hath sent Me, and I live by the Father; so he that *eateth Me*, the same also shall live by Me' (John vi. 58).

'O res mirabilis, manducat Dominum pauper servus et humilis!'

Such is the Church's song of joy and wonder. And this is the faith which to men like Macaulay is so utterly incomprehensible, that they can only refer to it in order 'to point a moral or adorn a tale.'

Should any one of my readers have hitherto shared Lord

Macaulay's prejudices, I would ask him to be candid with his own soul. Let him read once again the passage just quoted from Exodus. Is it not true that, if such a thing were reported to him as happening *now*, no matter what the evidence might be, he could not believe it? Does he, then, really believe that it happened in the time of Moses? Or is not his belief in such Old Testament wonders merely of that vague *unreal* kind that he attributes to Catholics with regard to the Real Presence? Has he ever inquired seriously either into the evidence of the Theophanies of the Pentateuch, or those of the Catholic Church? He has perhaps accepted the one and scorned the others. Was he guided by evidence or by prejudice? Such questions earnestly asked of his own conscience will probably excite a suspicion of inconsistency in the system of popular Protestantism.

There are many outside the Church who are beginning to open their eyes to this inconsistency; but they divide themselves into two parties, and come to exactly opposite conclusions.

Some cling fast to what they have read in Holy Scripture, which they believe to be inspired; and then they reason thus: The Jews were blessed with the special loving Presence of God in their tabernacles; can Christians be deprived of this privilege? And they look around, and they see that Protestant churches, however rich, are empty; they do not even profess to have a sanctuary or a visible Presence of God. They look at Catholic churches, and they see that over the tabernacle, when the Blessed Sacrament is reserved in it, hangs a lamp, and the lamp burns day and night, and tells them of the faith of the Holy Catholic Church—a faith that has never varied for eighteen hundred years, a faith that is shared by all nations; that day and night reposes there the Presence of the King of kings, more real, more substantial, and more permanent than any given to the Jews. And many Protestants are becoming aware that the Catholic doctrine is in harmony with the Holy Scriptures which they have been taught to revere, while the doctrine of their own Church contradicts them, and they are exclaiming, like Jacob, 'Truly God is in this place, and I knew it not. How terrible is this place! This is no other than the house of God, and the gate of heaven.'

But there is another school of Protestants who seek to be consistent by a contrary process. They start, not from their belief in the Holy Scriptures, but from their bisbelief of Catholic doctrine. They have made up their minds that miracles are now out of the question; that apparitions must, in the present age, be set down as delusions; that God now lets the world go its way, and does not visibly interfere to set it right. Having embraced these as incontrovertible principles, they read the Old Testament Scriptures. But it must strike every one that, if those records are true, in the old days God worked countless miracles; He appeared continually to men; He was ever interfering with the course of the world.

And men are beginning to feel that so utter a change in God's providence towards the world is incredible. Having settled with themselves that miracles are next to impossible now, they naturally begin to doubt whether they ever took place; having made up their minds that visions and apparitions are now fancies and delusions, they are beginning to form the same judgment about the visions and apparitions of the Old Testament; having adopted the philosophy that the only providence of God now is that of natural law, they conclude that it was ever so, and that the seers and prophets and historians of the Old Testament spoke only according to the conceptions of their own times when they represented the Invisible as controlling visibly the course of events.

The views of such men, from their starting-point, are logical enough. If there are no miracles in the Christian Church, it is consistent to say that there never was one in that of the Jews. If there is no infallible voice to set men right now, there never was a divinely-commissioned messenger on earth. If Jesus Christ is not present in the tabernacle of Catholic churches, there never was a sensible Presence in the tabernacle of the Jews.

And the force of logic has been felt by poets no less than by theologians. It is enough to compare Milton with Wordsworth on the subject that now occupies us, to see the progress in negation which the necessity of consistency has forced upon men's minds. We have no reason to question the sincerity of Milton's belief in the literal truth of the Mosaic narrative. A man of his sensibility, and who had given a special study to the subject, could not but feel that in the sensible Presence of God in Paradise Adam had enjoyed a singular favour. It was therefore but natural that the poet should represent Adam as lamenting his loss.

> 'This most afflicts me : that departing hence
> As from His face I shall be hid, deprived
> His blessed countenance ; here I could frequent
> With worship place by place where He vouchsafed
> Presence Divine, and to my sons relate—
> On this mount He appear'd ; under this tree
> Stood visible ; among these pines His voice
> I heard ; here with Him at this fountain talk'd.
> So many grateful altars I would rear
> Of grassy turf, and pile up every stone
> Of lustre from the brook, in memory
> Or monument to ages ; and thereon
> Offer sweet-smelling gums, and fruits, and flowers.
> In yonder nether world where shall I seek
> His bright appearances, or footstep trace?
> For though I fled Him angry, yet, recall'd
> To life prolong'd, and promised race, I now
> Gladly behold, though but His utmost skirts
> Of glory ; and far off His steps adore.'

Could anything be more natural than this pathetic lament of Adam ? What a beautiful opportunity would have been here for a Catholic poet endowed with Milton's genius ! Adam's complaint is made to the Archangel Michael. He who knew the future might have consoled Adam with the promise that the great boon of God's sensible Presence should be more than restored to his posterity. He might have told of the day when, throughout every country of that 'nether world' to which Adam was exiled, altars with 'stones of lustre' should be raised, and 'sweet-smelling gums and flowers' poured out, not merely to commemorate God's passing visits, but to receive and honour His abiding Presence.

But Milton knew not of this Presence. His country had renounced it ; and when he wrote, every Catholic priest who dared to erect an altar was treated as a felon and a traitor. So

Milton, after putting in the heart and mouth of Adam the feelings and expressions of Catholic Ritualism, has to fall back on his Protestantism for his reply. And cold comfort indeed it is that Adam receives. He is told that

'God's omnipresence fills
Land, sea, and air, and every kind that lives.'

One would have thought that Adam knew this already. But Protestantism had taught Milton its own theory of spirituality, and it led him into the blunder that Adam, in the days of his innocence, knew God's nature less perfectly than the youngest child of his fallen posterity.

Wordsworth, whose beautiful account of God's Presence, taken from Holy Scripture, has been already quoted, also felt the difficulty of the Protestant view. He first, therefore, suggests a doubt as to the literal interpretation of the sacred text. He is not sure whether the 'pure heights' of man's primeval intercourse with God were

Of actual vision, sensible
To sight and feeling, or that in this sort
Have condescendingly been shadow'd forth
Communications spiritually maintain'd,
And intuitions moral and divine.'

He even goes further than this; and seems to class with the Divine Presence recorded in Scripture the fanciful theophanies of all the Pagans. Thus Adam walking with God in Paradise, though higher in degree, is put in the same category with the Grecian herdsman who,

'Stretch'd
On the soft grass through half a summer's day,
With music lull'd his indolent repose ;
And in some fit of weariness, if he,
When his own breath was silent, chanced to hear
A distant strain, far sweeter than the sounds
Which his poor skill could make, his fancy fetch'd
Even from the blazing chariot of the sun,
A beardless youth, who touch'd a golden lute,
And fill'd the illumined groves with ravishment.'

I do not know whither such theories can lead, except to Wordsworth's favourite doctrine, that the imagination is the ennobling faculty of man, and ultimately to Renan's impious assertion that God is nothing else than the 'category of the ideal.'

But whence did these theories arise? Wordsworth supposes an objection made that 'this scheme of fine propensities' would tend, if urged

> 'Far as it might be urged, to sow afresh
> The weeds of Romish phantasy.'

Alas, they have no such tendency. They spring from the ignorance of those divine *realities* that are the object of Catholic faith. That faith has been called 'phantasy' so long, and those realities looked upon as dreams, that at last our philosophic poets and poetical theologians, perceiving that the faith of the old scriptural times was of a kindred nature to that of Catholics, are beginning to look upon Scripture itself as little else than 'the weeds of phantasy.'

However, this Essay is not addressed to Rationalists. I have all along taken for granted that my readers admit, with the Catholic Church, the authenticity and inspiration of the Holy Scriptures both of the Old and New Testaments; and the object of the present chapter is to show to the Protestant who admits the wonders of the Old Testament, and denies the wonders of the Catholic Church, that he is inconsistent—that from his point of view there is no harmony in the providence of God. In the belief of Catholics, there is one grand and harmonious development from the first day of the world to the end. The notion of most Protestants seems to be, that just as in the early days of the world there were mastodons and ichthyosauri, that have now passed away and given place to a more diminutive race, so, in the ancient times, God's dealings were more marvellous, the proofs of God's providence more clear, and the tokens of His love more frequent, than in these latter days of the world. But this is surely not the doctrine of Scripture. The prophets looked forwards, not backwards, for the great manifestation of God's power and love. The crust of the earth may have cooled in the lapse of ages, and the giant productions of primitive times have been replaced by a more puny animal and vegetable kingdom; but God's love has not grown cool, nor has the grandeur of the religion of patriarchs and prophets shrunk into the petty sectarianism of an unsupernatural Christianity.

Though God changes not, yet His scheme of revelation was one of continuous progress. Jesus Christ came that men might have life more abundantly, and the kingdom of God that He established was to comprise, develop, and bring to perfection whatever was good in the dispensations which preceded it. Among these good things, one of the most excellent, most beneficial, most loving of the inventions of God was that of a special sensible Presence in the midst of men; and—O, that Protestants could know it!—the very triumph of the love of God, the most fertile source of every virtue, the strength, the hope, the beauty, the glory of the Christian Church, whose worship is spirit and truth, is that Real Presence so flippantly bandied about by controversialists, and so fearfully blasphemed in the last three centuries.

The Holy Eucharist is the noblest of the sacraments, and the end to which the others lead. It is the life of the whole ecclesiastical year. It is the victim in the daily sacrifice at which all assemble. It is the fountain of the Church's poetry. It is the source of the love and adoration that built those mighty cathedrals at which the modern world wonders. And yet this external memorial, which is the central point of everything external, is itself preëminently the Mystery of Faith. Faith is the keystone of the whole arch of Catholic Ritualism. Alas for the clever but sceptical essayist who could scoff at such a mystery! Happy the gay but earnest-hearted Chancellor who was willing to lay down his life for such a faith!

If in noticing this great fountain-head of Catholic Ritual—the Real Presence—I have glanced back into Old Testament history, it is not because the words of the New Testament are too weak to bear up the weight of Catholic doctrine and practice, but partly because I refer to other writers for the full proofs of the great mystery, and partly because the prejudices against Catholic doctrine are for the most part quite independent of the interpretation of the words of Scripture. Those who hold the popular Protestant views of spirituality and prejudices against Catholic worship are almost sure antecedently to explain away words like those of our Lord's Institution; for they cannot, they will not admit the consequences contained in them. Let any one who doubts this read the following words of Macaulay, which follow those quoted in the beginning of this chapter. He is saying that, through some singular fatality or delusion, there are likely to be great and good men to the end of time, who will believe in the Real Presence, like Sir Thomas More. 'The text, "This is My body,"' says Macaulay, 'was in Sir Thomas More's New Testament as it is in ours. The *absurdity of the literal interpretation* was as great and as obvious in the sixteenth century as it is now. No progress that science has made, or will make, can add to what seems to us the overwhelming force of the argument against the real presence... A faith which stands that test will stand any test.'

Macaulay does not pretend, like one of the Articles of the Church of England, that transubstantiation is 'repugnant to the plain words of Scripture.' No, he is candid enough to admit that the literal sense is the Catholic sense. Then what makes him reject the literal sense of our Lord's words? It is the absurdity, the overwhelming absurdity of this sense, as it appears to him. No possible form of words in which the doctrine could have been stated by our Lord would have convinced him. The case is the same with most Protestants. If they enter into questions of grammar or exegesis, it is merely in self-defence. Their own conclusions are quite independent of such processes. The Real Presence is known to involve a priesthood, the priesthood a hierarchy, the hierarchy a perpetual, visible, and indefectible Church. The Real Presence involves a whole view of the Providence of God, or in other words, of God Himself. It brings us face to face with Him as a living God, and takes us out of the realm of vague abstraction and of Pantheism. This is the real source of much of the opposition to it. These are the 'overwhelming arguments' against it.

With men whose minds are thoroughly made up to believe in no God but the Unknown and Unknowable of modern scientists, there is little use in arguing either for the Church or for the Bible. But there are many whose minds are not thus resolved, and yet they are full of prejudices against the Church, though not against the Bible. I trust that what has been said may help them to see the unity of God's Providence in both—that they may reflect how the current of popular prejudices, against such mysteries as that of the Real Presence, is gradually undermining the Scriptures, and threatens to sweep them away utterly, and that they may recoil before such consequences. Catholics do not of course rest their faith in the Real Presence on the argument from analogy which has been here considered. But it is an aid to faith to see the harmony of God's Providence; while it is a sad confirmation of our ancient belief to see how those who have so long and so fiercely contended against us are now at length, through the sheer need of consistency, turning against that Bible which they had declared to be our enemy.

CHAPTER VII.

COMPENSATION AND REPARATION.

IN order to explain still more fully the spirit of Catholic worship, I must now enter into some detail regarding another of the pervading principles which have helped to mould it.

This principle or instinct is that of compensation. It is mainly the result of the Incarnation, and therefore preëminently characteristic of the religion of Jesus Christ. When the inspired writer, before the Incarnation, gave a reason for the splendour of God's worship, he found it in the majesty of God. 'What shall we do to glorify Him? for the Almighty Himself is above all His works. The Lord is terrible and exceeding great, and His power is admirable. Glorify the Lord as much as ever you can, for He will yet far exceed, and His magnificence is wonderful' (Ecclus. xliii. 30-32). But if we be asked now to give a reason for using all possible splendour, and all possible exactitude, in the worship of God, we shall find that reason not merely in the Majesty of God, but in His humiliations—and the worship of Christians is not merely adoration, but it is compensation.

Compensation and reparation are instincts natural to the human heart. When a man has been to some expense, or gone through labour, or endured suffering, or submitted to humiliation for the sake of another, if the latter has any feeling of generosity, he resolves to make some return to his benefactor. This is not the unwillingness of a proud heart to lie under an obligation; it is the unwillingness of a humble and a sensitive heart that he, who has conferred an obligation that it accepts, should be a loser or sufferer on its account. Thus, when a man has exposed his life, or devoted his energies, or spent his fortune for his country or his native city, a grateful and generous people try to make him some compensation; he receives a decoration, he is raised to the baronetcy or the peerage, or a public monument is erected to his honour. It would be strange, indeed, if this instinct of the human heart found no place in the worship of Jesus Christ.

A writer whom I quoted at the beginning of this Essay uses an argument in favour of 'simplicity' in religious worship that betrays an almost incredible confusion of mind; and yet it is often urged as if invincible. 'Our Lord's whole life on earth,' he says, 'was conducted in the very simplest and plainest manner. Should we not try to imitate His walk, if we are really anxious, for religion's sake, to act rightly?' I reply, that to imitate our Divine Master's poverty in what regards ourselves is a sublime evangelical counsel; but to retain our riches for our personal use, and refuse to employ them in His worship, on the plea that for our sakes He became poor, is as sordid a sophism as ever entered the human heart. The reasoning should stand thus: 'My Lord has embraced poverty for me; then I will pour out my riches at His feet: for me He has humbled Himself; then I will exalt Him: for my sake He has exposed Himself to men's neglect; then will I redouble my homage and adoration.'

But when I read such passages as the above, I cannot help recalling our Lord's saying about 'the children in the marketplace.' The Church may pipe to men, and they will not dance: she may lament, and they will not mourn (Matt. xi. 17). 'Let the worship of Jesus Christ be rich and splendid,' she says. 'No,' men answer; 'He loved poverty on earth, He must love it still.' 'Well, then,' cries the Church again, 'if Jesus Christ loves poverty now, imitate Him in your own lives. 'No,' again answers the world; 'it is enough that Christ was born in a manger; His children are not always to tabernacle there. Christ is not to be the pauper of the universe for ever; He is to be the King of Glory.'[1]

I will accept these words in a nobler sense. No; 'Christ is not to be the pauper of the universe for ever.' We will not

[1] Henry Ward Beecher.

treat Him as a pauper because for our sakes He became poor. Was not that the thought of the Wise Men of the East when they found Him in the crib of Bethlehem? Because He seemed weak and lowly, they prostrated themselves at His feet; because He seemed so poor, they opened their treasures and offered their gifts. Had theirs been the modern Protestant theory, how would they have acted? When they found the King of the Jews in such unexpected circumstances, they would have conferred together. They would have said, 'We have made a gross mistake; we thought, before setting out on our journey, according to our traditional notions, that God should be worshipped by prostrations, and by the offering of gifts. Yet does not the spectacle now before our eyes convince us of the contrary? Look at that little Infant wrapped in poor swaddling-clothes: what can be more "simple and plain," nay, abject and miserable, than His appearance? If He has chosen poverty, let us not insult Him with our treasures: if He loves to be humble, let us not contradict Him by our prostrations.' Such language sounds ludicrous and irreverent; yet what is it but the Protestant theory tested by the Gospel to which it appeals? Let us, then, repeat it again : 'Christ is not to be the pauper of the universe for ever.'

When the fathers were assembled at Ephesus for the consideration of the teaching of Nestorius, the heresiarch, in the presence of several bishops, exclaimed that he could never bring himself to adore as his God a Child laid in a manger, nourished at a woman's breast, and seeking refuge from His persecutors by flight. As this pretended reverence for the majesty of God had made impression on some gross minds, whose notions of the Godhead were more Pagan than Christian, several bishops undertook to explain the mystery of the Incarnation to the people. Amongst others was the learned Theodotus of Ancyra. He preached before an immense concourse in the Church of the Blessed Virgin. The importance of the occasion, the magnificence of the place, and the dignity of the assembly, inspired animation to his words, and after having shown that the humiliations of the Son of God, being chosen voluntarily, were a proof, not of weakness, but of clemency in God, and a manifestation, rather than a contradiction, of the divine attributes, he confirmed what he had been saying by an appeal to what was passing before their very eyes. 'That little Child,' he cried, 'who by His secret and ineffable power drew, then, the Magi to His crib, is the same who has gathered now this venerable assembly and brought about this glad festivity; now not laid in the manger, but exposed for veneration on this altar. That crib indeed is the parent of this holy table. He was laid in that, that He might be distributed from this, as the life-giving food of the faithful. Yes, that crib was a prophecy of this magnificent altar; the Virgin who knelt there has become the mother of the choirs of consecrated virgins who worship here; the squalor of the stable of Bethlehem has built this glorious temple, and the swaddling-clothes which bound those infant limbs have purchased for us the loosing of the bonds of sin to-day.'

His words were received with applause; for in those days, when the memory of the days of persecution was still fresh, and the conversion of the Empire had but recently allowed the Church to develop the magnificence of external worship, Christians did not look on the new order of things as a contradiction, but as a compensation for the constraint and poverty of former years. They saw in the change that the mustard-seed had grown into a tree; that the leaven was penetrating and raising the whole mass of human institutions.

Cardinal Newman, in one of his Anglican sermons, eloquently developed the same thought to which Theodotus gave utterance at Ephesus. The passage is too beautiful and appropriate that I need apologise for quoting it. 'The Son of God,' he says, 'was in the world from the beginning, and man worshipped other gods; He came into the world in the flesh, and the world knew Him not; He came unto His own, and His own received Him not. But He came in order to *make* them receive Him, know Him, worship Him. When He came, He had not a place to lay His head; but He came to make Himself a place, to make Himself a home, to make Himself houses, to fashion for Himself a glorious dwelling out of this whole world, which the powers of evil had taken captive. He came in the dark, in the dark night was He born, in a cave under ground; in a cave where cattle were stabled, there was He housed; in a rude manger was He laid. There first He laid His head; but He meant not, blessed be His name! He meant not there to remain for ever. He did not resign Himself to that obscurity; He came into that cave to leave it. . . . And He gave not sleep to His eyes, or slumber to His eyelids, till He had changed His manger for a royal throne, and His grot for high palaces. Lift up your eyes, my brethren, and look around, for it is fulfilled at this day; yea, long ago, for many ages, and in many countries. Where is the grot? where the stall for cattle? where the manger? where the grass and straw? where the unseemly furniture of the despised place? Is it possible that the Eternal Son should have been born in a hole of the earth? Strange condescension undergone to secure a strange triumph! . . . . He was not born in the Temple of Jerusalem; He abhorred the palace of David; He laid Himself on the damp earth in the cold night, a light shining in a dark place, till, by the virtue that went out of Him, He should create a Temple worthy of His name.

'And lo! in omen of the future, even in His cradle, the rich and wise of the earth seek Him with gold and frankincense and myrrh as an offering. . . . Pass a few generations, and the whole face of things is changed: the earth is covered with His temples. Go where you will, you find the eternal mountains hewn and fashioned into shrines where He may dwell, who was an outcast in the days of His flesh. Rivers and mines pay tribute of their richest jewels; forests are searched for their choicest woods; the skill of man is put to task to use what Nature furnishes. Go through the countries where His name is known, and you will find all that is rarest and most wonderful in nature or art has been consecrated to Him. Kings' palaces are poor, whether in architecture or in decoration, compared with the shrines which have been reared to Him.'

But let us continue our study of the Gospel.

When Magdalen poured out her precious ointment on our Saviour's head, there were some who had indignation within themselves, and said, 'Why was this waste of the ointment made?' The word 'waste' here seems exactly to express the view of men like the writer whom I have quoted. It implies that such an effusion of expensive ointment might have been suitably made in the case of an earthly king, who took delight in pomp and splendour, but that it was evidently out of place and thrown away when offered to Jesus Christ, who, by the plainness of His manner of life, showed how much He disdained whatever was rare and costly. To these murmurers it appeared that Mary's manner of worship was too ceremonious and unspiritual.

What was our Blessed Lord's answer? 'Let her alone; why do you molest her? She hath wrought a good work upon Me..... She is come beforehand to anoint My body for the burial. Amen I say to you, wheresoever this Gospel shall be preached in the whole world, that also which she hath done shall be told for a memorial of her' (Mark xiv.). The Spirit of God had revealed to the affectionate heart of the Magdalen the great principle of reparation—'She is come beforehand to anoint My body for the burial'—and Jesus foretells that when the true worshippers shall worship throughout the world in spirit and in truth, then shall this principle be fully recognised.

And was it not on the same principle of compensation that the chief external glories of our Blessed Lord's life surround just those parts of it which in themselves were most humiliating?

At the time that He was teaching the multitude, healing the sick, raising the dead, He appears generally to have disregarded the external homage of men. But in the humiliation of His childhood, when no words of grace had yet fallen from His lips to draw after Him admiring crowds, no miracle obedient to His command had manifested His omnipotence, then He called His ministers from heaven, and their angelic voices resounded on the hills of Bethlehem; then the shepherds knelt around His crib; while the Eastern sages, with greater pomp, though with hearts as simple, fell prostrate at His infant feet, and spread their offerings before Him, gold and frankincense and myrrh.

Again, when the time of miracles was past, and that of

His Passion and ignominy was beginning, the Spirit of God went out among the children of Jerusalem, and they came forth to meet Him; they cut branches from the trees, and spread their garments in His way, and as the procession entered Jerusalem they made the walls give back the echo of their cries: 'Hosanna to the Son of David! Blessed be He who cometh in the name of the Lord! Hosanna in the highest!'

But there were then, as now, men who considered all these external marks of homage as uncalled for and improper, and they took offence because our Blessed Lord seemed to tolerate them. 'Hearest Thou what these say?' they asked (Matt. xxi. 16), and they bade Him rebuke His disciples (Luke xix. 39). To whom He said: 'I say to you that if these shall hold their peace, the stones will cry out.' Yes; had there been no hearts found to render homage, external homage, and by that homage to make reparation to Jesus Christ in the day of His humiliation, the very stones pressed by His feet as He went about doing good, the stones soon to be wet with the blood He would shed for the souls of men,—those stones would have found hearts and voices to praise the Majesty of which He had emptied Himself for our sakes, and the love which had brought Him down so low.

I conclude, then, that if the Supreme Majesty of the Eternal and Invisible God afforded a reason to the Jews for doing their utmost to render His worship beautiful and splendid, Christians have an additional reason in the ineffable humiliation of the Incarnation for laying at the feet of their God, so great and yet so lowly, so ineffable in His abasements, as well as so mysterious in His perfections, all the homage that nature and art can furnish, that lively faith and burning love can devise.

We have now obtained a key wherewith to unlock much that is mysterious to Protestants in Catholic worship. Why so many genuflections and prostrations? they ask; why so much pomp and splendour? Is not all this empty and meaningless, or at least, is it not excessive? Yes, we reply; *empty* when faith does not show you the Presence that fills our ceremonies with life; *meaningless* till love supplies its interpretation; *excessive* to those who have not learnt the excessive abasements which it is designed to compensate.

It is the worship in spirit and in truth which Jesus Christ foretold; but you who criticise and scoff, you do not know the *truth*, and you have not the *spirit* that inspires those hundreds of worshippers whose evident devotion so bewilders you: you see nothing but the altar and the priest, the candles and the genuflections; you see only with the eyes of the body, not with those of the soul, and therefore you laugh and mock, or you wonder and deplore. Turn, then, from what you cannot yet understand; turn and look at the worshippers; watch the faith, the piety, the love, apparent in their postures, or written on their faces; and it may yet happen to you, as to many before, 'There cometh in one that believeth not, ... and he is convinced of all, he is judged of all, and so, falling down on his face, he will adore God, affirming that God is among you indeed' (1 Cor. xiv. 24).

To any candid intelligent inquirer, I offer this key to the spirit of Catholic worship. The Lord of Glory—it is thus the Church believes—for the sake of men, remains in a state of voluntary humiliation in the Blessed Sacrament of the Eucharist. Shall He be a loser by it? 'No,' she answers, 'not if I can prevent it.' Let the architect task his greatest skill; let the sculptor and the artist come to his aid; let the richest stuffs be brought from the produce of the loom; let the mines give up their gold, their silver, and their jewels; let the rarest flowers display their hues and shed their fragrance round His altar; let clouds of incense express the homage of men's prayers, while hundreds of tapers declare the light of their faith and the gladness of their hearts. Our God is in a state of humiliation for our sake! Then let Him be lifted up on high; let men fall on their knees and bow their faces low to earth; let Him be carried in procession; and let us tell the world that if our God seems to be a prisoner, He is a 'Prisoner of love,' and that even in His prison-house He is the Sovereign of our hearts. He is silent. Then let us raise our voices; let the sound of melody be heard; let us proclaim in antiphon and hymn this great truth—that the more He has humbled

Himself for our sake, the more should we delight to honour Him. 'Tanto Deus ab hominibus dignius honorandus est, quanto pro hominibus et indigna suscepit,' says St. Gregory.

I have heard men, who ought to have known better, make a scoff of the Blessed Sacrament because of the care which the priest had to take of it. They asked : ' Is your God senseless or helpless, that His priest must be so anxious for Him?' They reminded me of a scene on Calvary : 'They that passed by blasphemed Him, wagging their heads and saying, Vah ! Thou that destroyest the temple of God, and in three days buildest it up again, save Thyself by coming down from the cross ' (Mark xv. 29). While the Catholic worship, both in spirit and in form, reminds me of what St. John saw in heaven —the adoration of the Lamb : 'And I beheld, and I heard the voice of many angels round about the throne, and the living creatures, and the ancients ; and the number of them was thousands of thousands, saying, with a loud voice, *The Lamb that was slain* is worthy to receive power and divinity, and wisdom and strength, and honour and glory, and benediction. And every creature which is in heaven, and on the earth, and under the earth, and such as are in the sea, and all that are in them, I heard all saying, To Him that sitteth on the throne, and to the Lamb, benediction, and honour, and glory, and power, for ever and ever. And the four living creatures said, Amen ; and the four-and-twenty ancients fell down on their faces, and adored Him that liveth for ever and ever ' (Apoc v. 11-14).

There is a chivalry in things divine as well as in things human. As the weakness of women and the helplessness of children appeal to the generosity of the strong man, so the *voluntary* helplessness of the Son of God appeals to the devotion and generosity of the faithful ; and the minute prescriptions with which the Church guards the Blessed Sacrament are not, as some think, the cold formalities of a worship that has no life ; they are the delicate attentions of Christian chivalry, the loving expressions of worship in spirit and in truth.

CHAPTER VIII.

THE PATTERN ON THE MOUNT.

St. Paul reminds us, in his Epistle to the Hebrews, that the appurtenances of Jewish worship were framed by Moses according to a pattern that was shown to him in heavenly vision on the Mount (Heb. viii. 5), and that the priesthood of the law and its functions were a shadow of heavenly things. By these heavenly things St. John Chrysostom understands not what are invisible, but the sacrifice and sacraments of the Catholic Church on earth; and he enumerates especially the sacrament of Baptism, which opens the kingdom of heaven, the sacrament of Penance, which has the keys of the kingdom of heaven, the Altar and its Sacrifice, which receives the King of Heaven Himself, and the Divine Office, in which the Church on earth emulates the heavenly choirs. And St. Chrysostom does not exaggerate. For the worship of the Catholic Church is nothing else than a perpetual contemplation, adoration, and reproduction of that life of the Son of God by which heaven was brought down on earth.

In answer to an objection that there is in the New Testament no code of Ritual corresponding to that which occupies so conspicuous a place in the Old Testament, I replied, in an early part of this Essay, that no such written code was necessary, because the Christian Church has the Spirit of God, which supersedes it. Our High Priest, says St. Paul, in the chapter from which I have just quoted, is not like Moses: 'He is the Mediator of a better testament, which is established on better promises.' The Apostle then quotes those promises from Jeremias: 'This is the testament which I will make to the house of Israel after those days, saith the Lord. I will give My laws into their mind, and in their heart I will write them; and they shall not teach every man his brother, saying: Know the Lord; for all shall know Me, from the least to the greatest of them.'

We shall consider this great promise again. I now call attention especially to the words *all shall know Me.* The knowledge, then, of our Lord Jesus Christ—one easily attained, and universal, the gift of the indwelling Spirit of God—will be to the Christian Church in the place of a written code, which was the testament to the Jews. The 'PATTERN,' on which the eyes of the Christian Church are ever fixed, is the life of her Divine Spouse.

The worship of the Church was not the creation of a day, it was not a system organised according to some theory by Pope or Council. It was the growth of ages, of multitudes of minds and hearts, regulated indeed and reduced to order by authority, yet in itself the result of the working of a supernatural instinct; and that instinct was the contemplation, love, and adoration of Jesus Christ. The Church has fixed her eyes incessantly on the mysteries of His Life, and Death, and Resurrection. Seeking to recall to the minds of her children each of these events in its turn, she has created the great cycle of fasts and feasts that make up the ecclesiastical year. Distributing to her children the graces that her Divine Spouse has intrusted to her, she has naturally adopted the words and forms which He used Himself. Any one who examines the Ritual and Pontifical, the Missal and Breviary, will see how minute and tender has been the Church's memory; and he will understand that art and splendour have been employed by the Church, not to destroy 'the simplicity of the Gospel,' but vividly to represent its most touching scenes. He will see that if the character of her great days varies, it is because of the variety with which God Himself surrounded the Divine Object of her contemplation. If the churches blaze with lights on Christmas night, it is because 'the brightness of God' shone in the fields of Bethlehem. If the churches are draped in black and purple on Good Friday, it is because God Himself covered the earth with a pall of darkness while His Son hung on the Cross of Calvary. If the churches display all their riches on Easter Day, it is because the angel hosts wore robes of snowy splendour on the morning of the Resurrection.

It has been objected that the Church's system is a kind of 'spiritual drill,' repugnant to natures having any spontaneity of action, and that real religious joy and sincere religious sorrow will not adjust themselves by happy accident to the proper days of the week and seasons of the Christian year.[1] This may be so in those who have no living faith in Jesus Christ. But it is too late, after eighteen centuries of Christian experience, to bring forward *à priori* theories like this. Even Wordsworth bears testimony to 'a stir of mind too natural to deceive,' produced by the 'due return' of those few rites and usages which Protestantism has retained. And to call in question the depth and reality of this stir of mind, and of heart too, when the vivid ceremonies of Catholic worship appeal to the faith of Catholic populations, is to deny the testimony of history and experience.

It may be superfluous, after all that has now been said, to notice any more objections. Yet my rule in this controversy has been that truth is often made more apparent, at least to those who have learnt to object against it, by the statement and refutation of the errors opposed to it.

Dr. Vaughan knew that Catholics appeal to the divine wisdom given to the Church to create Ritual. He attempts to meet this by a very singular argument. 'Could the Christian Church,' he says, 'be shown to be competent to create such a Ritual, she could furnish no stronger evidence of being in a state in which it behoves her to do without it—inasmuch as the power to devise such a representative system supposes such a knowledge of the truth to be presented, as to make it clear that the end which all such systems are designed to subserve has been already gained. The power which can give the truth to the intelligence and the heart is forgetting its high obligation in attempting to give it through marble or upon canvas.' I commit this last sentence to the consideration of

---

[1] Miss Power Cobbe, in the *Theological Review*.

all admirers of art. It is evident that the principles upon which the Catholic mode of worship is attacked would destroy all art, if not all beauty, from the universe.

But let us examine Dr. Vaughan's reasoning. If the Church, he says, possesses that fulness of the knowledge of God which the creation of Ritual presupposes, she stands in no need of Ritual, since Ritual is a means of learning about God. Is there not here a strange confusion of ideas—a confusion of the teacher with the learner—a confounding of society itself with the individuals who compose it? If a society possesses a full tradition, does it follow that no individual requires to be taught by the society of which he is a member? Or does it follow that the society needs not to hand on its tradition, while its living members are perishing, and giving place to new ones?

If a nation is distinguished by a martial spirit, would any statesman say, 'The national courage is sufficient. No public monuments need be erected to commemorate past exploits, no pomp and pageantry of war need be used to kindle the hearts of the citizens. Each individual possesses the full spirit of the nation, and the next generation without any external aids will inherit all our fiery valour. A nation that is capable of martial display cannot be possessed of real courage'? No nation ever acted on a theory like this. It is neither written in human nature nor in the Gospel. 'Do this for a commemoration of Me,' is the language of Jesus Christ. It was but a higher application of an ancient and universal instinct.

Moses had said to the Jews, 'These words that I command thee shall be in thy heart; and thou shalt tell them to thy children. . . . And thou shalt bind them as a sign on thy hand, and they shall be and shall move between thy eyes, and thou shalt write them in the entry and on the doors of thy house' (Deut. vi. 6-9). Was this a carnal and sensual mode of teaching? Was it imposed on the Jews because they were merely the slaves of external forms? It would be folly to say so. These external means were to be used because the words were *in the hearts* of the fathers, and in order that they might be in the hearts of the children. 'And when thy son shall ask thee to-morrow, saying, What mean these testimonies and ceremonies and judgments? thou shalt say: We were bondmen,' &c. (ver. 20).

The Catholic Church was to have deeper knowledge and more fervent love, but the Spirit that should impart these would not abolish, but vivify, that mode of teaching which was founded on human nature. It had been foretold by the prophet Zacharias, 'I will pour out upon the house of David, and upon the inhabitants of Jerusalem, the spirit of grace and of prayers; and they shall look upon Me whom they have pierced' (Zach. xii. 10). St. John affirms that these last words were fulfilled in the Passion of Jesus Christ. But the 'spirit of grace and of prayer' was given to the adorers, not to the blasphemers, of Jesus crucified. We must look in Christian history to see how these words were accomplished. The Church has carried out in a Christian form that which Moses commanded to the Jews. The cross of Jesus Christ has been to her what the words 'thou shalt love the Lord thy God' were to them. The cross is engraven on her heart, and therefore she is ever talking of it to her children. She bids them wear it as an ornament around their necks, and she places it in the entry and on the doors of the house.

A minister sees this fulfilment of prophecy; but he can see what is Catholic only to criticise and to suspect. 'Their thoughts,' he cries, 'are ever about the Man who is suffering, bleeding, dying—a sensuous thought—rather than about the grand idea of the Atonement.' In this captious mood men can neither hear the voice of grace nor that of nature. Yet there are moments when nature makes itself heard. Then the heart speaks the very language of Catholic Ritual. Dr. Watts, who was certainly not favourable to Catholics, forgot the traditions of controversy under the influence of the humanising spirit of poetry. Alluding to the real or supposed custom of lovers carving their mistresses' names on the trunks of trees, he says he will do the same out of love for Jesus Christ:

> 'I'll carve our passion on the bark;
> And every wounded tree
> Shall drop and bear some mystic mark
> That Jesus died for me.

> The swains shall wonder when they read,
>   Inscribed on all the grove,
> That Heaven itself came down and bled,
>   To win a mortal's love.'

Dr. Watts spoke but the language of affection, and he expressed unconsciously the very thought that once covered our land with crosses and wayside crucifixes. Yet, according to his brother minister, he is guilty of a sensuous thought; and Dr. Vaughan would remind him, in his pedantic way, that, if he was competent to carve memorials of his faith and love, he could furnish no stronger evidence of his being in a state in which it behoved him not to do so—inasmuch as the power to devise such a representative system supposes such a knowledge of the truth as to make it clear that the end has been already gained.

Let men only learn to love rather than to protest, and the whole conduct of the Catholic Church in the matter of worship will be no longer to them the riddle that it now is. It is altogether founded on the love of Jesus Christ. But love must interpret the conduct of love; cold hearts cannot discover its secrets. The words spoken by Jesus Christ, when instituting the first and noblest of all Rites, 'This do for a commemoration of Me,' are the key to the whole of Catholic worship. It is to commemorate Him that the Church's doctors have written, that her poets have sung, that her architects and artists have laboured, that her musicians have composed. All her efforts have ever been to keep alive in the minds and hearts of her children an affectionate remembrance of what their Redeemer taught, did, and suffered for their sakes.

And this will explain the form that her Liturgy has gradually assumed in the course of ages. Although the essential features of Ritual are anterior to the inspired writings, yet the possession of these writings by the Church has moulded it subsequently in many details. The Church, ever studying, ever meditating on the Gospels of her Spouse, has culled every flower from them to adorn her Ritual. Every word that our Blessed Lord spoke, every action that He performed, the least details of His actions, the very sigh of His heart, or glance of

His eye, have found attentive observation and affectionate remembrance; and have been interwoven in some prayer of her Liturgy, or commemorated by some ceremony of her Ritual.

The proofs of all this can only be apparent to those who will study and try to understand her books. Alas, in the present day how few even of her children do this as it was done in those ages when the preparation to take an intelligent part in the divine worship was deemed no inconsiderable portion of the training of a Christian gentleman! However, even the stranger who has eyes to see and ears to hear cannot altogether miss the spirit of her worship. As I have so often had to quote the words of Protestants only to refute them, I am glad to conclude this chapter with words that will form a pleasing contrast.

The celebrated Lavater thus writes his impressions of a Catholic church: 'He doth not know Thee, O Jesus Christ, who dishonoureth even Thy shadow. I honour all things where I find the intention of honouring Thee. I will love them because of Thee. What, then, do I behold here? What do I hear in this place? Does nothing under these majestic vaults speak to me of Thee? This cross, this golden image, is it not made for Thy honour? The censer which waves round the priest, the Gloria sung in choirs, the peaceful light of the perpetual lamp, these lighted tapers, all is done for Thee. Why is the Host elevated, if it be not to honour Thee, O Jesus Christ, who art dead for love of us? Because It is no more, and Thou art It, the believing Church bends the knee. It is in Thy honour alone that these children, early instructed, make the sign of the cross, that their tongues sing Thy praise, and that they strike their breasts thrice with their little hands. It is for the love of Thee, O Jesus Christ, that one kisses the spot which bears Thy adorable blood. For Thee the child who serves sounds the little bell, and does all that he does. The riches collected from distant countries, the magnificence of chasubles, all that has relation to Thee. Why are the walls and the high altar of marble clothed with tapestry on the day of the Blessed Sacrament? For whom do they make a road of flowers? For whom are these banners embroidered? When the Ave Maria sounds is it not for Thee? Matins, vespers, prime, and nones, are they not consecrated to Thee? These bells within a thousand towers, purchased with the gold of whole cities, do they not bear Thy image cast in the very mould? Is it not for Thee that they send forth their solemn tone? It is under Thy protection, O Jesus Christ, that every man places himself who loves solitude, chastity, and poverty. Without Thee, the orders of St. Benedict and St. Bernard would not have been founded. The cloister, the tonsure, the Breviary, and the chaplet render testimony of Thee. O delightful rapture, Jesus Christ, for Thy disciple to trace the marks of Thy finger where the eyes of the world see them not! O joy ineffable, for souls devoted to Thee to behold in caves and on rocks, in every crucifix placed upon hills and on the highways, Thy seal and that of Thy love! Who will not rejoice in the honours of which Thou art the object and the soul? Who will not shed tears in hearing the words, "Jesus Christ be praised"? O the hypocrite who knoweth that name, and answereth not with joy, "Amen!" who saithnot, with an intense transport, "Jesus be blessed for eternity, for eternity!"[2]

[2] Lavater, quoted by Digby in *Mores Catholici*, book v. ch. 2.

PART II.

THE ORIGIN OF CATHOLIC RITUAL

JUSTIFIED BY THE NEW TESTAMENT.

CHAPTER I.

RITUAL CONSIDERED AS TRADITION.

FROM all that has preceded it will have been gathered by the attentive reader that a great part of Catholic Ritual is of ecclesiastical institution, and that the Church appeals to the New Testament not for the origin of each particular rite and ceremony, but for the principles that guide her in her development of divine worship.

It will also have been observed that the Church claims to possess certain Rites, altogether supernatural or beyond her own power to institute or her authority to abrogate. She professes to have received these from her first founders, the Apostles, and believes them to have been instituted by her Divine Head, Jesus Christ.

In the first part of this Essay we have been considering what support the New Testament gives to some of the principal characteristics of Catholic Worship. We have now to examine how far the Rites themselves, as well as their form, are of Christian origin.

The Catholic Church does not profess to have derived her Ritual from the New Testament. She believes it to be founded, in a great measure, on events of which there is more or less record in the New Testament, and therefore to be in perfect harmony with those records. But she believes it, in its essential parts, to be more ancient than the New Testament; and she has never maintained that the New Testament gives a full and detailed account of all that is of divine or apostolic origin in her Ritual.

In a word, Catholics believe that Ritual is founded on Tradition, and is itself no inconsiderable part of what is called divine or apostolic Tradition.

When St. John had completed his supplemental Gospel, he wrote these words: 'There are also many other things which Jesus did, which, if they were written every one, the world itself, I think, would not be able to contain the books that should be written' (John xxi. 25). The Rev. Mr. Beecher has made the following reflection on this saying of the Apostle: 'These words,' he says, 'affect me more profoundly than when I think of the destruction of the Alexandrian Library, or the perishing of Grecian art in Athens or Byzantium. . . . . The leaving out of these things from the New Testament, though divinely wise, seems, to my yearning, not so much the unaccomplishment of noble things, as the destruction of great treasures, which had already had oral life, but failed of incarnation in literature.' This is certainly a most true and natural thought, and may to some extent be shared by all. But a Catholic knows that there are words of Jesus Christ, not written in the New Testament, yet not therefore lost; for they were incarnate in a tradition which subsists to this day, and will subsist while the world lasts.

It may be said that I have promised to confine myself to Scripture. I have not forgotten, nor do I intend to violate my promise; for I am not going to consider the testimony of Tradition to Ritual, but the testimony of Scripture to the Tradition of Ritual. In the present chapter we are to consider what is meant by this word Tradition, and how Tradition and Ritual are related in the Catholic theory.

1. First, then, what is Tradition?

Various misconceptions exist respecting the meaning of this word, even among educated men,—misconcen ions that would seem wilful were it not for the notorious confusion of ideas engendered by the Babel of controversies amidst which we live. Thus Dryden, in his *Religio Laici*, written when he was a Protestant, contrasts Tradition with Scripture as 'oral sounds' with 'written words :'

> 'If written words from time are not secured,
> How can we think have oral sounds endured?
> Which thus transmitted, if one mouth has fail'd,
> Immortal lies on ages have entail'd.'

To take a modern instance, the author of a treatise on the Bible, called *Liber Librorum*, says that those who appeal to Tradition forget 'that everything to which man attaches importance he desires to have in writing; that all we know of history comes down to us in books; that books live when Tradition dies; and that letters remain unchanged when institutions have altogether lost their original character.'[1] He is mistaken. We do not forget such elementary truths. But he forgets that Tradition is not necessarily unwritten.

We do indeed maintain that oral teaching has many advantages over teaching by writing; but, again, books are of the greatest help to oral teaching, and may sometimes be necessary. When St. John wrote to Gaius, 'I had many things to write unto thee, but I would not by ink and pen write to thee, but I hope speedily to see thee, and we will speak mouth to mouth' (3rd Epistle of St. John v. 13, 14), he recognised the superior facility of oral communication. When he wrote his Gospel, he by the very fact recognised the great utility of written records.

The question of Scripture and Tradition is not one merely of the respective advantages of written or oral teaching, for Tradition is not necessarily unwritten. 'Unwritten Tradition' is a technical phrase. It does not mean Tradition committed to memory, and which it is unlawful to put on paper; it means Tradition not written down *in the canonical books of Scripture* by the inspiration of the Holy Ghost,—Tradition intrusted by the Holy Ghost to the Church, to be transmitted in other ways, of which writing is of course one of the principal.

[1] *Liber Librorum : its Structure, Limitations, and Purpose*, p. 84.

The distinction is, in many respects, precisely the same as that between the unwritten or common law, and the written or statute law, in British jurisprudence. What should we think of an educated Englishman who should write and publish an attack on the common law, without having ever read in Blackstone, or any equally accessible manual, that some of our laws are called unwritten, not because they are merely oral, or communicated from former ages to the present by word of mouth, but because their original institution and authority are not set down in writing, as Acts of Parliament are?[2]

On the other hand, with more plausibility, though not with justice, the same accusation has been brought against unwritten traditions that is often made against the common law of England, that there is far too much writing. 'What is called with us unwritten or customary law,' says Dr. Phillimore, 'is in truth to be collected from a vast and increasing number of written volumes. Fortescue said that in his time they required the lucubrations of twenty years. Whether the life of an antediluvian patriarch would now suffice to attain a perfect knowledge of it may, perhaps, be a question.'[3] So, too, it has been said that it would require more than a lifetime to read through the writings of the Fathers and other sources of Catholic Tradition; and it has been objected that whatever difficulties there may be in gathering one's religion from the Bible, there are tenfold more in gathering it from such multitudinous sources as those of primitive antiquity.

But here again the objection, as regards religion at least, is founded on a total misconception of what is meant by Tradition. The Apostolic Traditions have been handed down in a living and continuous society, and in ten thousand forms, from the day of their origin until now; and a member of that living society enters into possession of its Traditions by means of his education in, and intercourse with, the society itself. I need not know my genealogy in order to derive my blood from my ancestors, because it has been transmitted to me by a living succession. I need no more read St. Cyprian or St. Augustine

---

[2] *Blackstone*, Introduction, sect. iii.
[3] *Principles and Maxims of Jurisprudence*, p. 327.

in order to know the mystery of the Blessed Trinity, or the necessity of Baptism, than I need read Coke or Blackstone to know my right of being tried by my peers, or my duties as a juror. These are simple truths or facts, constituting the very life-blood of the society in which I live. And just as the multitude of channels by which such facts are handed down in civil society, instead of making the knowledge of them more difficult, makes it infinitely more easy, and makes ignorance of them almost impossible; so, too, in the Catholic Church, the multitude of the writings of the Fathers, the multitude of monuments of every age remaining to attest the apostolic faith, the multitude of the institutions, rites, and usages of the Catholic Church, does not make the knowledge of the faith difficult of access, but makes ignorance of it utterly inexcusable. The proof of this is in the plain and undeniable fact, that the simplest and most unlettered Catholic, if he is in any kind of living communion with his Church, does know perfectly well what she teaches on all the elementary truths and duties which it is necessary for him to know; while the most learned Protestants do not know, or do not agree in declaring, what the Holy Scriptures teach, even on the most important and fundamental subjects.

By Tradition, then, we mean either the handing down of truths and facts, or the truths and facts themselves which are handed down. And in this latter sense, by unwritten Traditions, Catholics mean all those truths and facts, whether identical with what is recorded in Scripture or not, which are handed down from one generation to another by any means besides the inspired Scriptures themselves. By Apostolic Traditions we mean such as are derived from the teaching and actions of the Apostles, and are not of later and merely ecclesiastical origin. Among Apostolic Traditions, and among the channels of Apostolic Traditions, Ritual holds a very prominent place.

It will be sufficient, in the present chapter, to state clearly the question at issue between Catholics and Protestants. The proof of the Catholic position will be reserved for the next chapter.

2. There are, doubtless, many Protestants who write *as if*, before the Apostles separated on their respective missions, they had written out the New Testament in its present form, multiplied copies of it, as is done at the present day, and distributed everywhere these copies to their disciples.

The controversies of the day, however, with Rationalists, have forced the attention of the Protestant world to the formation of the canon of the New Testament. The truths on this subject, which till lately seemed known only to the learned, have at length become popular.

A recent writer on the Protestant side, who is so far from having either ' High Church ' or Catholic tendencies, that while he speaks of Anglicans with scorn, he can scarcely bring himself to call the Catholic Church by any other name than ' the apostasy,' or ' the mystery of iniquity,' says on this subject : ' It was, without doubt, *long* before the written word occupied any position at all resembling that which it now holds. Nor is this surprising. For as the gospel had been at first proclaimed orally, a vivid tradition of this teaching would naturally take the place of any book or books in which it might be embodied. Indeed, for the first hundred and fifty years, the apostolic writings, although in separate circulation, do not seem to have been regarded in any sense as forming one authoritative book. The first catalogue of the books of Holy Scripture, drawn up by any public body in the Christian Church, which has come down to us, is that of the Council of Laodicea (A.D. 365). The application of the term Bible to the *collective volume* of the sacred writings cannot be traced above the fourth century.'[4]

But lest these facts should seem to favour the Catholic view of Tradition, the same writer adds : ' No one disputes that the Church (that is, a company of living believers in Christ) was called into existence by the Lord and His Apostles *before* the New Testament was written ; but it owes this existence to the Word which the Scriptures *contain*.' And then he quotes the following passage from Bernard's *Bampton Lectures :* ' The Word was antecedent to the existence of the Church, as the cause is to the effect. The *writing* of that Word, and its

[4] *Liber Librorum*, p. 79.

reception when written, were subsequent to the formation of the Church, but the writing only *made permanent* for future time the Word by which the Church had been created; and the reception of the writings only *recognised* them as the same Word in its form of permanence. Thus, while the Church is *chronologically before* the Bible, the Bible is *potentially* before the Church; since the *written* Word, which is the ground of faith to later generations, is one in origin, authority, and substance with the *oral* Word, which was the ground of faith to the first generation of Christians.'

There are those who assume as a first principle requiring no proof that the written Word was coextensive with oral teaching. This assumption we shall consider in another chapter. They also assume that, if they are coextensive, the written record will necessarily replace oral teaching. This may be so sometimes. If you were engaging a clerk, and had come to an agreement in conversation, and then the terms of the contract were put on paper and signed by the partners, no doubt the document would replace the verbal communication as more explicit, certain, and permanent. But a written instruction is not always a complete substitute for other methods. A watchmaker, watch in hand, directs his apprentice verbally how to construct the machinery. He then writes down every rule thus orally given, but at the same time leaves with the apprentice the model watch itself, to elucidate those instructions. May the apprentice, on the pretext that he has his master's writing, disregard and put aside the watch as now superfluous? Assuredly not. The watch would be a part of that apprentice's tradition. The written paper might—we will suppose—be coextensive with the conversation and the watch; it might explain its every detail. Yet the watch would be coexistent with the paper, both its own witness and the paper's interpreter, as much as the paper would be its exponent. Let us put the Church and her institutions in the place of the watch, and we see the office of Tradition.

Even if there were explicit and detailed and undisputed authority in Scripture for every doctrine and practice of the Catholic Church, which is a thing we do not assert, yet, even if there were such, we should still make use of Tradition, still defend it as a divine appointment, still consider it as an authentic, authoritative, and divine witness to God's revelation. The Scriptures alone, however full or explicit they might be supposed to be, would require something more than themselves, not by way of explanation, but of result or fulfilment. If I found all the decrees of all œcumenical councils, in so many words, in the pages of the New Testament, I should still require something more. I should look not in Scripture, but outside Scripture, for the things of which it spoke—for the rites and the sacraments, and the priesthood and the hierarchy, just as I have to look for these things now, not in the shelves of my library, not in the writings of the fathers and doctors of the primitive or mediæval Church, but in the living Catholic Church.

But the continued existence of such things as I have mentioned constitutes a part of what we call Tradition. Things have a voice as well as books. Institutions not only exist but speak. They are witnesses. 'The heavens show forth the glory of God,' says the Psalmist, 'and the firmament declareth the work of His hands.... Their *sound* is gone forth into all the earth, and their *words* into the ends of the world' (Ps. xviii. 1-4). God's creatures, then, are God's witnesses. God's supernatural works—the Christian Church with its constitution and its Ritual—have also a sound which is gone forth into all the earth. As the continued existence of the universe is God's tradition of the Creation, so is the continued existence of the Church the tradition of the Redemption.

Tradition, then, is neither confined to the memories and mouths of men, nor to the pages of books. It is also the voice of Ritual. Let me take as an illustration the one sacrament of Baptism. Its form of words teaches of the Blessed Trinity, Father, Son, and Holy Ghost. The pouring of the water teaches of the stain of sin, original or actual, and indirectly of the first father of the human race, from whom original sin is derived, and, consequently, of the unity of the human race. It teaches also of the second Adam, the Redeemer, by whose authority this rite is administered; it teaches of grace and justification, and of the death and resurrection of Jesus Christ, through which, and according to which, the death to sin and resurrection to grace are conferred. It teaches also of a visible Church, to which it is a visible entrance. Of all these things it speaks by its very nature. How much more clearly when the rites and ceremonies of ecclesiastical institution are added to it, the exorcisms and unctions, the profession of faith and the promises, the white robe and the lighted candle, and the rest! So is it with regard to the other sacraments. To quote the words of the Archbishop of Westminster:[5] 'The sacrament of Baptism incorporates, so to say, the doctrines of original sin and of regeneration; the sacrament of Penance, the absolution of sin after Baptism, the cleansing of the precious blood, the power of contrition, the law of expiation; the sacrament of Confirmation, the interior grace, and the seven gifts of the Holy Ghost; the sacrament of Order, the divine authority, unity, and power of the hierarchy of the Church; the sacrament of Matrimony, the unity and indissolubility of Christian marriage, the root of the Christian world; and so on. Each one embodies, teaches, and requires faith in a constellation of Christian truths; and the seven sacraments of the Church are a record, or Scripture of God, anterior to the written Gospels of the Evangelists. Much more the divine worship of the universal Church, of which one of these seven sacraments is the centre, namely, the sacrifice and sacrament of the Body and Blood of Jesus Christ. The incarnation, redemption, and consubstantial union of the Mystical Body with its Head, the communion of saints and of souls departed, are therein incorporated and manifested. All truths congregate around the altar, as all truths radiate from Jesus Christ. The whole revelation of Christianity is reflected in it.'

I am as yet rather stating the Catholic theory than proving it. But to complete the statement, another important consideration must be added. The Protestant supposition seems to be, that Christianity is a divine philosophy, that can first be delivered orally, and then committed to writing. I do not mean that Protestants deny its living power, its influence on

[5] *Temporal Mission of the Holy Ghost*, p. 180.

life, its tendency to realise itself in action, and to pervade and transform society. Still they look on it as a philosophy, doctrinal or moral. Its acceptance, and consequently its influence, might be interrupted for a time, even for ages; yet if it were consigned to a book, it might, after such interruption, find fresh readers, and a new and even greater realisation. This is what Protestants believe really to have happened.

In the Catholic theory, such an interruption in the tradition of Christianity would be its destruction. A doctrine or precept, like that of almsgiving, for instance, may be conceived to lie dormant in a book for ages, and then to strike root in the congenial soil of a better generation of readers, and bear fruit a hundredfold. But a *supernatural* Ritual does not admit of interruption. Any breach of continuity would be its destruction. Like the heaven-descended fire on the Jewish altar, it must never be allowed to die out, or it cannot be rekindled, except by a miracle.

A supernatural Ritual, such as that in which Catholics believe, presupposes divine institution. The Catholic Church does not claim any power to institute fresh sacraments. Those that she possesses she believes to have been given to her by her Divine Founder. Among them is one to perpetuate the priesthood, without which some of the other sacraments could not be administered. Her Ritual, therefore, involves a priesthood; her priesthood, a hierarchy; her hierarchy, a divinely-founded, perpetual, and indefectible Church.

All these things, if so be, may be read of in the Bible, but they cannot by any possibility be originated from the Bible, any more than—to compare human things to divine—an electric battery can be originated from a mere treatise on electricity. As an experiment in chemistry requires, besides the book, the possession of Nature's forces, so Ritual requires, besides the Bible, the transmission of heavenly grace. The power to forgive sins, for example, must be derived from the breath that Jesus Christ breathed eighteen centuries ago, not from men who read of it eighteen centuries after it has been breathed. If it did not start into existence then—if it has not continued in existence ever since—if the Holy Ghost, imparted to men, as Catholics believe, by that breath, has not been imparted to men in unbroken succession from that day till now, then the sacrament of Penance can never begin to exist. From this statement of Catholic belief it will be clear that, even if we granted that ' the written Word was one in origin, in authority, and in substance with the oral Word,' yet we could never admit the substitution of the former for the latter in any epoch of the Church's history.

In a word, Ritual, as Catholics understand it, is not merely a system of ceremonies or observances of human institution, but contains, besides these, sacraments of divine origin, some of them at least requiring a supernatural priesthood and an uninterrupted Apostolic succession, and each of them presupposing and expressing a cluster of divinely revealed doctrines. Such a Ritual as this cannot be based on Scripture alone. It involves Tradition, for it *is* Tradition.

For the same reason, therefore, the Protestant rule of faith is the negation of Ritual such as this. For if Ritual is a teacher, when the authority of *sole* teacher is claimed for Scripture, Ritual is thereby repudiated. And this, be it remarked, must be the case, quite independently of, and antecedent to, any testimony of the Scripture itself as to Ritual. I have said that if the Scriptures gave the fullest and clearest possible testimony to every part of Ritual (as understood by Catholics), still the Scriptures could not be our only informants, for they would thereby refer us to another and independent source of knowledge. Channels of grace must be channels of truth also. On the other hand, if the Scriptures gave testimony of the clearest nature to the divine institution of a supernatural Ritual, yet Protestants could not receive this testimony, without thereby abandoning the exclusive position they assign to Scripture. Were a Protestant, for example, starting from the principle that the Bible is the sole divinely appointed source of knowledge of God's will, to conclude from the study of his Bible, that it taught the Real Presence of Jesus Christ in the Eucharist, and of a divinely appointed succession of men to consecrate the Eucharist till Jesus Christ's second visible coming, he would then be obliged to seek for those men who are supposed to be already in existence. But if they are in existence, and in the exercise of their heaven-received functions, they must be in possession of the truth he has just discovered. They must be not only possessing it, but teaching it by word and by act, and must be doing so by their very office. His divine teacher then, the Bible, by being faithfully listened to, has brought him to another equally divine teacher, Tradition; and he finds that he was mistaken in supposing that Scripture was the sole divinely instituted channel of truth. If he is unwilling to make this admission of his mistake, he has but one alternative. He must so interpret Scripture, whether it is willing or not, as that it *shall* not refer him to any divine institution outside itself—it shall not tell him of sacraments, of a priesthood, of a teaching and indefectible Church. Thus, then, the first principle of Protestantism, or 'Scripture alone,' is destructive of its second principle, or 'free and unbiassed interpretation.' Perhaps this connection between Ritual and Tradition may explain some of the opposition which the former has had to encounter. Ritual was originally rejected by the Protestant reformers, not from deficient testimony to it either in Scripture or in Tradition, but from the necessity of the position they had taken up.

The function here assigned to Ritual as channel of Tradition will at least serve to explain why, having appealed to the New Testament as a witness to Ritual, I am obliged to consider its testimony with regard to Tradition itself. This will not involve a repetition of an old and hackneyed controversy. Though the importance of Ritual as a monument and channel of Tradition is an old Catholic topic, yet I am not aware that the subject has been treated with any minuteness in its relation to Scripture; and I hope that the considerations which follow will help to illustrate both the origin of Ritual and the structure of the New Testament.

CHAPTER II.

SCRIPTURE SENDS US TO RITUAL AND TRADITION.

TRADITION has a full right to be heard in its own defence; yet in this Essay I am appealing not to Tradition but to Scripture. I ask, not what does Ritual say about its own origin, or what do fathers and ecclesiastical writers say about Ritual, but what does the New Testament say about the tradition of Ritual. Do the Scriptures of the New Testament altogether condemn Tradition and class it among the lying inventions with which the spirit of darkness deludes his followers, as some men pretend? Or do they allow that it may serve a temporary purpose, and then yield place to themselves and become obsolete, as others maintain? Or do they suppose that it has a perpetual office, and is essential, by the will of God, to the transmission of Christianity, as Catholics teach? These are the questions now to be answered.

1. And first, does the New Testament entirely condemn Tradition? Among the many charges made by Dr. Vaughan against Ritualists (under which name he includes Catholics) is one which is often repeated by Protestants, and which I therefore notice. It is well known that our Blessed Lord severely denounced the Pharisees, because 'they made void the commandment of God that they might keep their own tradition' (Mark vii. 9), and He applied to them the words of the prophet, 'In vain do they worship Me, teaching doctrines and precepts of men' (v. 7). It is asserted then that Catholics and Pharisees are in this respect just alike. Dr. Vaughan even considers that Catholics were aimed at by Jesus Christ still more than His contemporaries. I will not deprive him, however, of whatever benefit his argument may derive from his own statement of it. I will give it in full.

'Our Lord knew,' he says, 'that the sin of the Pharisees

had been a besetting sin of human nature in all past time; and He knew that it would remain a besetting sin of human nature through long centuries to come. He knew that the great sin of the world hitherto had been creature-worship. He knew that the next sin to that, and a sin naturally connected with it, had been a superstitious reliance upon ceremonies. He knew, moreover, that the course of multitudes to whom His Gospel was to be sent would be, not to reject it, so much as to corrupt it, and to corrupt it after the Pharisaic manner. His lessons on this subject, accordingly, were designed, not so much for a few men then living, as for the generations of men to whom His words would pass to the end of time. He knew that the Christian Church would have her Elders as the Jewish Church had them; that she would have her traditions as that Church had them; and that she would have her Ritual superstitions bearing a strong resemblance to those then prevalent. On no other ground can we understand why the Gospels should have given us this everlasting Pharisee. We know that the Pharisee who comes up thus in the pages of the Gospel, comes up after the same manner in the pages of church history, presenting the same type, and filling about the same space.'

This pretended resemblance between Catholics and Pharisees has been examined in a former chapter. Let us confine our attention to the question of Tradition. The answer to the objection is very easily found. Our Blessed Lord does not condemn the Pharisees for following Tradition, but for following *their* traditions, human traditions, false traditions, traditions contrary no less to the real and authentic tradition of the Jews than to the written law.

The religion of the Jews was at no time a mere book-revelation. Antecedent to and concurrent with the writings from time to time given to them by their legislator and their prophets, was the great national tradition—their polity and worship. At the time of our Lord, sects and heresies had been formed, like those of the Pharisees and Sadducees, some taking from, others adding to, the ancient and authentic tradition. What Jesus Christ blames in the Pharisees is, that they magnify their sectarian traditions, and by so doing undermine the moral law. What is there in this that bears the slightest resemblance to the conduct of Catholics? We follow no sectarian traditions; we call ourselves by no party names; we admit no human precept in opposition to the law of God.

We admit Tradition, we attach great importance to Tradition; therefore we are like the Pharisees! Do Protestants then deny all traditions? Is it maintained that Tradition is essentially evil? But even Protestants admit, as we have seen, that the Christian faith was taught first traditionally, that several generations of Christians, and those the most heroic, had little besides Tradition to instruct and guide them. Is it possible that educated and earnest men should argue, from the condemnation of false and immoral traditions, that all traditions are false and immoral? Because the Pharisees prayed at the corners of the streets, is all prayer condemned? Because the Pharisees disfigured their faces when they fasted, is all fasting hypocritical? Because the Pharisees sounded a trumpet before them when they gave alms, are we never to relieve the poor? It would be as reasonable to maintain this as to say that, because the Pharisees followed false traditions, we are not to follow those that are true. Examine our traditions; prove them to be false, to be human, to be immoral, and then triumph over us and call us Pharisees; but do not use the childish argument of a mere play upon words, as if all traditions are bad because certain traditions were condemned by Jesus Christ.

But before we take leave of the argument against Tradition, which has given occasion to these reflections, it is but fair to see whether the words of our Blessed Lord have no application to Protestants. It is certain that Protestants, no less than Catholics, go by Tradition, though Protestant traditions are modern, local, changeable, not ancient and universal and immutable like those of Catholics. 'The truth is,' says Mr. Gladstone, 'that we are all of us *traditioners* in a degree much greater than we think. What we suppose to be from Scripture is really, as a general rule, from the Catechism, or the schoolmaster, or the preacher, or the school of thought, in immediate contact with which we have been brought up.'[1] A Protestant

---
[1] Remarks on *Ecce Homo*, by Mr. Gladstone.

may repudiate Tradition; may try to exercise his private judgment on Scripture, unfettered by the school or sect with which he has been associated; he may study Scripture without note or comment, yet even then he will not escape the influence of Tradition. He cannot put from his mind his past thoughts and character; and these have been in a great measure formed by the Tradition in the midst of which he has lived. It has been most truly said: 'Our real commentators are our strongest traits of character; and we usually come out of the Bible with all those texts sticking to us which our idiosyncrasies attract.'[a]

We have a painful example of this in the very accusation against Catholics that I have copied from Dr. Vaughan. How came he to see the Catholic in the Pharisee? How came he to see a condemnation of the Catholic mode of teaching in that of the Rabbinical traditions? The explanation is, that he was himself under the influence of Tradition—of the Tradition of *his* Elders, of Calvin, Luther, Cranmer, Knox, and the rest. It was these elders who originated such preposterous interpretations.

Among the Jews the Rabbinical traditions were of a later origin than either Scripture or the real Mosaic and prophetic traditions; so, too, among Protestants these traditions of their elders are not yet four hundred years old. And these new and false traditions render illusory the precepts and promises of God as contained in Holy Scripture. If there is no profanity in imitating the conduct of Dr. Vaughan and applying our Divine Master's words to modern controversy, I would venture to address writers like those with whom I am engaged in this manner. 'Jesus Christ said, "Preach the gospel to every creature.... I am with you all days to the consummation of the world.... He that heareth you heareth Me, and he that despiseth you despiseth Me.... But the gates of hell shall not prevail against My Church." But *you* say, " The gates of hell did prevail for eight hundred years and more; Jesus Christ is not with the Church but with the Bible; he that reads the Bible may despise the living teachers." Thus do you make

[a] Henry Ward Beecher.

void the word of God by your tradition that you have given forth.'

2. Moreover, Tradition, so necessary at first, became even more necessary afterwards for the preservation of the Christian faith.

We are told that towards the beginning of the fourth century the Canon of the New Testament was at length completed and generally accepted, and that thereupon the old rule of faith, oral Tradition, became antiquated. It had been a transitory form of communicating the knowledge of the truth, and truth now took its only permanent form in the promulgated canon; and this became the sole rule of faith to later generations, as oral Tradition had been to the first. But history tells us that, almost immediately after the period appointed by this supposed providence of God for the substitution of the Book for the Church, the civilisation of Greece and Rome, in which the use of books was comparatively easy and general, was swept away by the incursions of barbarian hordes, and gave place to that state of ignorance and anarchy in which the individual possession and study of the Bible was a sheer impossibility to the immense majority of Christians.

And besides this, Tradition is no less needful to restrain the fancies of those who read than to instruct the ignorant. It is the guardian of unity as well as of perpetuity. It was foretold by the prophet Jeremias, as the distinguishing mark of the Church of the latter days, that there should be one universal faith, easy of access to all. 'I will write My law in their hearts, and they shall teach no more every man his neighbour and every man his brethren, saying, Know the Lord; for all shall know Me, from the least of them even to the greatest, saith the Lord' (Jer. xxxi. 34). I need not say that this promise of the Interior Teacher is not to be understood as if no exterior teacher, whether Book or Church, would be requisite. It is a promise of a Spirit that shall simplify and vivify other modes of teaching. It cannot be interpreted as if contrary to the commission given to the Apostles, 'Go and teach all nations.' It is, however, a clear promise that the knowledge of God in the Christian Church shall be a common property, and that where the Spirit of God is, there the din of sects shall not be heard, as it is among Protestants, each sect exclaiming to the other, 'Know the Lord!'

It seems almost needless to prove here that this unanimity of faith is not, and never has been, the result of the Protestant use of the Bible. It is equally certain that it is, and has been, the result of the traditional method of teaching used in the Catholic Church. If we conclude, then, that the Spirit of God —the interior Teacher—was promised to the traditional method, we are but interpreting prophecy by its manifest fulfilment.

But let me here point out how Ritual helps to make unity easily attainable; how it summarises, so to say, a doctrine, in so palpable a manner, that it is known alike to the simple and the learned. An illustration from what is before the eyes of all will make this clear. What disputes have agitated the Protestant world of late years in England and America regarding the Eucharist! What a Babel of voices, each crying, 'Know the Lord!' and yet not only they do not succeed in convincing opponents, but they are scarcely able to make clear to others what it is that they believe themselves. In spite of the multitude of books, it is almost impossible to discover what doctrine each sect even *wishes* to teach. This is not so in the Catholic Church. It is perfectly well known to every one what *she* wishes to teach. She has so clear a method of expressing her faith, that it is known alike to her children and to her enemies. That method is Ritual. Every part of her Ritual of the holy Eucharist proclaims her belief in the Real Presence. The most simple cannot mistake it, the most subtle cannot evade it.

3. But did Jesus Christ, did His Apostles, intend that the Gospel should be made known to men by means such as these? I ask not, was the doctrine I have just mentioned taught by Him? for the solution of that question depends upon a previous one. Before we can know what are the doctrines and the practices of His religion, we must know by what means He intended such knowledge to reach us. Protestants appeal to Scripture: what does Scripture say?

It says not one word to indicate that the Christian faith

and life are ever to be derived from a book independently of Tradition. Though Jesus Christ intended to confer upon His Church the inestimable treasure of the Gospels, Epistles, &c., of the New Testament, no such intention is expressed among His recorded sayings. If He gave personally any precept to any of His Apostles to write, it could only be among the 'many things' which the Gospels do not state. What they *do* state is, that He chose Tradition as the means of making known His precepts to the world, and that in speaking of Tradition He laid a special stress on Ritual: 'Teach ye all nations, *baptising* them' (Matt. xxviii. 19): 'Taking bread, He gave thanks and brake, and gave to them, saying, This is My Body which is given for you. *Do this for a commemoration of Me*' (Luke xxii. 19).

That the Apostles of Jesus Christ intended their writings to be used in the Christian Church is evident from the mere fact of their writing; and of the value and importance of their writings there never could be a question among those who believe in their divine commission. And St. Paul imposes on the Thessalonians the precept: 'I charge you by the Lord that this epistle be read to all the holy brethren' (1 Thes. v. 27), and again on the Colossians, 'When this epistle shall have been read with you, cause that it be read also in the Church of the Laodiceans, and that you read also that which is of the Laodiceans' (Col. iv. 16). The importance, then, of Scripture, as superadded to oral Tradition, is self-evident, and has been defined by the Council of Trent; but in vain would you seek in the pages of the New Testament for proof or hint that any Apostle contemplated a time when Scripture should supplant Tradition, and when, by the promulgation and acceptance of Scripture, Tradition should lose its authentic character and authoritative force. St. Paul tells the Thessalonians to 'stand fast, and hold the traditions which they have received, whether by word or by epistle' (2 Thess. ii. 14). A modern writer on the Canon admits that 'there is nothing to indicate that the Apostles regarded their written remains as likely to preserve a perfect exhibition of the sum of Christian truth,' and even affirms that they were 'perhaps unconscious of the position they were destined to occupy.' He seeks to account for this on the ground that 'the mission of the Apostles was essentially one of preaching, not of writing; of founding a present Church, not of legislating for a future one.'[3] But the Apostles did legislate for the future, and were perfectly conscious both of God's provisions and the Church's duties. Let us hear St. Paul: 'O Timothy, keep that which is committed to thy trust, avoiding the profane novelties of words ... Hold the form of sound words which thou hast heard of me in faith, and in the love which is in Christ Jesus. Keep the good thing committed to thy trust *by the Holy Ghost*, ... and the things which thou hast heard of me by many witnesses, the same commend to faithful men, who shall be fit to teach others also. .... Evil men and seducers shall grow worse and worse, erring and driving into error; but continue thou in those things which thou hast learned, and which have been committed to thee, knowing of whom thou hast learned them. .... All Scripture inspired by God is profitable to teach, to reprove, to correct, to instruct in justice, that the man of God may be perfect, furnished to every good work. I charge thee before God and Jesus Christ, who shall judge the living and the dead, by His coming and His kingdom, preach the Word,' &c. (1 Tim. vi. 20; 2 Tim. i. 13, 14, ii. 2, iii. 14, iv. 1).

Here is an Apostle of Jesus Christ making express provision for the transmission of the faith and discipline of his Master, now that he himself is near his death. He looks forward to the future, even to the distant future, the latter days; he foresees errors, profane novelties, evil men, and seducers. What means does he provide for the safe custody of the religion he has planted with so much labour? What precautions does he take against the dangers that threaten it? Does he say that Tradition is an unsafe guardian, that it has nearly done its work, that it must soon yield to Scripture? Does he tell Timothy to multiply copies of the epistles he has received, and of all other portions of Apostolic writings which he can collect, and to spread them among the people? Does he speak of the printing-press or of Bible Societies? No. He

---

[3] Smith's *Dictionary of the Bible*, art. 'Canon.'

Scripture sends us to Ritual and Tradition. 195

speaks of the fulfilment of a sacred trust; and that trust is to preach the doctrine received, and to hand it on as a sacred trust to other men.

The subject is well illustrated by comparing the conduct of Moses with that of St. Paul, both on this and on other occasions. When the Jewish lawgiver was drawing near his death, 'he gathered unto him all the ancients and doctors,' and read out to them a solemn canticle; but as 'he knew that after his death they would do wickedly, and would quickly turn aside from the way he had commanded them,' he made another provision. He 'wrote the words of the law in a volume, and finished it; and he commanded the Levites, . . . Take this book, and put it in the side of the ark of the covenant of the Lord your God, that it may be there for a testimony against thee' (Deut. xxxi. 24-29).

When St. Paul deems his end drawing near, he, too, 'calls together the ancients of the Church,' and gives them a last and touching exhortation (Acts xx.). He also foresees future scandals and rebellions. 'I know that after my departure ravening wolves will enter in among you, not sparing the flock. And of your own selves shall arise men speaking perverse things, to draw away disciples after them.' But he does not make the same provision as Moses had done. He writes down no statement or summary of the law of Jesus Christ. He delivers to them no volume to remain as a memorial against them. Against the dangers that threaten he refers them to his oral teaching: 'I have not spared to declare unto you all the counsel of God.' He solemnly charges them: 'Take heed to yourselves and to the whole flock wherein the Holy Ghost hath placed you bishops, to rule the Church of God, which He hath purchased with His own Blood;' and, lastly, he 'commends them to God and to the word of His grace, who is able to build up.'

This solemn mention of the Holy Ghost explains the conduct of the Apostle. There is a tone of hopelessness in the address of Moses that is not in that of St. Paul. Both, indeed, foresee and foretell evil days. But whereas Moses can only look back to the threats and terrors of Sinai, St. Paul remembers how the prophecy of Jeremy was fulfilled in the descent of the Holy Ghost on Pentecost, and is strengthened and consoled by the great promise of Jesus Christ: 'I will ask the Father, and He shall give you another Paraclete, that He may abide with you for ever, the Spirit of Truth, whom the world cannot receive, because it seeth Him not, nor knoweth Him; but you shall know Him, because He shall abide with you and be in you' (John xiv. 16, 17). Therefore, though St. Paul knows that each of those whom he addresses is fallible and may prove unfaithful, though he fears for individual souls, he fears not for the Truth, nor for the Church. It is purchased by the Blood of God, and ruled by the Holy Ghost. 'It is founded on a Rock, and the gates of hell shall not prevail against it.'

Dr. Whately, in a sermon on the above passage of the Acts of the Apostles, observes that St. Paul, in his previsions and provisions for the future, says nothing of Popes or of Councils. The remark is a foolish one, and might be retorted on himself by the equally correct but equally foolish remark that neither does the Apostle say anything of the Bible. The truth is, that St. Paul relied neither on Book nor on Tradition, considered as mere human means of preserving truth. His trust was in the Holy Ghost, and the Holy Ghost, the interior Teacher, makes use of many external means, of which inspired Scripture is one, and all the rest are called Tradition. It was the Holy Ghost who had appointed the Bishops assembled at Ephesus to rule the Church (Acts xx. 28). It was, therefore, to Him that Paul commended them, that He might make them faithful guardians of the oral lessons they had received.

So also, in writing to St. Timothy, he reminded him that the 'good thing' had been committed to his trust by the Holy Ghost (2 Tim. i. 14), and exhorted him, aided by that divine Assistant and Protector, to teach the doctrine he had learnt, to use the inspired Scriptures which he possessed, and to hand down the whole deposit to the future teachers of the Church. As to the epistle in which he conveys this advice, he assigns to it a temporary purpose: 'These things I write to thee, hoping that I shall come to thee shortly; but if I tarry long, that thou mayest know how thou oughtest to behave thyself in the house of God, which is the Church of the living God, the pillar and ground of the truth' (1 Tim. iii. 14, 15). Let me not be misunderstood. I do not insinuate that the Epistle to St. Timothy was designed by the Holy Ghost, who inspired it, to serve only the temporary purpose of the personal instruction of St. Timothy, for which St. Paul declares that he wrote it; nor do I intend to deny—though no proof to this effect can be brought from Scripture—that St. Paul himself was aware of the future and perpetual use of his epistle. I cannot doubt that St. Paul intended both St. Timothy and St. Timothy's successors, as he did the Thessalonians, to 'stand fast, and hold the traditions which they had received, whether by word or by epistle.' The Apostle also had declared that all Scripture, which is inspired, is useful to the Christian minister, the appointed guardian of the 'deposit' and the teacher of the flock, for the fulfilment of his various duties. Of course, therefore, as time went on, the faithful successors of St. Timothy would make the same use of the New Testament, or of those portions of it which they possessed, that St. Timothy had made of the Old. But how utterly different is this from the substitution of Scripture for Tradition, and of the private reader for the public and authoritative teacher!

That the Holy Ghost and the Apostles intended that Scripture should be of great and inestimable service to the Church is, then, a legitimate conclusion from facts; but that Scripture should ever depose Tradition or supersede the living teacher is contrary to its own express declarations. The Church is still the pillar and ground of the truth; but Tradition and Ritual form the basis of this pillar no less than Scripture. It is hard to see how an unprejudiced man, whose mind is not already possessed by the axiom, 'The Bible alone is the religion of Protestants,' could, from the words addressed by St. Paul to Timothy, come to the conclusion that, in the course of a century or two, the Church of the *living* God would grow sick and die, the pillar and ground of the truth would totter and fall. Yet what else is the Protestant theory?

When Jesus Christ stood before Pontius Pilate, and was

interrogated as to His Kingship, He replied: 'For this was I born, and for this came I into the world, that I should give testimony to the truth' (John xviii. 37). The kingdom, then, of Jesus Christ is one of which truth is the constitution, truth the wealth, and the diffusion of truth the very purpose of its existence. The kingdom of Jesus Christ, or the Church of the living God, as St. Paul calls it, is the very 'pillar and ground of the truth.' Truth can no more fail from the Church than Jesus Christ can have been born in vain. The preservation of this truth whole and undefiled is the perpetual work of the Holy Ghost. In this work the Apostles and their successors are His coöperators. In fulfilling their trust they are not left to their own discretion. The same mode was doubtless prescribed to others as to St. Timothy and to the Bishops at Ephesus. What they had received orally and personally before many witnesses from the Apostles, they committed orally and personally to faithful men. Together with copies of Apostolic writings they handed down Apostolic doctrine, Apostolic discipline, Apostolic ritual, Apostolic succession. Those faithful men were commanded to do the same to another generation of faithful men after them. When was this to cease? Was it, indeed, ever to cease? No hint of such a thing is given by the Apostle. It was a trust for which they were to render an account to God. Would they have been faithful men, had they considered that their trust had lapsed, without an express declaration of the will of God?

No. If that charge of St. Paul was given by divine authority, then it is certain that had those men who received the deposit in direct succession from the Apostles—*quasi per manus*—relinquished that deposit, no matter when—at the end of the first century, when the Canon was completed; in the fourth century, when it was generally promulgated; in the fifteenth, when printing was invented; in the sixteenth, when their authority was challenged; in the nineteenth, when Bible Societies claimed to do their work—had they at any period, without a new revelation of God's will, declared that their authoritative guardianship of the faith and worship, discipline and government, of the Church had now had its time, they would have sinned against the Holy Ghost, who had committed to them the deposit, and set them to rule the Church, and would have betrayed the Blood of Jesus Christ, with which the Church was purchased.

CHAPTER III.

RITUAL A KEY TO SCRIPTURE.

Section I. How Ritual helped to edit the New Testament.

The late Dr. Whately, in his Annotations on Bacon's Essays, wrote as follows: 'Many defend oral tradition on the ground that we have the Scriptures themselves by Tradition. Would they think that, because they could trust most servants to deliver a letter, however long or important, therefore they could trust them to deliver its contents in a message by word of mouth? Take a familiar case. A footman brings you a letter from a friend, upon whose word you can perfectly rely, giving an account of something that has happened to himself, and the exact truth of which you are greatly concerned to know. While you are reading and answering the letter, the footman goes into the kitchen, and there gives your cook an account of the same thing, which he says he overheard the upper servants at home talking over, as related to them by the valet, who said he had it from your friend's son's own lips. The cook relates the story to the groom, and he in turn tells you. Would you judge of that *story* by the letter, or of the *letter* by the story?'

When this publication of Dr. Whately appeared, a writer in a Catholic periodical made some remarks on this passage, which I abridge. 'Consider,' he says, 'what this argument supposes. There is the individual soul to which God wishes to make a communication; He therefore sends to it a letter by a footman. Now who or what is this footman? It is no other than the Church, of which the soul may perhaps aspire to be a member—say the billionth part. Yet this soul, forsooth, is the master, and the millions are the footman. This soul has direct communication with God, and the other millions have simply received from Him a *sealed* letter, and have only learned its contents from the kitchen conversation of the valet and the cook! These millions obsequiously bring to the soul, enthroned in its solitary pride, the sealed book, and say, " O, happy soul, to whom it is reserved to look on that which is forbidden to our eyes, receive this book ! To you only is it given to peruse its contents. Open it and read, and judge for yourself about the meaning thereof." And then the soul, after it has received, and studied, and understood, and believed the book, and become a member of the Church, and in union with God, and a scholar of the Holy Spirit, and a partaker of the unction whereby wisdom is given, must dissemble all this knowledge—must become an infinitesimal fraction of a footman ; and must, as one of the deputation, carry the same book to the next soul, pretending to know nothing of it, never to have seen the inside, and to have only indirect evidence of the contents.'[1]

Such is Dr. Whately's conception of the Christian Church.[2] His knowledge of the nature of Holy Scripture is of much the same stamp. He compares the New Testament to a letter, written for the purpose of communicating full information regarding a most important occurrence, of which the reader hitherto knows nothing, but of which he will desire to know the 'exact truth.' Yet the New Testament, on the very surface of it, is the exact contrary of all this : it is a letter intended for a reader who knew almost everything already ; containing, therefore, together with some further details, references and hints of which the reader only had the key.

Dr. Whately's illustration, however, sins far more grievously still against the facts of the case. He speaks of the New Testament as of a letter. A letter is an individual document. The New Testament, it is true, at the present day and for centuries

[1] *Rambler*, March 1857.
[2] He seems to have borrowed his comparison from Dryden :
' The welcome news is in the letter found,
The carrier's not commission'd to expound.'
Nothing, however, is more clear in Scripture than the carrier's commission.

back, has become also a separate and individual book, a distinct collection of documents; and as such at the present day it might perhaps be spoken of as 'a letter' from God, provided the illustration were not faulty in other respects. But then Dr. Whately thoughtlessly assumes that, in the same complete and distinct state in which it now exists, the New Testament was put by God in the hands of the Church, to be carried by her as by a messenger to generation after generation of readers. If this is not supposed, his whole comparison of the footman and the letter is grossly and ludicrously inadequate.

Let us seek an illustration more in accordance with the facts of the case. An engineer, wishing to arrange his affairs, opens a chest containing a multitude of letters and other documents. Many of these are papers of his father's; and these he wishes to gather into a separate packet. They are not, however, originals, but copies. Neither the handwriting nor the signature of his father is there to guide him. Mixed up with his father's papers are many contemporaneous letters and documents of others, treating of the same or of kindred subjects. How is he to sort out the genuine letters of his father? He and he alone can do it. He reads them all carefully. He knows his father's style and tone of thought. He remembers the family history of some of the papers. He detects phrases or allusions which could have come from his father alone, and which the son alone would have noticed. In some of these papers there are references to machinery that his father was constructing; but these very machines are now in the son's possession, and by comparing them with the papers—the completed work with the rough sketch or the partial detail—he can assure himself that these papers are his father's. It is evident that no one but the son, or one in a similar position, could make this selection. It is evident also that when it is made no one else could properly *edit* those letters—*i.e.* interpret them aright, illustrate them, supplement them. And this because he is not merely the possessor of his father's letters, but he was the confidant of his labours, and is the inheritor of his constructions.

Such are the true relations of the Church and the Bible.

The sacred books of which it is composed came into the hands of the Catholic Church, together with many other treatises on the same subjects. When the time came for making the separation, the Catholic Church alone could have made it. In her traditions she possessed the Apostolic doctrine; she was formed by the Apostolic discipline; she worshipped according to Apostolic example. She had in her possession, in daily use, the Sacrifice and Sacraments given her by the Apostles. Though some Apostolic writings had perished, and of the others only copies were in existence, yet she had her family history of these documents, and she therefore, but she alone, could have compiled the Canon of the New Testament.

And for the same reason she only can *edit* it—*i.e.* explain it correctly, interpret its allusions, supply its omissions, and explain its purpose. And all this she can do, because, besides the Bible, she possesses in her Tradition, and particularly in her Ritual, a divine legacy, coeval with or anterior to the Bible—its key, and sometimes its supplement.

When we say that the Church gives us the Bible, we do not mean that the Church hands down the Bible just as society hands down any other ancient books. For so natural and material a work as the safe transmission of a written or printed volume the continual presence of the Holy Ghost would not be required. This presence is claimed for a far higher work—for the verifying the sacredness of the books no less than for the safe custody and defence of them. But we mean that the primitive Christian society, or the Church, received from the Apostles the full tradition of the Christian revelation before the New Testament was written; so that the Apostles, before they left the earth, could say to all their disciples, as St. Paul to the clergy of Ephesus, 'I take you to witness this day that I am clear from the blood of all men, for I have not spared to declare unto you all the counsel of God' (Acts xx. 26, 27). This he said at a time when three of the Gospels were not yet written, and few of the Epistles; and when certainly those Epistles that had been written were quite unknown at Ephesus. The 'whole counsel of God' was known, therefore, before the New Testament was written; and the most ardent advocates of Bible Societies must admit that several generations of Christians lived and died practising the most heroic virtue without the Bible, by means of Tradition ; so that St. Irenæus, writing in the middle of the second century, says : 'What if the Apostles had not left us writings ? would it not have been needful to follow the order of that Tradition which they delivered to those to whom they committed the Churches ?—to which many of the barbarous nations who believe in Christ even now assent, having salvation written without paper and ink, by the Spirit in their hearts, sedulously guarding the old Traditions.'

Now it was this society, thus moulded, penetrated, and informed by the Christian faith, worship, and discipline, that received the New Testament. Those books were not put, collected and bound in a volume, into the custody of the Church in the same way that they came from the hands of the Catholic Church into the hands of the society to which Dr. Whately belonged, and which handed them down to him by a mere natural and, as it were, manual tradition. The early Christian society received the writings of the Apostles together with a multitude of other writings of various degrees of excellence. St. Luke says, that even in his day '*many* had taken in hand to set forth in order a narration of the things that have been accomplished among us, according as they have delivered them unto us, who from the beginning were eye-witnesses' (Luke i. 1). There were then many Gospel histories in circulation: doubtless there were also many treatises on Christian doctrine and discipline. Many of these, as we know, were read, together with the writings of the Apostles, in the assemblies of the faithful. By degrees the Spirit of God, who guided the Church, made known that it was time to distinguish between the writings that bore authority, and those that were merely read for edification, as well as between the latter and those that were unworthy and were to be rejected.

How was this sorting to be made ? What was the test to be applied ? Was it a mere historical and critical question as to the genuine writings of Apostles ? This certainly was not the judgment of the primitive Church, since it selected the

Gospels of St. Mark and St. Luke, who were not of the Twelve. The verifying faculty by which the Church formed the Canon was the spiritual consciousness created in her by the presence of the Holy Ghost, and the possession of Apostolic Tradition regarding the whole circle of revelation, together with the various local Apostolic Traditions regarding the inspiration of each particular book. The certainty we have that the Church then judged aright is founded on our belief in the continual indwelling of the Holy Ghost, and the accomplishment of the promise of Jesus Christ: 'I am with you all days.' But if any man holds that the Church of the nineteenth century can err, or that of the sixteenth, he has no guarantee that the Church of the third or fourth century did not err in rejecting books that contained part of the deposit, and admitting books that have no divine authority.

SECTION II. WHAT KEY WILL OPEN THE NEW TESTAMENT.

I HAVE now to show that the New Testament, at least in its allusions to Christian rites, requires a key; that it was meant to be read with a key; and that the key intended was the Apostolic Ritual, which was independent of and antecedent to such allusions.

It has been warmly maintained that the New Testament needs no other key than such as we should employ in interpreting Plato or Thucydides; that is, a critical knowledge of the language, and a certain familiarity with the political, philosophical, or social circumstances, in which the author wrote.

This is indeed to some extent true, if by familiarity with circumstances we understand those of the Christian Church; but this would be equivalent to interpreting the Christian Scriptures by Christian traditions; and this is not what is meant by those to whom I refer. They repudiate such tradition, and regard it as the main source of erroneous interpretations. The knowledge by which they think to attain to the real sense of the Gospels is familiarity with the state of the Roman or Jewish society at the time Christianity made its appearance, not that of the Christian society that resulted from the Apostles' preaching.

'The question really demanding a settlement is this,' says a recent author: 'whether the rules and gifts which qualify a man for the right understanding of ordinary written language are, or are not, sufficient for rightly understanding the Bible?' He maintains that they are; and that 'the interpretation which, in spite of all ecclesiastical opposition, ought to be adopted as the only true one, is unquestionably that which has in modern times been styled the Historico-Grammatical.'[3]

This writer supposes that the only reason why any one contests this method of interpretation is that the Bible, having been written under the direct guidance of the Holy Ghost, is not to be measured by common rules. To this he replies, 'Surely it will be allowed that if God has deemed it desirable to reveal His will to mankind by means of intelligible books, He must have intended that the contents of those books should be discovered in accordance with those general laws which are conducive to the right understanding of documents in general. For if this were not the case, He would have chosen insufficient and even contradictory means inadequate' to the purpose He had in view, which cannot be supposed.'

Since, however, the New Testament nowhere asserts that it was written in order 'to reveal God's will to mankind,' as the words are understood by Protestants, we cannot argue from the will of God to the intelligibility of Scripture, but rather must conclude from the nature of Scripture, whatever it may be, to the will of God.

Certainly the Bible must be intelligible when used as it was intended to be used. This is a self-evident axiom for all who believe the Bible to come from God. It may be obscure, and its obscurities will have a divine purpose; but generally or in a great measure unintelligible it cannot be. The question, then, is one of fact: is the New Testament, in all its main features at least, an intelligible document when submitted to historico-grammatical processes, and to those alone? Let us consider plain historical facts. Will the opponents of Tradition under-

[3] *Liber Librorum*, p. 166.

take to prove that candid and intelligent men do, as a matter of experience, attain to such a generally-accurate and universally-admitted interpretation of the facts and doctrines of the New Testament as they do, for example, of the life and opinions of Cicero? Is it not, on the contrary, an undeniable fact that learned men, candid men, men eager for truth, men who spend their whole lives in the study of the New Testament in quest of truth, come to utterly different conclusions as to the most fundamental doctrines and practices of the Christian religion? What pretext, then, is there for supposing that the documents of the New Testament are to be interpreted just like all other documents? Is there any similar diversity with regard to other documents? If it were no more difficult to ascertain the meaning of the Gospels than it is to interpret the Roman historians; if the sense of St. Paul's Epistles could be ascertained by the same means by which we read and understand the epistles of Cicero, then no history ought to be more generally admitted than that of Christianity, no facts of antiquity ought to be so universally agreed upon by the learned as the opinions and acts of St. Paul; for certainly more patient labour has been spent on the study of the Bible than on that of all other ancient documents put together. But is there any such unanimity amongst learned men? Are we gradually approaching to it? Does not almost each year witness some new attempt to reconstruct Christianity out of Scripture? Three hundred years and more of Protestantism have been devoted to the study of the Bible without Tradition. There has been no lack of learning nor of earnestness. If at the end of that time there is even more diversity than at the beginning, it is not rash to conclude that the experiment has failed, and that truth is unattainable by this means.

It is impossible, then, on the one hand, to deny the utter diversity of the results of individual interpretation of the Bible, and, on the other hand, it would be grievously unfair to attribute it in all cases to moral perversity in the individual interpreters. The fault is in the method. I will choose an illustration of this in the matter of Ritual; and certainly I shall not be accused of making much of a trivial matter if I allude to the controversies concerning the Sacrament of unity, or the Holy Eucharist.

That there is such a Sacrament or Rite is a point admitted on all hands. Thus far, though perhaps no farther, there is agreement. Now, according to Protestant principles, we must learn the meaning and practice of this rite by independent investigation of the Bible. What will be the result? I will quote a passage from Locke in answer, for he reasons logically from his principles, and admits the result candidly. He is pleading, not for unity, but for toleration of diversity, and this is his argument:

'Every Christian,' he says, 'is to partake of that bread and that cup which is the communion of the body and blood of Christ. And is not every sincere Christian indispensably obliged to endeavour to understand these words of our Saviour's institution, "This is My body, and this is My blood"? And if, upon his serious endeavour to do it, he understands them in a literal sense—that Christ meant that that was really His body and blood, and nothing else—must he not necessarily believe that the bread and wine in the Lord's Supper are changed really into His body and blood, though he doth not know how? Or if, having his mind set otherwise, he understands the bread and wine to be really the body and blood of Christ, without ceasing to be the true bread and wine; or else, if he understands them that the body and blood of Christ are verily and indeed given and received in the Sacrament in a spiritual manner; or lastly, if he understands our Saviour to mean by those words the bread and wine to be only a representation of His body and blood—in which way soever of these four a Christian understands these words of our Saviour to be meant by Him, is he not obliged in that sense to believe them to be true, and assent to them? Or can he be a Christian and understand these words to be meant by our Saviour in one sense, and deny his assent to them as true in that sense? Would not this be to deny our Saviour's veracity, and consequently His being the Messiah sent from God?'

I see no flaw in this reasoning. If the method of individual search, which Locke presupposes, is once admitted; if contradictory conclusions necessarily result from that search, from whatever morally innocent cause—the nature of the truth, the structure of Scripture, or the 'set' of men's minds—then those contradictions must be accepted as the inevitable, innocent, and divinely-intended fruits of Christianity.

Yet in what a *reductio ad absurdum* are we landed! Jesus Christ is acknowledged to be the great Deliverer from error. Every follower of His is bound to use his best endeavours to ascertain his Teacher's meaning. But either Jesus Christ could not make His Apostles understand in what sense He gave His Body and Blood, or the Apostles, if they knew it, could not transmit their knowledge to their disciples. And thus, in the seventeenth century of Christianity, the meaning of one of its central institutions was still to be discovered, or rather never to be discovered with certainty, though always to be sought after with anxiety.

I have selected this example, not because of any eccentric opinions of Locke (for he does not state his own opinions), but because Locke, with a rare candour, prefers to vindicate for each man the right of private judgment, rather than to convince others of the fruits of his own private judgment. But I, for my part, will never believe of my Divine Master, that on the last evening of His life, while He was apparently providing a sacrament of union and of love, He was in reality casting among His disciples an apple of discord, an insoluble enigma, over which they might hopelessly quarrel till time should be no more. If this is the necessary result of the Protestant method of interpreting Scripture—and I do not see how, in the presence of three centuries of Protestant history, this can be denied—then that method must be an erroneous one. By means of it the cement of Christianity has been changed into a dissolvent; the bond of union has become the bone of contention. In the system of religion thus explained by Locke, the discovery of truth is a mere accident, while heresy or individual choice is a duty; and, by a climax of paradoxes, contradiction never rages more fiercely than around the central rite of unity and love.

Of course all this was foreseen by Jesus Christ, and in a certain sense willed by Him. It was willed as the punishment of those who should turn their backs upon His Church. God has so inspired the Holy Scriptures as that they shall be a mystery and a secret to the learning that scorns submission. He will not allow them to give up their meaning to those who have forsaken unity and broken charity. He gave the New Testament, a shrine containing an inestimable treasure, and He gave the key of Tradition wherewith to unlock it; but He will not suffer the lock to be picked, and the treasure to be possessed by those who reject the key.

If we now look for the source of the peculiar obscurity of the New Testament, both with regard to Doctrine and Ritual, it is not difficult to discover. It is this—that the New Testament, having been written for men well instructed in Christianity, naturally and providentially omits whatever it was superfluous to say to such men; and that, also providentially, there is absolutely no other means of supplying these omissions but by Christian Tradition.

When we examine a history, the first question to be settled is, whether it was written for men previously ignorant of the facts it professes to narrate, or conversant with them: for to read a history correctly, we must read it with the eyes of those for whom it was written. If we discover that they were in ignorance of the facts narrated, we shall expect to find a full and precise information in the history. Our only preparation in such a case will be acquaintance with the language and with the tone of thought of the readers. If we can succeed in attaining to this, we shall read as they read, and obtain the same amount of information that they obtained—that is, a full and precise knowledge of the matter of the history.

If, on the other hand, we discover that the original readers were conversant with the facts, we shall expect to find the writer passing over many things of importance, dwelling on more recondite details, and dealing in hints and allusions. In such a case we may or may not be able to put ourselves in the place of the first readers; that is, we may or may not be able to attain to their previous knowledge, and so to read as they read. If some particular history we are examining is of this supplementary structure, we cannot seek from it alone the necessary information; yet there may be many other histories or channels by which to supply deficiencies; or the subject-matter may be such that our familiarity with similar events may enable us to make many probable conjectures.

What is the case with the New Testament? It was certainly written for well-informed readers, conversant with the events it relates. It therefore naturally omits much that would have been set down had it been written to instruct the ignorant. It probably omits the most familiar points, which in this case would be the fundamental doctrines and daily practices. Can we supply this information? By Christian Tradition we certainly can. But without it there is no means whatever of doing this. The Gospels contain the only detailed record, besides Tradition, of the origin of Christianity. We can throw little light on their obscurities from conjecture; for in the whole history of the world there are no similar circumstances to give us any clue; and God's ways are too mysterious for us to attempt to measure them by our own reasonings. Hence it is that if we reject the only key which God has provided, we may try to pick the lock, but it will resist all our efforts.

We need not be surprised at this peculiar structure of the New Testament. If Jesus Christ came on earth to establish a Church; if He wished that the members of that Church should be known to be His disciples by their union, then He would take the means to secure this union. Such means we find by experience to be a common faith delivered by a living authority, and the bonds of the same worship and sacraments. And we find, in fact, neither in the written nor in traditional records of our Lord's life, any other means appointed by Himself. The living Church is ever acting on the commission she received from Him previously to the recording of it in the Gospels. 'Go and teach all nations, baptising them.' Tradition and Ritual are the great features of her charter. The Scriptures she has received as a help to Tradition. In her hands alone are they intelligible and consistent.

But He who inspired them for the use of His Church has taken precautions to prevent His truth from falling into the hands of those who abandon unity. He has inspired, not indeed a riddle, but a document that requires a key; and has intended that the vain efforts of talent and learning to dispense with the Church, and yet retain truth, should convince us still more of the value that He sets on humility and charity—that is, on submission to and communion with His Church.

Section III. Baptism and Communion.

In the present section I shall confine myself to those two sacraments which are generally admitted by Protestants, Baptism and Communion: I shall put aside for the moment all the conjectures to which they have given rise, and the controversies of which they have been the subject. I shall ask my reader to suppose that he knows as yet nothing more of them than the name. I shall then invite him to turn to the New Testament, not merely as Protestants profess to do, to see what it says about these rites; but also to notice what it omits to say, and what was the *intention* of the writer either in statement or omission.

1. We will begin with Baptism.

A careful collation of the four Gospels would convince us that in the Christian religion there was to be some important practice called Baptism. But what more should we learn? We should conjecture that it was a ceremony, and an initiatory ceremony into the Christian Church; and we should be left in doubt and darkness as to its precise nature.

All the Evangelists relate that our Lord received baptism from John. John, however, contrasts his baptism of water with the baptism which Jesus should confer 'of the Holy Ghost and of fire.' We look for an account of this wondrous baptism. The water of John's baptism was figurative, but it was a material reality, not a metaphor. What is the 'fire' of the baptism of Jesus? Is it only a figure of speech, or is it the element so called? The Evangelists do not answer the question. We find that St. Luke and St. John do not even allude to the institution of Christian baptism. St. Mark barely mentions it in recording the words, 'He that believes and is baptised shall be saved' (Mark xvi. 16). St. Matthew is the most explicit. He relates the precept to baptise believers 'in the name of the Father, and of the Son, and of the Holy Ghost.' But He does not say what these words mean, though the formula occurs nowhere else in his Gospel; nor does he say precisely that these words are to be used; nor whether the ceremony is to be performed with oil, fire, or water.

The necessary conclusion from the examination of these passages is, that it was not the intention of the Evangelists to teach the nature of baptism to their readers, and that they all suppose their readers well instructed on the subject. They had all been baptised; they had all seen that rite administered, probably many times; many of them had administered it themselves; they knew the character of its ceremonies, and were thoroughly instructed in the doctrine concerning it. They knew, of course, that it had been instituted by Jesus Christ Himself. But it was interesting to them to be told the precise occasion on which He promulgated it. Under such circumstances, it was natural for St. Matthew to tell them just what he does, and to pass over everything that he would have recorded had he been writing for strangers.

This explanation of the reticence of the Gospels is fully borne out by an examination of the remaining books of the New Testament. Take, for example, the following passage from the Acts of the Apostles : ' Paul came to Ephesus, and found certain disciples, and he said to them, Have you received the Holy Ghost since ye believed? But they said to him, We have not so much as heard whether there be a Holy Ghost. And he said, In what then were you baptised? Who said, In John's baptism. Then Paul said : John baptised the people with the baptism of penance, saying, That they should believe in Him who was to come after him, that is to say, in Jesus. Having heard these things, they were baptised in the name of the Lord Jesus. And when Paul had imposed his hands on them, the Holy Ghost came upon them' (Acts xix. 1-6). This is certainly a glimpse of a religious system in which Ritual holds no insignificant place. But everything is told by allusions. St. Paul's astonishment at the answer of the disciples, and his expressing his astonishment by the question regarding the form of their baptism, are not explained, nor are they supposed to need explanation, to St. Luke's readers. They had the key to all this in their own baptism. Those who, like Catholics, know that Christian baptism can only be conferred validly in the name of the Blessed Trinity, will understand at once St. Paul's question. Those who do not know this have been puzzled by the phrase, 'They were baptised in (or into) the name of the Lord Jesus,' and have raised a question whether the invocation of the Blessed Trinity is necessary. The help of Tradition would have taught them that the words of St. Luke were a *technical* phrase, well known to the first Christians.

We have another example of a similar technical phrase in the eighth chapter of the Acts of the Apostles. The historian, relating the interview between the deacon Philip and the eunuch of Ethiopia, sums up a long conversation in these words: 'He preached unto him Jesus.' Those to whom Jesus has not been preached, in the same way that He was preached by Philip, could not possibly know the meaning of this phrase, or how much is contained in the word 'Jesus.' Had a Catholic affirmed that it contained any doctrine regarding sacraments, and been unable to adduce direct Scripture proof for his affirmation, his word would not only have been questioned, but ridiculed. This, however, is now evident from the context; for as Philip and the eunuch journey on, the eunuch exclaims: 'See, here is water; what doth hinder me from being baptised?' Philip, then, in 'preaching Jesus' had preached the necessity and nature of baptism. Of course, in this case, Scripture is thus far the key to itself. It is Scripture that tells us that 'preaching Jesus' means, among other things, preaching baptism. Yet this only comes out incidentally; and it was not the intention of St. Luke to instruct his readers, by means of this circumstance, in the meaning of the word 'Jesus.' 'To preach Jesus' was evidently a technical phrase, of which the meaning was well known to those for whom St. Luke wrote. How much more does it imply besides baptism? This is a question that could never be answered from Scripture alone—that can never be answered at all unless we have the key possessed by those first disciples.

If the nature of baptism cannot be gathered with certainty even from the historical books of the New Testament; if the authors of those historical books had no such design as to teach their readers the external form, the meaning, the obligation of baptism, one can scarcely expect to find these things in the other writings of the Apostles. The silence of the Epistles regarding matters of Christian worship in general is insisted on by some as a strong argument against Ritualism. But nothing can be more fallacious than negative arguments, especially arguments drawn from omissions in epistolary correspondence. 'The Epistles,' says Locke, 'were writ to those who were in the faith and true Christians already, and so could not be designed to teach them the fundamental articles and points necessary to salvation. . . . . And they were writ upon particular occasions, and without those occasions had not been writ, and so cannot be thought necessary to salvation, though they, resolving doubts and reforming mistakes, are of great advantage to our knowledge and practice. I do not deny but the great doctrines of the Christian faith are dropped here and there, and scattered up and down in most of them.'[4]

In the preface to his paraphrase of St. Paul's Epistles, Locke speaks still more to the purpose. 'The nature of epistolary writings in general disposes the writer to pass by the mentioning of many things, as well known to him to whom his letter is addressed, which are necessary to be laid open to a stranger, to make him comprehend what is said; and it not seldom falls out that a well-penned letter, which is very easy and intelligible to the receiver, is very obscure to a stranger, who hardly knows what to make of it. The matters that St. Paul wrote about were certainly things well known to those he writ to, and which they had some peculiar concern in, which made them easily apprehend his meaning, and see the tendency and force of his discourse. But we having now, at this distance, no information of the occasion of his writing, little or no knowledge of the

[4] *Reasonableness of Christianity*, Locke's Works, vol. viii. pp. 152-4, ed. 1823.

temper and circumstances those he writ to were in, but what is to be gathered out of the Epistles themselves, it is not strange that many things in them lie concealed to us, which, no doubt, they who were concerned in the letter understood at first sight.'

Now if this is the case even with regard to points of faith that are, directly or indirectly, the subject-matter of these letters, how much more will it be true of those rites that were not in any way the scope of the Epistles? 'You may read Epistle after Epistle of St. Paul,' says Dr. Vaughan, 'and not find a word touching upon anything of a Ritual nature. It should be remembered,' he adds, thinking to give additional force to his argument, 'that the Epistles of St. Peter, and in fact nearly all the other Epistles, are completely silent touching the worship of the early churches.' The conclusion he would draw from this is, that in those days Ritual had but little significance. As if it would not be easy to make a collection of hundreds of letters of the Popes in which there is not even a distant allusion to Ritual! The only conclusion that can fairly be drawn from the fact that the Epistles seldom, directly or even indirectly, treat of Ritual is, that the Christians to whom they were written were well-instructed in such matters of daily life, and therefore required few admonitions, and that in consequence it is not to the Epistles we must look for information regarding subjects on which they hardly touch.

But let us remember that we are in search now for information regarding a sacrament that even the most anti-ritualistic Protestants acknowledge to be of divine institution and of perpetual and universal obligation. If the Protestant theory of the sufficiency of Scripture be correct, we *ought* to find all necessary information, regarding this sacrament at least, in the New Testament.

We have sought in the Gospels and in the Acts of the Apostles. We have found that they do not give the information we seek, but suppose their readers to be already in possession of it. Do the Epistles supply the deficiency?

We have in them many allusions to Christian baptism. We are told that there is 'one Lord, one faith, one baptism' (Eph. iv. 5), which shows the importance of the rite, but not its nature. The Corinthians are reminded, 'In one Spirit were we all baptised into one body, whether Jews or Gentiles,' &c. (1 Cor. xii. 13), which is an appeal to their knowledge of a fact personal to themselves, regarding which they were consequently well informed, but which conveys little information to those who have not a similar experience. There are passages where more doctrinal teaching is conveyed, but it is only by allusion to what was already known. Such, for example, is the exhortation to the Colossians : 'As therefore you have received Jesus Christ the Lord, walk ye in Him. . . . . . Buried with Him in baptism, in whom also you are risen again,' &c. (Col. ii. 6, 12). The Apostle is not giving the instruction we seek, but referring to instruction already received orally. Or again, in the Epistle to the Romans : '*Know you not* that all we that are baptised in Christ Jesus are baptised in His death,' &c. (Rom. vi. 3). This, with the words that follow, is the most explicit teaching regarding the nature of baptism in the Epistles ; yet it is still an allusion to knowledge possessed previously ; and clear as it must have been to those to whom the letter was written, it has been interpreted in the most contradictory manners by men who persist in reading Scripture without its key. I need say nothing of such passages as that of St. Paul to the Corinthians: 'What shall they do that are baptised for the dead, if the dead rise not again at all?' (1 Cor. xv. 29) because it is evident that the allusion was quite clear to the Corinthians, and it is acknowledged that it is quite obscure to us.

But I observe regarding all these passages, and any others that remain which I have not quoted, that they give but very scanty information as to the external form of the sacrament.

From this review we may draw some important conclusions.

a. Neither St. Matthew when he wrote his Gospel, nor St. Luke when he wrote his history of the Apostles, nor the Apostles when they wrote their letters, had any design that their respective readers should gather for themselves either the doctrine of baptism or the form of administering it. Why indeed teach them what they knew already?

b. If it was not intended that such information should be gathered from any one of these writings, taken alone, much less was it intended by their authors that it should be obtained by a collation of them all.

Such a collation was impossible until a collection of the various writings had been made, and their authority settled; and as this was not done till many years after the death of the writers, Christians for several generations would have been without an accurate knowledge of a rite that each and all of these documents allude to as of the utmost importance.

c. It seems now to be maintained by Protestants that, though it never entered into the design of the authors, singly or collectively, to inform the Church by their writings of what she ought to know regarding baptism, yet the Holy Ghost so overruled their minds and pens, that the collected writings do now supply her with that rule of faith and practice which the Apostolic Church had in oral Tradition; that though each writer, taken alone, is obscure, yet one supplies what is wanting in another, and one clears up what in another is doubtful.

The overruling Providence of God in the formation of the New Testament is a Catholic Tradition; but this supposed Providence, which makes the collected Scriptures into a perfect and sufficient rule of faith and practice, Catholic Tradition rejects, and Scripture itself supplies no evidence of it. If Protestants want us to believe that we are to gather our information about baptism by collating all the books of the New Testament, let them begin by proving that, without the help of Tradition, *any* satisfactory information on which they themselves can agree can be gathered from those books. They will then have to prove, in the second place, that the original mode of transmitting revelation, instituted by Jesus Christ and His Apostles, was afterwards to be set aside in favour of this new one, which is of an utterly different nature. Until they have proved these two points, the theory or assumption—for it is nothing else—of the sufficiency of Scripture is not even plausible.

2. We will now examine whether the New Testament gives us more complete information regarding the other rite that Protestants accept, than it does regarding Baptism. They call it 'The Lord's Supper.' It matters not to inquire whether

this expression is used in Scripture of the Communion instituted by Jesus Christ, or only of those love-feasts observed by the first Christians in connection with the Holy Communion, or whether, as some appear to think, these are one and the same rite. Call it what we may—Holy Eucharist, Holy Communion, Blessed Sacrament, Holy Mass with Catholics, or Lord's Supper with Protestants—in what way did its Institutor, Jesus Christ, intend that His disciples in future ages should learn its nature and its manner of administration?

From an accurate and critical collation of all the texts concerning it in the various books of the New Testament—such is the Protestant answer.

This was evidently not the primitive method, for such a collation was of course impossible until the various books of the New Testament had been sifted, their authority settled, and the Canon drawn up. No one will maintain that for so many generations Christians were without the means of celebrating correctly one of the principal rites of Christ's institution.

Should it be said that this method of learning our Lord's will was only intended for later ages, I would reply that there is not a trace, in any one of the books of the New Testament, of any design on the part of their authors to teach men how to celebrate the Lord's Supper, or to explain its meaning to those who are in ignorance.

St. John says not one word about its institution. St. Matthew and St. Mark record our Lord's own act, but they say nothing from which their readers could conjecture that the ceremony which Jesus Christ then performed was to be an institution among Christians. They do not record the words: 'This do for a commemoration of Me.' They give neither command, counsel, nor even permission to repeat the action. And no man who read those Gospels alone, without any other knowledge on the subject, could have gathered in any way that there was to be a Christian rite called the Lord's Supper, or Holy Communion. The recipients therefore of those Gospels, had they not possessed Tradition, far from seeking more full and detailed information, would not have seen any need whatever to concern themselves about it.

Those to whom St. Luke's Gospel came would indeed have discovered that their Master, after breaking the bread, and saying, 'This is My body,' added, 'Do this for a commemoration of Me.' They would therefore have studied attentively his account of the rite, in order to know how to perform it. They would probably have noticed that St. Luke, in speaking of the cup, does not renew the injunction. They might therefore not unnaturally have supposed that this was no part of the future rite. Perhaps at some later period of their life the Epistles of St. Paul to the Corinthians might have fallen into their hands, and then they would have discovered their mistake, since he tells us—what no Evangelist records—that Jesus Christ commanded the cup also to be used in the commemoration. But did no one know this until he wrote his Epistle, about twenty-four years after our Lord's ascension?

Certainly he did not write with the intention of making it known; for he says that he had delivered to them the doctrine orally before; and the reason why he again recalls the institution is, not that they may learn to celebrate correctly, nor to teach them the doctrine of the Holy Eucharist, but that from that doctrine, already perfectly well known to his readers, he may urge upon them certain moral conclusions: first, as to the eating of meats offered to idols (in the tenth chapter), and then as to the abuse of the love-feasts (in the eleventh chapter); and for these reasons he introduces the mention of this rite by these words: 'I speak as to wise men, judge ye what I say' (ch. x. 15); *i.e.* you are well instructed, reflect then on the truths of faith, consult your own reason, your own consciences, and see if my conclusions are not just.

St. Paul, as the Anglican Brett has correctly observed, does not write to inform his readers what is necessary for the consecration of the Eucharist. 'It is an instruction to them to consider what is administered to them, and how they ought to receive it, but does not appear to be any direction to the ministrator how or in what manner he was to consecrate the elements, or with what words he was to bless, eucharistise, or give thanks, over them. He plainly supposes that the administrators of the Eucharist had rightly performed their parts (bating their not excluding the ignorant and unworthy from partaking the divine mysteries); otherwise he would not have instructed the communicants only, but the administrators also. Neither would he have told the communicants that they received the Lord's body, though they did not discern it, if what had been given to them had not been consecrated in such a manner as to be made the Lord's body, in such a sense as Christ intended it should be understood to be so. Neither does St. Paul say what liquor was to be in the cup, which would have been necessary if he had intended to direct the minister of this sacrament what he was to say and do on this occasion.'[5]

Since not one of the writers of the New Testament wrote with any design of teaching men how to celebrate this great Christian rite, since they all suppose their readers well instructed in both the practice and the doctrine, what grounds have Protestants for their persuasion that, without the Tradition which the sacred writers presuppose, they can attain, by a general and critical collation of all these writers, to an accurate knowledge of what not one of them intended to teach?

The investigation we have been pursuing brings us to the conclusion that, with regard to Ritual at least, the New Testament requires a key, and that the key of Apostolic Tradition was possessed by those to whom the books of the New Testament were originally written. This Tradition was not merely a doctrine orally handed down. It was the Ritual itself received from the Apostles, and alluded to in the New Testament, though not derived from it. This Ritual must have embodied doctrines as well as facts. If men were baptised into the name of Jesus, they must have known who Jesus was; if they were baptised in the name of the Father, the Son, and the Holy Ghost, they must have known the signification of those three words; they must have known certain doctrines regarding the death and resurrection of Jesus Christ which St. Paul speaks of as symbolised by Baptism. They must have known the nature of the Church into which Baptism had introduced them, the kind of authority claimed by those who had baptised them, in a word the whole truth and discipline of Christ in its ele-

[5] Brett, *Dissertation on the Liturgies.*

mentary and essential facts. Those who had learned from Apostolic lips how to celebrate or how to receive worthily the Body and Blood of Christ knew well what was meant by those words. They needed no critical conjectures and collation of texts to inform them whether that Rite was a sacrifice or a sacrament, or both or neither.

In a word, they possessed in the doctrines they had been taught, and in the familiar Ritual with which those doctrines were intimately connected, a living and full Tradition, by means of which they were either able to dispense with Scripture altogether, if they had it not, or to use or interpret aright those portions they possessed.

Section IV. Other Rites.

THE two rites we have been considering in the last section were chosen by way of illustration of a principle. That other rites are mentioned in the New Testament is quite as clear as that Baptism and Communion are there to be found. The question, therefore, immediately suggests itself, do the Holy Scriptures without tradition tell us anything about the number and the relative importance of the various parts of Ritual? It is as necessary to know the place and importance of a rite as to know its nature and external form. If the New Testament mentions several rites, this is not sufficient for our instruction, unless we are told which of these is of temporary, which of permanent institution, which is intended for a class and which is of universal use, which is merely permitted or counselled, and which is of strict obligation. It is certain that the New Testament is either silent on such points, or conveys its information only indirectly and by inference. This consideration is of vital importance to Protestants, and it may be well to develop it by comparing together the Scripture testimony with the received Protestant traditions and usages.

There are ceremonies holding a conspicuous place in the New Testament narrative, which, rightly or wrongly, are omitted in ordinary Protestant Ritual. I choose as examples the Washing of the Feet, and the Anointing of the Sick. It is not my wish to suggest a new heresy to any lover of novelties, yet I will state my own conviction that a perfectly impartial, unprejudiced reader, confining himself strictly to the New Testament, would select the 'washing of feet' as one of the principal rites or sacraments of Christian observance, and that he would probably rank it with Baptism and Communion.

Let it not be said that it is mentioned only once by the Evangelists, and perhaps once alluded to in the Epistles (1 Tim. v. 10). It would be a most insulting treatment of any saying of God to judge of its importance by the number of times it is repeated. All words of God, being utterances of Truth and Wisdom, must be emphatic. A clear precept coming from God, though given but once, must be obligatory. If, then, any one reading St. John's Gospel should judge that our Lord Jesus Christ has instituted and commanded the practice of a mystical and ceremonial washing of the feet, the mere silence of the other Gospels, or of the other books of the New Testament, on the subject, could be no reason for disregarding a divine precept. Now what is the case? St. John records the history of the washing of feet in the most circumstantial detail. It is performed in a very striking and emphatic manner by Jesus Christ, on the very eve of His death. He seems to make it essential to fellowship with Himself. 'If I wash thee not, thou shalt have no part with Me' (John xiii. 8). He seems to impose a formal precept of its repetition. 'You ought also to wash one another's feet, for I have given you an example, that as I have done to you, so you do also' (ib. v. 14, 15). He seems to insinuate some mysterious meaning or virtue in it beyond what lies on the surface: 'What I do, thou knowest not now; but thou shalt know hereafter' (v. 7). Any one considering these things with a mind unprepossessed, and with no further knowledge on the subject, would assuredly assign to this rite an important place, if not the very first place, among the observances of Christianity.

It is evident, at least, that not from Scripture alone did Protestants derive their neglect of the ceremony so impressively performed by our Blessed Lord. No passage of Scripture is alleged to prove that His apparent precept imposes no real obligation. This is decided on conjecture alone. Washing of the feet, it is said, was an oriental custom, a token of hospitality and of kindness in our Lord's time and country. Therefore His action must be considered merely as an oriental mode of teaching a lesson of charity and humility. The lesson must be always taught, but not in the same symbolic form. But surely there is great rashness in such processes of reasoning. Could not our Lord have adopted a natural or oriental rite, and have elevated it to a supernatural dignity, and made it of universal obligation? Was not a supper on bread and wine a natural repast before our Lord's institution of Holy Communion? Was not Baptism an oriental usage when it was adopted and raised to new meaning and dignity, and promulgated for all nations, by Jesus Christ? Those, then, must have a great reliance on the certainty of their own reasoning, who, with no other foundation than conjecture, persuade themselves that our Lord's command entails no literal obedience on themselves. Can it be that they are emboldened to take this view from observing that the Catholic Church has never counted the washing of feet among the list of grace-conferring Sacraments? This is indeed the case; but then Catholics do not support their view by appeal to Scripture only. The words that our Blessed Lord spoke to St. Peter after washing his feet—'What I do thou knowest not now; *but thou shalt know hereafter*' (John xiii. 7)—point to a subsequent and supplemental information which was to be the key to what is recorded by St. John. We believe that that key was given to St. Peter and to the Apostles, and by them traditionally given to the Churches that they founded; and by it we know that the washing of feet, though an important rite for all ages, is not an eighth sacrament.

Let us turn now to the anointing with oil mentioned by St. James. The passage runs thus in the Protestant version: 'Is any sick among you? let him call for the elders of the Church, and let them pray over him, anointing him with oil in the name of the Lord; and the prayer of faith shall save the sick, and the Lord shall raise him up; and if he have committed sins, they shall be forgiven him' (James v. 14, 15). It is well known that both the Catholic Church, and the oriental sects separated from the Church for fourteen centuries, account this ceremony a sacrament instituted by our Lord to confer grace on His sick members till the end of time; whereas Protestants hold it to be a miraculous and merely temporary rite; and Anglicans call our repetition of it a 'corrupt following of the Apostles.' Yet what clear warrant of Scripture have they that their own neglect of it is not a corrupt disobedience to the Apostles? They do not even allege any such. They rely solely on their own critical conjectures. There is no need here to discuss the different interpretations given by Catholics and Protestants. Let us allow, for argument's sake, that the Protestant explanation, which supposes St. James to refer to the miraculous gifts of healing then possessed by certain Christians, is a plausible one; assuredly it is not so clear and certain as to leave no room for doubt. The Apostle seems to give a universal rule: Is *any* sick? whereas the grace of healing could be only exercised on certain occasions; he speaks of calling in the *elders*, whereas the power of healing was not granted to all of them or to them exclusively; he speaks of *forgiveness* of sins, which certainly seems to belong to an interior benefit conferred on all ages rather than to an external grace belonging to a certain epoch. And the Church throughout the world has so understood it and so understands it still. Protestants also have admitted that the institution of this sacrament, as understood by Catholics, would, 'if warranted, be matter of great comfort;' yet they only do so in order to add that 'if not warranted, it must be matter of as great presumption;'[6] and then they eagerly contend that it is not warranted, in order to deprive themselves of comfort, and prove us guilty of presumption. It is perfectly true that millions of Christians have been comforted in their last moments by a lively confidence in the promise here made by St. James, and have thanked Jesus Christ with their dying breath for that beautiful series of Sacraments, which had literally accompanied them from the cradle to the grave.

[6] Burnet, *On the Thirty-nine Articles*, art. 25.

Reader, death is coming on apace for you and me. It is my earnest hope and prayer, that the hand that traces these lines, and the eyes of those that read them, may be anointed with the Holy Oil of Prayer, as saints have called it, ere we go to render our account 'of things done in the body, whether good or evil.' Have you quite made up your mind to forego this consoling rite? And are you quite sure of the grounds on which you prefer to go before your Judge,

> 'Unhousled, disappointed, unanel'd'?

Have you carefully examined into the conduct of your forefathers who first discarded this hope of Christendom? Will you risk your salvation on the accuracy of their criticism of Scripture, and knowledge of the ways of God? Is it not perhaps true that you accept Baptism because the Reformers accepted it, and reject Unction because they rejected it, without having exercised in regard of either rite that independent judgment which is your boast? The rashness of Protestant criticism and conduct in respect to this rite is beginning to be acknowledged in different quarters. A learned Anglican clergyman, the Rev. Mr. Scudamore, acknowleges that 'it could hardly be right' (in the compilers of the Anglican Prayer-Book) 'to remove from the Formularies all recognition of a rite prescribed and practised by the Apostles.' 'As it is,' continues Mr. Scudamore, "the rite has dropped out of general knowledge in this country. But if a sick person, having faith in the prayers of the Church, were to send for his parish priest, or priests (the Presbyters, or "elders of the Church"), and, appealing to the Scriptures, were to request them, on its authority, to "pray over him, anointing him with oil in the name of the Lord," I do not see how they could refuse compliance without incurring the guilt of disobedience to the voice of God in Holy Scripture.'

But if it would be a sin in the 'elders' to refuse the rite when asked to confer it, can the neglect to ask for it be without guilt? Can a Church which has taught her children this neglect be the Church of the Apostles and of Jesus Christ? An Anglican writer, more bold than Mr. Scudamore, uses language very candid, yet very strange from one in his position. 'The

Roman Church,' he writes, 'has retained permanently as part of her system many things which are the common heritage of Christendom, but of which the English Church was burglariously despoiled by her own treacherous shepherds three hundred years ago. Some of these things, as, for instance, Unction of the Sick, are of Scriptural obligation, and their disuse cannot be described less gravely than as a heinous sin.'[7]

But here I would make a remark of great importance. The obligation of this Apostolic rite can be proved from Scripture, or at least cannot be disproved from Scripture, and therefore it cannot be neglected without rashness. Yet the manner of performing it cannot be derived from Scripture alone; and the attempt to revive it, without the traditions and the authority of the Catholic Church, is little less rash than was its first abandonment contrary to her tradition and authority. Surely no one will maintain that St. James was writing of something hitherto unknown and unpractised by those to whom his Epistle was addressed—that he was giving such full information as would be required in the promulgation of an entirely new rite. There is scarcely a word in the whole passage that does not suggest a question, and has not been the subject of a discussion.

'*Is any one sick?*' What degree of sickness is required? If a painful or serious sickness, must there be imminent or at least remote danger of death? If recovery has taken place once or twice, must the same recourse to God and to the 'elders' be had in every subsequent attack, and even where the case seems desperate, as, for example, in extreme old age?

'*Let him call.*' Must the patient himself express the desire; or, if through insensibility he is incapable of this, may his will be interpreted by others?

'*The elders.*' Is this word to be interpreted literally as the old men, or has it a technical meaning like our modern Senators and Aldermen? If a technical meaning, who are these 'elders,' and how do they become such? The Apostle uses a plural form; is, then, the presence of more than one necessary,

[7] Leading article in *Church Times*, Sept. 13, 1872.

or is the expression to be understood as pointing out the class, without reference to number?

'*Let them pray over him.*' Was there any prescribed form of prayer? Must the patient join in the prayer? Does its efficacy depend solely on the faith of the 'elders'? The Anglican Church teaches that 'the unworthiness of the minister does not hinder the validity of the Sacraments.' Could this doctrine be applied to the rite in question?

'*Anointing him.*' The whole body? Or what part?

'*With oil.*' Supposing olive oil, such as was used by the Apostles, cannot be obtained, would it suffice to use colza oil, or train oil, or petroleum, or grease?

'*In the name of the Lord.*' Does this phrase signify that this unction is an institution of our Lord, or does it mean that His name is to be explicitly invoked?

'*The prayer of faith.*' This has been taken to mean the whole rite performed in obedience to God's will. Is this its meaning? Or does it refer to that special faith to which our Lord promised miracles, so that the promise would be conditional on the possession and exercise of such faith by the elders?

'*Shall save.*' Is this salvation or cure to be understood of soul or of body, or of both?

'*The Lord shall raise him up.*' Is the restoration of bodily health intended, or is it a raising up of the soul by strength and confidence? If of the body, is it a promise of a sudden and clearly miraculous cure, or of a gradual one? Is the promise of bodily health absolute, or conditional on its being profitable to the soul?

'*If he have committed sins.*' All have committed sins. Of what sin, then, does the Apostle speak? Of all sins as yet unforgiven? And if so, on what conditions of repentance? And how can Protestants explain the connection between forgiveness of sin and the ministry of 'elders,' or an external rite? Or does the Apostle speak only of such sins as have been the cause of the sickness, as some have conjectured? And in this case, is the connection to be real or only surmised? And how are rash judgments and superstition to be avoided? Does the forgiveness extend only to the punishment, the temporal pain or sickness which is the consequence of the sin, on condition that the sin itself has been already pardoned; or does forgiveness include the guilt also? And once more: immediately after the words already quoted from St. James, he adds: 'Confess therefore your sins one to another, and pray one for another that you may be saved.' Have these words any connection with the foregoing? And if they have, is confession of sin a condition or a means towards the promised forgiveness? Must the confession be made to the 'elders,' and is this the meaning of 'confess one to the other,' *i.e.* the sick man to the elders, just as 'pray one for another' means the elders for the sick man?

Here are a multitude of questions, not started for the love of controversy, but suggesting themselves necessarily and requiring solution before the exhortation of St. James could be carried into practice. The answers to them can neither be safely derived from conjecture, nor are they contained in any parallel passage of Holy Scripture. Those for whom the Apostle immediately wrote had the answer in the living Tradition of their Church. Has God given to us no such key?

CHAPTER IV.

THE CANON AND THE CODE.

WHAT has been said will be sufficient to explain the Catholic stand-point. The Church has a vast system of Ritual, which she has developed during the centuries. Of this system, one part is divine and immutable, the other is her own creation, and subject to her will. That part which is of ecclesiastical institution has to some extent been derived from the study of Scripture, or has sprung from the action of principles that are recognised and approved in Scripture. This was the subject of the first part of the Essay. But that part of Ritual which is of divine origin is necessarily older than the New Testament, and independent of it, though the Ritual as existing in the Church not only harmonises with the written record, but explains it.

Two difficulties occur in this view which deserve some answer.

1. First, then, it may be said that if even divine Ritual need not be gathered from Scripture, or even, strictly speaking, proved thereby, there can be no test whereby to distinguish between divine institutions and human additions and corruptions. Thus it is the popular notion among Protestants that under the name of Tradition a door is opened for every kind of innovation. Besides this, even suppose that we could succeed in tracing back a doctrine or a practice or a ceremony to the very earliest ages of the Church, what guarantee do we possess of its apostolicity? Might it not be a primitive corruption, or at best a merely human element introduced amidst what is divine? This has led some Protestants, while admitting Tradition as an *initial* source of the knowledge of Revelation, to deny its authority, unless it be confirmed by clear proofs from

Scripture. They would assign to it somewhat of the position that theologians hold towards the Bishops assembled in Council. It prepares the matter on which Scripture alone can pass judgment.

This is not and cannot be the Catholic view. Divine Tradition is the word of God no less than Scripture. The written and unwritten Word may support and explain each other, but they have equal authority.

I reply, then, to the difficulties proposed, that we have the very same means of sifting traditions and verifying those that are authentic, and assigning their proper character—as divine or apostolico-divine, or merely apostolic, or ecclesiastical[1]—that we have of sifting early Christian writings, and discerning between those that are inspired, those that are good though human, and those that are bad. The apocryphal gospels and epistles, that abounded in early ages of the Christian Church, do not disprove the authentic writings of the Apostles. Neither do apocryphal traditions throw discredit or doubt on those traditions that are authentic and divine.

Our Canon of Scripture and our Code of Ritual are drawn up by the same means, by the same authority, and with the same certainty. There are doubtless, at the present day, difficulties attending the historical evidences of both. The oral testimony of apostolic men died with them. The living Tradition of apostolic Churches, though it survives in its results, can no longer be tested in itself. Many important historical documents have perished. Neither individuals nor the Churches have the materials at hand on which the Churches of the third or fourth centuries passed judgment. That judgment can never be revised. We must accept it, whether as to our Canon of Scripture or our Code of Ritual, as final and divine, or we must lapse into hopeless scepticism. There are no greater historical difficulties about the seven Sacraments than about the fourteen Epistles of St. Paul. Those who decline to admit the Church's infallibility, or in other words the fulfilment of God's promises to her, will seek in vain for literary or scientific certainty. They

---

[1] On these distinctions, and on the whole subject of Tradition, consult Franzelin, *De Verbo Dei*.

will become the sport of caprice or of fashion; and we shall have, on the one hand, Luther proclaiming the Epistle of St. James to be an 'Epistle of straw,' and on the other the Church of England calling the Sacrament of Extreme Unction 'a corrupt following of the Apostles.'

2. A second difficulty might be thus stated: Does not the Catholic view of Tradition make the New Testament an incomplete work? or can any plan be assigned according to which God has drawn the limits between Scripture and Tradition?

Before replying directly to this question, I may observe that the rejection of Tradition would not free Protestants from difficulty. The completeness of Scripture could only be a conjecture, an assumption, or a trust. Even if all apostolic writings had survived, Protestants could have no certainty that the whole Christian Revelation had been embodied in them. But it is admitted that apostolic writings have perished.[2] We do not know what they contained. Catholics have just as much right to conjecture (if they so please) that a lost epistle contained details regarding the *Sacrifice* of the Eucharist, or the *Sacrament* of Holy Orders, identical with the testimony of primitive Tradition, as Protestants have to contend that the lost epistles would have added nothing to those we possess. Let any one consider what would be the effect, on those who look to Scripture only, of the absence of one or other book of our present Canon. If what we now call the First Epistle to the Corinthians had perished, instead of that which was really the first written, some one might have told us that there is not a tittle of evidence in any apostolic epistle that the Apostles practised, or even knew, of such an ordinance as 'the Lord's Supper' or Communion;[3] and we should have had a great negative argument framed against the Eucharist, similar to that we hear so much of against the devotion to the Blessed Virgin. It would have been said: Could St. Paul be in the habit of celebrating the Eucharist, and yet never say one word about it in any one of his Epistles? This cannot now be said, because

---

[2] In his *first* Epistle to the Corinthians St. Paul alludes to a previous one. 1 Cor. v. 9.

[3] Many Protestants refuse to see any allusion to the Eucharist in Heb. xiii. 10.

by means of the First Epistle to the Corinthians we have his own testimony to the fact. Yet—except on the assumption of an overruling Providence of God compelling St. Paul to record every part of his faith and practice *at least once*—what more value is there in a negative argument derived from the silence of fourteen Epistles than in one derived from the silence of thirteen? Or, on the other hand, if the fourteenth, being preserved, throws quite a new light on the other thirteen, who can tell but that the fifteenth, which is lost, would, if preserved, have thrown a new light on the present fourteen? I do not say that this would have been so, for we know absolutely nothing as to the contents of the lost epistles; but to my mind, at least, there is no improbability in supposing that they would have *completed* the knowledge which we derive from Scripture on some points of doctrine, discipline, or ritual, just as it is now completed by the possession of Tradition.

Whatever may be thought of this, the completeness of the New Testament as a record of Revelation is a mere assumption. Catholics deny it; and if they are asked for what reason, or on what plan God gave Tradition as a complement to Scripture, or Scripture as a complement to Tradition, I would answer as follows:

In many cases we must be satisfied with knowing the fact of God's Providence, without being able to attain to its intrinsic reason; and this appears to be partly the case as regards the Canon of the New Testament. It is the Catholic belief that God inspired the sacred writers both as to what they say and as to what they omit; and there are many cases when we can discover deep and beautiful wisdom in an omission. But there are many cases when we shall be at a loss to know why great prominence is given to certain things and others are passed over.

However, I think that a careful examination of the structure of the historical books will reveal to us the method which directed the historians in their statements and omissions. They seem to have entered into detail with regard to those things that were transitory, and to have passed lightly over those things that were to be permanent, and that would therefore speak for themselves. The birth, death, and resurrection of Jesus Christ were transitory actions; they were to take place once only. They were ever to be remembered, but never to be repeated. Now, though these great facts are commemorated in unwritten Tradition, and bound up with the Ritual of the Church, yet the circumstances which attended them were such as could scarcely have been transmitted safely and in detail without writing. As God wished these circumstances to be remembered, He inspired the Evangelists to enter into the fullest detail in relating them.

So also with regard to the words of Jesus Christ. Many besides those now known may have been in the mouths of the first Christians, like that which St. Paul quoted to the elders at Ephesus; but for ages the memory has perished of all but such as are recorded in the Gospels. We conclude that God inspired the Evangelists to record all such of the words of His Divine Son as it was pleasing to Him to communicate to future ages.

But when we turn to the second class of things, those that are in their own nature permanent, we find a different plan pursued. 'The things of the kingdom of God' are referred to (Acts i. 3), but not related in detail. The government and hierarchy of the Church, the Church's worship, her sacraments and rites, were to be visible and imperishable institutions. They would bear witness to themselves—tell their own tale. They would thus be familiar and well known to all those for whom the historians wrote. It was natural therefore to omit these things, or merely to mention their first origin, or to refer to them by an allusion.

Again, amongst familiar things were the great doctrines of the faith. These are everywhere supposed, seldom spoken of explicitly. Perhaps of all matters connected with Scripture this is the most important to bear well in mind.

Let us take, for an example, the method of writing used by St. Luke in the Acts of the Apostles. When he gives an abridgment of an Apostle's discourse in a Jewish synagogue, or in a heathen market-place, he merely details the process by which the Apostles insinuated themselves into their hearers' minds. As this process would vary according to circumstances, it would not be known to St. Luke's readers. They would remember how the Apostles succeeded with themselves; they would be glad to know how they had succeeded with others. This, therefore, would be exactly the kind of information St. Luke would be likely to give. But when once the Apostles had found docile hearers, their instruction would be of the same tenor in every place. St. Luke's readers had personal experience of that instruction: there was no necessity to repeat it to them. It would have been wearisome to do so. Locke has noticed that when St. Paul preached to the Jews or to proselytes of the Jews, he said nothing to them of the believing in one true God, Maker of heaven and earth; which he did when preaching to heathens; and the reason he assigns for this difference is a good one: 'It was needless,' he says, 'to press this truth about God to those who believed and professed it already.' Now, a precisely similar account may be given of St. Luke's manner of abridging the Apostle's sermons. As St. Paul thought it unnecessary to teach the unity of God to Jews who knew it already, so St. Luke thought it needless to tell Christians that the Apostle taught his converts the Trinity of Persons; because his Christian readers knew the Apostle's doctrine already. He says it equivalently when he relates that the converts were baptised; for he is writing to Christian converts, who had themselves been baptised 'in the name of the Father, and of the Son, and of the Holy Ghost.' It would have been almost an impertinence in St. Luke, had he wearied his readers with the first elements of Christianity, and with repetition of the facts of their daily experience.

If Christians in those days had been, like Protestants now, divided into a multitude of sects—one affirming, the other denying, Jesus Christ to be God; one adoring, the other rejecting, a Trinity of Persons; one believing Baptism to be an efficacious sacrament, the other regarding it as a mere figure; one believing in and worshipping the Real Presence, the other calling such worship idolatrous—if such had been the condition of those first Christians, then St. Luke would most probably have adopted a very different method in his narrative. He would have passed rapidly over the Apostle's adventures, and dwelt little on his preliminary preaching, while he would have enlarged on the precise meaning given to the articles of faith controverted among his readers.

But St. Luke was writing to men who, like Catholics of the present day, were united in faith. To his readers the facts and the truths of Christianity were objective, undisputed realities, clearly and universally admitted. He therefore adopts exactly the style that Catholics make use of under similar circumstances. If two converts to the Catholic faith compare notes regarding their conversion, they will dilate on the points in which they differed, on the events or the train of reflections that led them respectively to seek admission into the Church; but they will never waste time in asking each other about the nature of the creed they were taught, and which they professed, or the form of their reception. They know they were both taught the same creed, and both admitted by the same rites.

If a missionary writes home to Catholics, he dwells on his adventures, and the arguments by which he convinces the ignorant savage or the learned bonze; he does not tire his readers by repeating the Apostles' Creed on the occasion of each conversion that he narrates. You might read through a volume of the Annals of the Propagation of the Faith without meeting a single passage in which the missionary informs his fellow-Catholics at home that he believes in seven sacraments, and teaches his converts to believe the same. It may crop up incidentally, but it will be only incidentally; and the last book, perhaps, from which a reasonable man would think of gathering a full and precise notion of the Catholic creed and discipline, would be those very historical letters that everywhere presupposes them.

Some most important consequences follow from this structure of Holy Scripture both as to Catholic and Protestant theology.

a. Though Catholics contend that all or nearly all their doctrines and practices are to be found in the Bible either explicitly or in allusion, in germ or in principle, yet they have never denied that much that is plain in Councils is obscure in

Scripture, nor have they affirmed that the relative importance of certain doctrines or practices in the Catholic Church always corresponds to their relative prominence, or to the space they occupy in the New Testament.

This admission is no source of embarrassment to an instructed Catholic, nor of triumph to an unprejudiced Protestant. There is nothing whatever to perplex a Catholic in the fact that nowhere in the New Testament is it explicitly stated that there are Three Persons in God, distinct, yet of one nature; or that the Son of God is God the Son, or that Confirmation is a sacrament, or that the sacrament of Penance is the only plank after making shipwreck of baptismal innocence, and the rest.

We feel no more embarrassed at such omissions than we should be if we found it nowhere explicitly stated in a gardener's life and journals that the sun rises and sets, that there are four seasons in the year, that rain is necessary to the fertility of the soil, with similar truisms. One would scarcely expect such well-known facts to be set down even in a formal treatise on gardening; though they doubtless would be so stated were any person found to deny them. But in the life or correspondence of a gardener, we should expect to find them everywhere taken for granted and alluded to as too familiar to writer and to reader to require more distinct mention. Now, neither the Gospels nor the Acts of the Apostles nor the Epistles are formal treatises on the Christian faith and discipline. Therefore Catholics do not look in them for formal statements of elementary truths. We take, not from them, but to them, our belief in the Blessed Trinity, and it unlocks many a passage; we take to them our belief in the Divinity of Jesus Christ, and it makes everything plain; we take to them our belief in the Sacraments, and we find just those indications that we should expect to find under the circumstances in which they were written.

b. And next as regards Protestant theology. Were it true that the Bible was intended by God to be the sole source of knowledge to mankind regarding the Christian religion, then not only would all necessary doctrines and practices of that religion find explicit statement there, but they would hold the relative prominence that they do in the mind of God, and ought to do in reality. But will Protestants maintain that this is the case? Will those who believe in the Divinity of the Holy Ghost, and in the duty of offering Him worship, maintain that these doctrines are taught as formally in the Bible as in their own pulpits? Or does the observance of the Sabbath stand out in that relief in the New Testament which it obtains in the doctrine and discipline of most Protestants? Protestants no doubt are continually discovering these inconsistencies, and discarding doctrines and practices of their forefathers on the plea of greater conformity to the Bible. But if what has been said of the structure of the New Testament is true, then this very attempt to build on it alone may only lead to wider departure from real and primitive Christianity. For, when a creed or rule of life is drawn exclusively from a document in which the essential parts of the system are omitted or mentioned only in allusion, while minor details occupy an ample space, there is every likelihood that the minor points will get an undue importance, while the essential things will be put in the background, or be neglected altogether.

St. Paul, for example, complains to the Hebrews that they are still children requiring to be fed with milk, that is, to have the rudiments of Christian faith and morals repeated to them. He thinks the oral instruction they have received ought to have done this. He does not want to occupy himself with it again. In a word, he wants to write an epistle to men, not a catechism for children. He determines to do so: 'Wherefore,' he says, 'leaving the word of the beginning of Christ' (as Catholics would say—' What every Christian ought to know'), 'let us go on to things more perfect, not laying again the foundation.' He does not want to repeat in his Epistle the foundation, or fundamental truths of Christianity. He merely indicates what that foundation is: 'Not laying again the foundation of penance from dead works, and of faith towards God, of the doctrine of baptisms, and of imposition of hands, and of the resurrection of the dead, and of eternal judgment' (Heb. vi. 1, 2). He here places the doctrine concerning Ritual as among the very foundations of Christianity, those elementary truths and facts that ought to be familiar to every disciple of Christ by the living and traditional teaching he has received, *and which ought therefore to find no place in his Epistles.*

Now is it not evident that if men, forgetting this structure of the Epistles, go to them as to a catechism for an exposition of the whole Christian system, or look in them for the fundamental things, they will expose themselves to the most serious mistakes? Allusions will certainly be misunderstood; and even when the meaning of what is clear is attained, it will be perverted by the unnatural position that is assigned to it.

This will help us to understand the words of St. Peter. He says that in St. Paul's Epistles are certain things hard to be understood, which the unlearned and the unstable wrest, as they do also the other Scriptures, to their own destruction. And he adds immediately the following warning: 'You, therefore, brethren, knowing these things before, take heed, lest being led aside by the error of the unwise, you fall from your own steadfastness. But grow in grace, and in the knowledge of our Lord and Saviour Jesus Christ' (2 Pet. iii. 16-18). The existence of the obscurities here alluded to proves them to be designed by God. We must believe that God inspired St. Paul to write thus obscurely. But the fact of the danger to which these obscurities expose the unlearned and unstable ought to convince any one that God has provided a remedy against the danger. The exhortation of St. Peter shows what this remedy is. He tells his disciples not to let the interpretation of difficult passages of Scripture which may either occur to themselves, or be suggested by others, make them 'fall from their steadfastness,' *i.e.* abandon their steadfast adherence to the doctrine and discipline of Christ, which they have received orally from their teachers. If they hold fast to Tradition they may 'grow in grace and in the knowledge of Jesus Christ,' by reading the Scriptures. If they have not Tradition, Scripture will only make still broader for them the road that leads to 'destruction.' To those who are steadfast to the Tradition they have received, the very difficulties of Scripture will be a powerful help to grow in grace. They will exercise their patience, excite their attention, and provoke a most fruitful labour in their solution. But of course these are exercises not for the unlearned and unstable, but for those who are settled in the faith.

CHAPTER V.

VIEWS OF HISTORY.

THE history of religion, according to the ordinary Protestant view, is an immense anti-climax. Judaism is a half-success. Christianity is a catastrophe. In the twelfth book of Milton's *Paradise Lost*, the Archangel Michael draws out for Adam the long history of his posterity. In grand pictures taken from Scripture, the four thousand years of preparation pass in review. Everything progresses in expectation of the promised Deliverer. He comes, He dies, rises triumphant, and ascends into heaven. Adam exclaims in rapture:

> 'O goodness infinite, goodness immense!
> That all this good of evil shall produce.'

But his raptures are premature; he has the curiosity to ask Michael what shall follow the preaching of the Apostles. Great and glorious things, doubtless, while Michael draws his prophecy from the Acts of the Apostles. He tells of the descent of the Holy Ghost, the gift of tongues and miracles.

> 'Thus they win
> Great numbers of each nation to receive
> With joy the tidings brought from Heaven; at length,
> Their ministry perform'd, and race well run,
> Their doctrine and their story written left,
> They die.'

But as soon as Michael—Milton's Michael, of course—leaves Scripture, and takes the Protestant view of history, how changed is the scene! Scarcely are the Apostles dead, when wicked men

> 'The truth
> With superstition and traditions taint,
> *Left only in those written records pure,*
> Though not but by the Spirit understood.
> Whence heavy persecutions shall arise

> On all who in the worship persevere
> Of spirit and truth ; the rest—far greater part—
> Will deem in outward rites and specious forms
> Religion satisfied.'

And so the world goes on, 'under its own weight groaning,' till the day of doom.

The reader must be of a very genial temperament who, with this philosophy of history in his mind, can exclaim with Adam —Milton's Adam, of course :

> 'Greatly instructed I shall hence depart,
> Greatly in peace of thought.'[1]

O, how different and how consoling is the Catholic view of God's providence ! How grand are the words with which Bossuet sums up his discourse on universal history ! 'Etre attendu, venir, être reconnu par une posterité qui dure autant que le monde, c'est le caractère du Messie en qui nous croyons.'[2]

It is strange that the same historical facts should have two such contradictory interpretations. It is stranger still that the advocates of each should appeal to the very same Scriptures in support of their views.

The truth is, however, that in both cases the view is antecedent to the interpretation of Scripture, consciously so with Catholics, unconsciously, though not less really, with Protestants. The Catholic Church reads Scripture in the light of her own history. Fulfilments interpret prophecies, and facts give meaning to words. With Protestants, the denial of the Church is also previous to the reading of Scripture, and gives to it its character. The testimony of history is deliberately set aside in favour of the private interpretation, and then the private interpretation necessitates a new view of history.

Now this Essay was undertaken in the hope that it might assist some Protestants in obtaining more reasonable and more cheerful views of history than those expressed by Milton. I

---

[1] Milton's *Paradise Lost*, book xii.

[2] Bossuet, *Discours sur l'Histoire Universelle*, 2 partie, c. 31. 'To be expected (from the beginning), to come (at the promised time), to be acknowledged by a posterity that lasts to the world's end, are the marks of the Christ in whom we believe.'

stated, in the introductory chapter, that it was intended for those who had no wish to believe evil of Catholic worship, but who thought themselves compelled to do so by their allegiance to Scripture. I had conceived that there would be among Protestants many who would desire to be faithful followers of Jesus Christ, yet who would not deem it essential to His honour to believe that the 'far greater part' of His nominal disciples in all ages have deemed 'in outward rites and specious forms religion satisfied.' I liked to think that many Protestants would rejoice in the thought, if it could be proved to them to be true, that the religion of Him who died for men has had historical realisation among men, and that it was not, after the death of the Apostles,

'Left only in the written records pure.'

In order to attain this end, I have endeavoured to place myself in the Protestant point of view, that I might discover the main source of the prevalent distrust of the worship of Catholics.

I believed that it arose from certain false principles assumed as axioms—principles regarding spirituality, and principles regarding Tradition. I have endeavoured to remove misconceptions and prejudices, by showing the real relations of Scripture and Tradition, and how Ritual is related to each of them. If the New Testament points to Tradition, that is, to historical Christianity, as the channel and exponent of Ritual ; if historical Ritual, when examined, is found to be in perfect harmony with the New Testament; and if the principles through which Ritual has been developed are also recognised in the New Testament, I do not know what farther proof can be desired that the Catholic Church and her worship are the work of Him to whom the New Testament owes its inspiration.

It has been objected that my argument, as drawn out in this volume, though perfectly conclusive against ordinary Protestants, who refuse all help from Tradition, is of no avail against those Anglicans, who appeal to the Traditions of the early Church—that I have only proved that Scripture should be interpreted or supplemented by the records of 'sub-Apostolic times,' not by the actual doctrines and practices of the Roman Catholic Church.[3]

It is true that I have not been controverting with Anglicans, nor attacking their peculiar position. Those with whom I have been concerned are the old-fashioned Bible Protestants. Nor do I fear that, if I can drive them from their intrenchments, they will take refuge in the Laudian camp. They acknowledge readily enough on which side antiquity lies. 'The plain truth is,' says Milton, 'that when any of our men, of those that are wedded to antiquity, come to dispute with a Papist, and leaving the Scriptures put themselves without appeal to the sentence of synods and councils, using in the cause of Sion the hired soldiery of revolted Israel; where they give the Romanists one buff, they receive two counterbuffs.'[4]

Besides this, if there is one point on which all antiquity is most certainly agreed, it is that Christians must look to the Church *of their own day* for the solution of controversies, for ecclesiastical discipline, and for the worship of God. The Fathers appealed to the past to defend, but never either to reject or to correct the present Church.

And again, if my arguments have been of any value, they have proved that the knowledge of Scripture Ritual was to be acquired from the *living* Ritual. What does it matter that the Ritual thus referred to was that of the Apostolic or sub-Apostolic age? It was the Ritual *before the eyes* of those who first read the Scriptures; the Ritual in which they had been baptised and in which they daily worshipped. If we who live in the nineteenth century are to go back to past ages, and to search among ancient monuments for a key that has been lost, we are certainly not following the method of those very men to whom we appeal, who held the key in their own hands; we are not following the method intended by the sacred writers. For who can conceive that when St. Paul referred to the 'cup of blessing which *we* bless' and the 'bread which *we* break,' he expected his readers to collate ancient liturgies before they could be sure about his meaning? or that when St.

[3] *The Guardian*, April 13, 1870.
[4] Milton, tract, *Of Prelatical Episcopacy*.

Views of History. 245

James exhorted the sick to 'call for the elders of the Church,' he expected them to get at the sense of his words from minute and critical comparison of Greek and Latin Fathers?

It may of course be maintained that such is the misfortune of our present position, that this is the only method left to us if we wish to get at the meaning of Scripture. This is an intelligible position. But it is an acknowledgment that religion has utterly changed its nature since the days of the Apostles. As for Catholics, when we profess our belief in a Catholic and *Apostolic* Church, we mean a Church whose method as well as whose doctrine is Apostolic; a Church now in the possession of Apostolic truth, Apostolic discipline, and Apostolic worship; not one that looks for these in the surviving fragments of a past tradition.

If, then, a Catholic is asked where the true religion of Jesus Christ may be found, he will certainly not refer the inquirer to the fifth or sixth century of Christianity, or talk about an undivided Church, past or future. He would reply in the words of the epitaph to Sir Christopher Wren in St. Paul's Cathedral, *Si monumentum quæris circumspice.* Look round you at the Catholic Church, which is the Building of Jesus Christ. Look well at her institutions, her government, her worship, her Ritual, and remember Who said: 'Heaven and earth shall pass away, but My word shall not pass away.'

There are other means of knowing a man's words besides hearing and reading. We may see what he said in the effects of his words. 'What was the architect of that cathedral talking about all those hours that he was closeted with the builder?' 'I know not,' you say, 'I did not overhear, and I have no record of his conversations.' 'Indeed, but you have a most certain record. There rises the cathedral before your eyes. Look up at its mighty towers, examine the tracery of its windows, go round it and admire all its details, and then you will know what the architect was busy about. "If you wish for a record of his labours, as well as a monument of his talent, look round you."'

St. Luke tells us that for 'forty days, after His resurrection, Jesus Christ appeared to His Apostles, and spoke to them of the kingdom of God' (Acts i.). You would wish to know what words He spoke to those minds at length prepared to hear. You seek for them in vain in Gospels or Epistles. Were they, then, spoken in the air? Did the breeze convey them away? If so, why were they spoken? They were spoken to the builders of the Church by the great Architect, who said: 'On this rock I will build My Church, and the gates of hell shall not prevail against it.' 'He spoke of the kingdom of God.' He drew up the chart of its constitution: He laid down its fundamental laws. Become a citizen of that kingdom, and you will not only know but enjoy the word spoken by its King.

This is the Catholic plan; it is that also of reason and of Scripture. But others will not adopt it. They say: 'I like not yonder building, though I venerate the architect. That building, indeed, bears his name, and immemorial tradition has ascribed it to him. But I hold him not responsible for it. The builders departed from his plan, and spoilt his work. See! here I have an unfinished ground-plan that is certainly his, and I have also an imperfect journal of his life. I have, therefore, put the building completely from my thoughts; I have sat down to a careful examination of these documents, and they have convinced me more than ever that the architect's intention has not hitherto been understood. He intended to build something far simpler. But the workmen he employed were dissatisfied with his design, and substituted their own ornate and monstrous projects in its place. Let us demolish this building, for it is unworthy of him; and then let us exercise our ingenuity on his plans, and build up a better church, such as he intended.' So they talk; but while each has his own private judgment about the architect's plan, and they disagree even in the outlines, they reconstruct nothing.

There is a second class of men who acknowledge that the builders worked according to the instructions they received. But they do not like the building as it *now* stands. Much has been added to it, they say, by later hands. It needs not to be demolished, but renovated. And to know how the restoration must be made, they go back to history, and they look to old drawings, and consult old descriptions. But neither are *they* agreed. Some would reform it back to what it was at one period; others prefer a later or an earlier stage; and respecting no one period are they united. For the accounts are so many, and they are so difficult to reconcile, that they are ever furnishing new matter of doubt.

Besides, all the accounts have some very troublesome omissions. It seems there was an agreement among the builders to speak very cautiously, and in very obscure terms, and such as could only be comprehended by the initiated, about certain parts of the building. This was called the 'Discipline of the Secret,' and it is a sore puzzle to our antiquarian reformers.

But what hinders them altogether from agreement is their peculiar way of studying. Since the present cathedral is before their eyes, it would be but natural to look at it, and by means of it to explain both the plan of the founder and the obscure allusions in the ancient records. But no; this might compel them to admit that the building has simply grown into what it was intended to be, and thus they could exercise no private judgment and attempt no reform. So they hold the architect's plan in one hand, and the description of some old builder or observer in the other, and they compare, and conjecture, and cry, 'I have found it,' to one another: but the other too has made his discovery, and they compare their discoveries, and they do not agree; and so they go back to make fresh conjectures.

And yet the Architect never said that His work should be spoilt or should want reforming; but simply, 'I am ever with you to the consummation of the world.'

But men say the Church is falling into decay, and they must erect again the old scaffolding to make the necessary repairs. Are they sure there remains enough of that old scaffolding to serve their purpose? If the Providence of God allowed the building to fall into ruin, are they certain that He has preserved the scaffolding that had been taken down and cast aside? In other words, if the living Church of the nineteenth century has lost primitive truth, abandoned primitive worship, and rejected primitive discipline, on what theory of Divine Providence can we expect that amid the immense destruction of early Christian writings and monuments which has taken place, God should have preserved just enough to enable antiquarian research to bring back His Church to her primitive model?

I am far, indeed, from despising the testimonies of the Fathers, the ancient liturgies, the monuments of the Catacombs, or whatever other fragments of primitive Christianity time has spared, and diligence and learning have recovered. They are of great interest to confirm our faith, of great use to defend it; but the faith itself must rely neither on the private interpretation of a divine but incomplete[5] record of God's Revelation like the New Testament, nor on the private interpretation of the equally incomplete remains of antiquity. The 'whole counsel of God' is declared only by the living Church, in whose hand alone both Scripture and Tradition, the Canon and the Code, are complete and fitted for their purpose.

It was intended by God that we should look back upon Scripture from the communion of the Church, not that we should measure the living Church, or build up a Church of the future, from our own conceptions of Scripture. O how different is the New Testament according as we adopt one or other of these two courses! If we give our own conjectural meanings to the words of Jesus Christ, then they are as words that were spoken for no purpose, except to have been the occasion of error and the subject of dispute. But if we believe that they are indeed God's words, words of power and life, creative words, words that shall never pass away,—and if in this belief we look for their meaning in their realisation,—how grand is the New Testament!

We see a Church that fills the world at present, and that has filled the history of eighteen centuries, against which every power is striving and has striven; and that Church proclaims, —My life is in my commission: 'Go, teach all nations;' my strength is in the promise, 'I am with you all days.' How wondrous are these words thus read in their fulfilment!

We see presiding over that Church one who claims descent

---

[5] *Incomplete* of course only in the sense before explained, as an exponent of the whole of Revelation; not incomplete for the purpose designed by God.

from Peter. He is the visible foundation of the Church, while he is the stone of stumbling to all her enemies. How the Catholic heart beats when it recalls the word, 'Thou art Peter, and on this rock I will build My Church, and the gates of hell shall not prevail against it'!

We read of the last words of Jesus Christ on earth, how He foretold that 'penance and remission of sins should be preached in His name unto all nations, beginning at Jerusalem' (Luke xxiv. 47). We put no interpretation of our own upon these words, for they are a divine prophecy, and we look for God's own interpretation in their historical fulfilment. And in that history we find that there was preached, not merely the doctrine of repentance, but also a sacrament of Baptism for the remission of sins, and a sacrament of Penance for the pardon of sins committed after Baptism. And we remember how another Evangelist tells us of a power conferred: 'Whose sins you shall forgive, they are forgiven; and whose sins you shall retain, they are retained' (John xx. 23); and we question not but that those words are the germ of the mighty tree which spreads its branches before our eyes.

We open the Church's catalogue of saints, and we find that they belong to every age and every clime, and we remember who said, ' Many shall come from the east and the west, and shall sit down in the kingdom of God' (Matt. vii. 11). We note among those saints one whose name is held in benediction above the rest. We remark how devotion to the Virgin Mother of Jesus Christ has struck its roots deep into the hearts of all the children of the Catholic Church. We do not lament or criticise, nor do we grow anxious lest the worship of her Son should suffer. We remember how, when God foreshowed to Mary this very devotion that we now see in historical fulfilment, Mary's spirit exulted in God her Saviour, 'because from henceforth all generations should call her blessed.' We remember that Mary foretold her own glories, as a part of the accomplishment of the promise that had been made to her: 'Thy Son shall be great, and shall be called the Son of the Most High;' and we too magnify the Lord, while we bless her who is all blessed.

Or, lastly, we see the worship which in every country has for ages been offered to God ; and we remember how eighteen hundred years ago the Son of God said, 'Woman, believe Me that the hour cometh when you shall neither on this mountain, nor in Jerusalem, adore the Father. But the hour cometh, and now is, when the true adorers shall adore the Father in spirit and in truth. For the Father also seeketh such to adore Him' (John iv. 21, 23). And we doubt not that the Father has found those whom He sought, that in every country He has found true adorers, and that the worship that we see offered to Him in every country, the worship of which Catholic Ritual is a part, is that worship in spirit and in truth which the Son of God foretold.

APPENDIX.

(See p. 146.)

It has been well remarked by an author who has written with much learning and originality on ancient sacrifices in their relation to the Holy Eucharist, that it has been too much the custom of certain writers 'to magnify unduly, and indeed to invent, points of *difference* between the Christian and Mosaic systems; to expound Christianity, especially in the matter of sacrifice, rather by contrasting it with the law of Moses, than by drawing out the parallel between them. Whereas the structure in the two cases is the same, and was declared by God to be so; modified only by the entering in, in the greater system, of the unique and inimitable elements of the Incarnation and its consequents.'[1]

Yet this author in his attention to one part of the parallel has himself overlooked another. Having remarked that throughout pre-Christian times worship was offered *by means of* sacrifices and not *to* them, he continues thus: 'There is no countenance then, from this quarter at least, for the mediæval opinion, lately reintroduced by some earnest minds among us, that the supreme purpose, or, however, a very principal one, of the Eucharist, is to provide in the ordained media of the rite—the consecrated Elements—an object of Divine Worship. However ingeniously it has been endeavoured to invoke the countenance of fathers and liturgies to such a view, it would seem absolutely fatal to it, that the ancient sacrificial system, divinely accredited to us as an exact type or copy of the Gospel scheme, gives not the remotest hint of such a feature as destined to have place in it.'[2]

Mr. Freeman has not remarked that his argument would prove too much, and, if valid, would be no less 'absolutely fatal' to the worship of Jesus Christ on Calvary than to His worship in the Holy Eucharist, since the sacrifices of the Old Law pointed as much to the death of Christ as to the unbloody commemoration of it. But the objection has in reality no force against either. The Incarnation introduces something 'unique and inimitable' into the Christian antitype. The worship due to Christ as Victim,

[1] Rev. Philip Freeman, *The Principles of Divine Service*, vol. ii. part ii. ch. i. sect. 9.   [2] *Ib.* sect. 2c.

whether on Calvary or on our altars, could not be prefigured in bulls and goats. If it was to be typified, it must have been in some other element of the ancient system; and I have already shown that that element was the Presence, which no less referred to Jesus Christ than the sacrifices. In Mr. Freeman's scheme of Christianity, the most important and striking feature of ancient worship—the sensible Presence—would find no counterpart. All the arguments of his learned volume would thus be undermined. He has shown that the visible sacrifices of antiquity were to be fulfilled in the visible though supernatural and divine Sacrifice of the Eucharist, to be offered by human hands and received by human lips, and not by faith only. But a Protestant of the ordinary type might reply to him, that if all the sensible manifestations of God's Presence are to result, first indeed in the Incarnation, but afterwards in the complete absence of any sensible object of worship, then there is no reason why, by a similar law, all the material sacrifices of ancient times should not end, first in the Sacrifice of Calvary, and then afterwards in the same Sacrifice, not renewed mystically on our altars, but commemorated and offered in the soul only of the believer.

Mr. Freeman's endeavour to be faithful to the negative teachings of his Church has caused him to mar one of the most beautiful positive teachings of Holy Scripture.

LIST OF THE PRINCIPAL PASSAGES OF HOLY SCRIPTURE MADE USE OF IN THIS ESSAY.

Gen. iii. 8	Apparition in Paradise, 137, 142, 147.
Exod. xix. 16	Apparition on Sinai, 139.
xxiv. 9-11	Vision of God, 149.
xxv. 22	The Propitiatory, 139-141.
xl. 33	The Majesty of God, 139.
Deut. iv. 7	God present to the Jews, 140.
vi. 6-9	Memorials of the great commandment, 170.
xviii. 15	The Great Prophet, 144.
2 Kings vi. 12-23 (*Prot.* Samuel)	David's pomp; Michol's scorn, 107.
3 (*Prot.* 1) Kings viii. 27	God's presence, 140.
4 (*Prot.* 2) Kings xix. 14-16	Prayer of Ezechias, 141.
Ps. xviii. (*Prot.* xix.) 1-4	God's works His witnesses, 182.
lvii. (*Prot.* lviii.) 5, 6	The deaf asp, 86.
lxxxiii. (*Prot.* lxxxiv.)	David's devotion to God's presence, 106, 140.
Prov. xxxi. 22	Purple and fine linen, 93.
Wisdom xiii. 1-5	Nature teaches of God, 68.
Ecclus. xliii. 30-32	God's Majesty a reason for splendour, 158.
Isa. xii. 4-6	Promise of God's presence, 142.
xxx. 29	Joyous solemnities of the old Law, 106.
lx. 13	Types of the Church, 99.
Jer. xxxi. 31-34	Promise of the New Testament, 167, 191.
Zach. viii. 3	God's Presence, 145.
xii. 10	Spirit of prayer promised to Christians, 171.
Mal. i. 11	The Christian oblation, 147.
St. Matt. ii. 9-11	Adoration of the Magi, 55, 160, 163.
iii. 11	Baptism of fire, 212.
xvi. 18	Promise to St. Peter, 249.
xvii. 2	Splendour of Transfiguration, 57, 106.
xxi. 16	Triumphal procession, 164.
xxiv. 30	Majesty of the Day of Judgment, 60.
xxiv. 35	Christ's word shall not pass away, 248.
xxvi. 26-29	Institution of Holy Communion, 219.
xxvii. 45	Darkness on Calvary, 57.
xxvii. 54	Earthquake at the Passion, 58.
xxviii. 3, 4	Angels in white, 58.
xxviii. 19	Command to baptise, 213.
xxviii. 20	Promise of Christ's presence, 248.
St. Mark i. 10, 11	Phenomena at our Lord's Baptism, 56.
vii. 7, 9	Traditions of the Pharisees, 187.
vii. 33	Cure of the deaf mute, 85, 107.
viii. 11	Promise of Catholicity and sanctity, 249.
viii. 23	Cure of the blind man, 86.
ix. 2	Bright robes at Transfiguration, 57, 95.
xi. 17	Piping and lamenting, 159.
xiv. 3-9	Magdalen's 'waste,' 66, 163.
xv. 29	Blasphemers of Jesus, 166.
xvi. 16	Promise regarding Baptism, 213.

St. Luke i. 1	Many primitive Gospels, 204.
i. 48	Blessed Virgin's prophecy, 249.
ii. 8-10	Apparition to the Shepherds, 55, 56.
xi. 39-42	Pharisaic observances, 82, 83.
xviii. 10-14	Pharisee and Publican, 83, 84.
xix. 30-40	Triumphal procession, 164.
xxii. 19	The great commemoration, 44, 147, 193, 208.
xxiii. 56	Embalming of our Lord's body, 73.
xxiv. 4	Shining apparel, 58.
xxiv. 47	Penance to be preached, 249.
St. John i. 26	Jesus in the crowd, 143.
iv. 19-24	Worship in spirit and in truth, 38, 147, 250.
v. 39, 40	Searching the Scriptures, 12, 14, 19, 60.
ix. 6, 7	Cure of the blind man, 83.
xii. 30	Heavenly voice, 57.
xiii. 6-15	Washing the Disciples' feet, 87, 223.
xx. 12	Angels' postures, 58, 96.
xxi. 25	Many things unrecorded in Gospels, 176.
Acts i. 3	Things of the kingdom of God, 234, 245.
i. 10	White garments, 58.
ii. 2, 3	Phenomena of Pentecost, 59, 91.
ii. 17, 19	Prophecy of Joel quoted, 59.
viii.	Simon Magus, 123.
viii. 35, 36	Philip 'preaching Jesus,' 214.
xv. 10	The old Law a burden, 105-107.
xvii. 11	Example of the Bereans, 13, 19.
xix. 1-6	John's baptism, 213.
xix. 12	St. Paul's relics, 95, 126.
xxi. 11	Agabus, 87, 97.
Rom. vi. 3	Doctrine of Baptism, 217.
xiv. 5	Holy days, 33.
1 Cor. x. 15, 16	Why St. Paul speaks of the Eucharist, 220.
xi. 2-16	Covering and uncovering the head, 85, 95.
xiv. 1-40	Unknown tongues, 110, 117.
xiv. 24	Worship of God, 165.
2 Cor. iii. 6	Letter and spirit, 27.
Gal. iv. 9-11	The Sabbath, 33.
Col. ii. 16	The Sabbath, 33.
2 Thess. ii. 14	Apostolic traditions, 193.
1 Tim. vi. 20	Oral teaching, 194.
2 Tim. i. 13	Oral teaching, 194.
Heb. v. 13	Spiritual infancy, 99.
vi. 1, 2	Ritual a fundamental, 238.
viii. 5	Pattern on the Mount, 167.
St. James v. 14, 15	Anointing, 224-229.
2 Pet. iii. 16-18	Obscurity of the Epistles, 239.
3 John, ver. 13, 14	Advantages of oral communication, 177.
Apoc. i. 10	Lord's Day, 31.
v. 11-14	Adoration of the Lamb, 166.
viii. 3, 4	Altar of incense, 100-102.
xix. 7	Fine linen, 94.
xix. 12-14	Vision of garments, 95.

THE END.

By the same Author.

SOULS DEPARTED:

Being a Defence and Declaration

OF THE

CATHOLIC CHURCH'S DOCTRINE

TOUCHING PURGATORY AND PRAYERS FOR THE DEAD.

By CARDINAL ALLEN.

FIRST PUBLISHED IN 1565, AND NOW EDITED IN MODERN SPELLING BY THE REV. T. E. BRIDGETT, C.SS.R.

Tastefully bound in black cloth, and embellished with a Portrait of CARDINAL ALLEN.

Price 6*s.*

"Nothing can be more complete, nothing more effective, nothing more moderate and scholarly than this treatise of the great English confessor and organiser on purgatory and prayer for the departed. Not only is it not out of date at the present day, but there is no modern work of the sort in English or French, so far as we are aware, which is either half so persuasive or half so eloquent."—*Dublin Review.*

"Having read it with unflagging interest, we can promise that, though it is a reprint of a long-forgotten treatise, it will fully recompense any fairly-educated reader."—*Tablet.*

"Well worth republishing. . . . The clearness of thought and vigour in assailing heresy will make the book attractive to every careful reader."—*Month.*

"At once a classic of the Roman Church in England and a standard exposition of the belief and doctrines of that Church on the subjects treated."—*Scotsman.*

"The book from beginning to end is solidly instructive and edifying."—*Freeman's Journal.*

"The substance of the work is admirable."—*Irish Monthly.*

BURNS AND OATES, LIMITED,
LONDON AND NEW YORK.

By the same Author.

DEFENDER OF THE FAITH: THE ROYAL TITLE
ITS HISTORY AND VALUE. Price 1s.

"Well worth reading; . . . singularly clear and satisfactory."—*Irish Ecclesiastical Record.*

"We commend this valuable little book to those Catholics who value historic research and truth, and also to those non-Catholics who are being misled by the shallow untruths which three centuries of apologetic ingenuity have devised to give a fair appearance to the error into which our forefathers were first driven or fell."—*Weekly Register.*

DISCIPLINE OF DRINK. Crown 8vo, cloth, 3s. 6d.

"The historical information with which the book abounds gives evidence of deep research and patient study, and imparts a permanent interest to the volume, which will elevate it to a position of authority and importance enjoyed by few of its compeers."—*The Arrow.*

"A learned and interesting book, and likely, we hope, to be really useful."—*Spectator.*

"A learned and deeply-interesting historical work. To non-Catholics as well as to Catholics the work will repay a thoughtful reading."—*The Temperance Record.*

OUR LADY'S DOWRY: HOW ENGLAND WON AND LOST THAT TITLE   Second edition, cloth, 9s.

"This book is the ablest vindication of Catholic devotion to Our Lady, drawn from tradition, that we know of in the English language."—*Tablet.*

SUPPLIANT OF THE HOLY GHOST: A PARAPHRASE OF THE "VENI SANCTE SPIRITUS." Now first printed from a MS. of the seventeenth century composed by Rev. R. JOHNSON, with other unpublished treatises by the same author. Second edition, cloth, 1s. 6d.

HISTORY OF THE HOLY EUCHARIST IN GREAT BRITAIN. 2 vols. demy 8vo, 18s.

BURNS AND OATES, LIMITED,
LONDON AND NEW YORK.

28 ORCHARD STREET, LONDON, W.

A SELECTION FROM

BURNS & OATES' PUBLICATIONS.

The complete Classified Catalogue (90 pages) will be sent post free to any applicant.

Meditations, Spiritual Reading, and Devotion.

A BISHOP AND HIS FLOCK. By the Rt. Rev. John Cuthbert Hedley, O.S.B., Bishop of Newport. Crown 8vo, cloth, gilt top. 6s.

This volume contains more than 30 of the Pastoral Letters addressed by Bishop Hedley to his flock during the past 22 years. It offers plain and practical instructions on a great variety of subjects, such as Worship, Sacraments, The Blessed Eucharist, Grace, Zeal for Souls, Devotion, and Ritual. There are important addresses on the Sacred Heart, on Mixed Marriages, on Attendance of Catholic Children at non-Catholic Schools, on Church Music, on Patron Saints, on the Christian Family, &c.

A DAILY THOUGHT, from the Writings of Father Dignam, S.J. Demy 32mo, bound in leather, gilt edges, 2/-

A FORM OF PRAYERS FOLLOWING THE CHURCH OFFICE. For the use of Catholics unable to hear Mass upon Sundays and Holidays. By John, Marquess of Bute, K.T. Limp cloth, 1/- net (postage 2d.) leather, 2/6 net (postage 3d.)

A GOOD PRACTICAL CATHOLIC. A Spiritual Instruction to people in the World. By Rev. H. Reginald Buckler, O.P. Second Edition, Revised and Enlarged. Wrapper. 6d.

A RETREAT: consisting of Thirty-three Discourses, with Meditations: for the use of the Clergy, Religious, and others. By Right Rev. Bishop Hedley, O.S.B. Cr. 8vo, half-leather. 6/-

AT THE FEET OF JESUS. Meditations by Madame Cecilia, of St. Andrew's Convent, Streatham. Cr. 8vo. 3/6.

A Voice that is Still. Words written or spoken by the late Father James Clare, S.J. With a sketch of his life by Father McLeod, S.J. Demy 32mo, leather, gilt edges, with portrait. 2/-

Characteristics from the Writings of Cardinal Wiseman. Selected by Rev. T. E. Bridgett, C.SS.R. Cr. 8vo. 6/-

Christian Perfection, On. By Ven. Father Alphonsus Rodriguez. For persons living in the World. 6/-

Devotional Library for Catholic Households. Containing—New Testament; Book of Psalms; Imitation of Christ, by Thomas à Kempis; Devout Life, by St. Francis de Sales; Spiritual Combat, by Father Scupoli. All neatly bound in cloth, red edges, with cloth case to match. 5/- net (postage 4d.)

Devout Life, An Introduction to a. By St. Francis de Sales. Translated by Very Rev. Dr. Richards. Cloth 1/6. Calf, 5/- Morocco, gilt edges, 5/6

Faber (Rev. F. W.). All for Jesus: or, the Easy Ways of Divine Love. Cr. 8vo, cloth. 5/-

Faber (Rev. F. W.). Growth in Holiness: or, the Progress of the Spiritual Life. Cr. 8vo, cloth. 6/-

Faber (Rev. F. W.). Notes on Doctrinal and Spiritual Subjects. Two Vols. Cr. 8vo, cloth. 10/-

Faber (Rev. F. W.). Spiritual Conferences. 6/-

Faber (Rev. F. W.). The Creator and the Creature: or, the Wonders of Divine Love. Cr. 8vo, cloth. 6/-

Faber (Rev. F. W.). The Precious Blood: or, the Price of our Salvation. Cr. 8vo, cloth. 5/-

Father Dignam's Retreats. With Letters and Notes of Spiritual Directions, and a few Conferences and Sermons. New and Enlarged Edition, with a Preface by Rev. Father Gretton, S.J. Cr. 8vo. 6/- net (postage 4d.)

Golden Words: or, Maxims of the Cross. Translated and Adapted from the Latin of Thomas à Kempis. By F. H. Hamilton, M.A. Sixth Edition. Beautifully printed in red and black. Cloth, gilt, bevelled boards, red edges. 2/-

Growth in the Knowledge of Our Lord. Meditations for every day of the Year. Adapted from the original of the Abbé de Brandt. By Mother Mary Fidelis. In Three Vols. Cr. 8vo. 21/- net (postage 6d.)

MEDITATIONS, SPIRITUAL READING, AND DEVOTION 3

HOLY WISDOM *(Sancta Sophia).* Directions for the Prayer of Contemplation, &c. By Ven. Father F. Augustin Baker, O.S.B. Edited by Abbot Sweeney, D.D. Cr. 8vo. Handsomely bound in half leather. 6/-

IMITATION OF CHRIST, OF THE. By Thomas à Kempis.
New Popular Edition for Distribution. Cloth, red edges, 6d. net (postage 2d.) Leather, red edges, 1/-
Superfine Pocket Edition. Fancy cloth extra, with red borders, 1/6. And in leather bindings, from 2/6 to 10/-
Presentation Edition (size, 6¼ by 4¾ inches). With red border on each page. Cloth extra, 3/6. And in leather bindings, from 7/- to 15/-

JEWELS OF PRAYER AND MEDITATION, FROM UNFAMILIAR SOURCES. By Percy Fitzgerald. Fcap. 8vo, cloth, gilt. 2/6

JOURNALS KEPT DURING TIMES OF RETREAT. By Rev. John Morris, S.J. Edited by Rev. J. H. Pollen, S.J. 6/-

LAYMAN'S DAY, THE. JEWELS OF PRACTICAL PIETY. By Percy Fitzgerald. Fcap. 8vo, cloth, gilt. 2/-

MANRESA: or, the Spiritual Exercises of St. Ignatius. For general use. Fcap. 8vo, cloth. 3/-

MEDITATIONS FOR EVERY DAY IN THE YEAR. By Bishop Challoner. Revised by Bishop Vertue. Cr. 8vo, cloth. 3/-

MEDITATIONS ON THE LOVE OF GOD. From the Spanish of Fray Diego de Estella, by Henry W. Pereira, M.A. Cr. 8vo, cloth. 3/6

PERFECTION OF MAN BY CHARITY, THE. A Spiritual Treatise. By Rev. R. Buckler, O.P. Cr. 8vo, cloth. 5/-

PRACTICAL MEDITATIONS FOR EVERY DAY IN THE YEAR, on the Life of Our Lord Jesus Christ. Chiefly for the use of Religious. By a Father of the Society of Jesus. In Two Vols. Cloth. 9/-

RETREAT MANUAL, THE. A Handbook for the Annual Retreat and Monthly Recollection. By Madame Cecilia, of St. Andrew's Convent, Streatham. With a Preface by the Rev. Sydney Smith, S.J. Fcap. 8vo. 2/-

SPIRIT OF THE CURÉ OF ARS, THE. Translated from the French of M. l'Abbé Monnin. Edited by Rev. John E. Bowden, of the Oratory. 32mo, cloth, with Portrait 2/-

SPIRITUAL COMBAT: together with the Supplement to the same, and the Treatise of Inward Peace. By Rev. Lorenzo Scupoli. (Size, 5 by 3¼ inches). Cloth, red edges, 1/- Leather, 1/6, 2/6, and 4/6

SPIRITUAL CONFLICT AND CONQUEST, THE. Edited by the Very Rev. Jerome Vaughan, O.S.B. Third and Cheaper Edition. Cr. 8vo, 580 pp. 5/-

ST. FRANCIS DE SALES' LETTERS TO PERSONS IN THE WORLD. Edited by Very Rev. Canon Mackey, O.S.B. 6/-

ST. FRANCIS DE SALES' TREATISE ON THE LOVE OF GOD. Edited by the Very Rev. Canon Mackey, O.S.B. 6/-

ST. FRANCIS DE SALES' LETTERS TO PERSONS IN RELIGION, with Introduction by Bishop Hedley on "St. Francis de Sales and the Religious State." Edited by Very Rev. Canon Mackey. O.S.B. Cr. 8vo, cloth. 6/-

ST. GERTRUDE, THE EXERCISES OF. 32mo, cloth, 1/6; leather, 2/- & 4/6

ST. GERTRUDE AND ST. MECHTILDE, THE PRAYERS OF. 32mo, cloth, 1/-; leather, 2/- & 4/6

ST. TERESA'S OWN WORDS: or, Instructions on the Prayer of Recollection. Arranged by the Right Rev. Bishop Chadwick. Cloth, 1/- net (postage 2d.)

ST. TERESA'S PATERNOSTER: A Treatise on Prayer. By Very Rev. Joseph Frassinetti. Translated by Very Rev. Canon Hutch, D.D. 18mo, cloth. 4/-

TOWARDS ETERNITY. By the Abbé Poulin. Translated by M. T. Torromé. Cr. 8vo, cloth. 5/-

"Your simple and nobly conceived meditations, so full of true piety and solid doctrine, offer to all sincerely generous souls the means of knowing God better by loving Him more."—*The Bishop of La Rochelle in a letter to the Author.*

ULLATHORNE (Archbishop), CHARACTERISTICS FROM THE WRITINGS OF, together with a Bibliographical Account of the Archbishop's Works. By Rev. M. F. Glancey. Cr. 8vo, cloth. 6/-

ULLATHORNE (Archbishop). CHRISTIAN PATIENCE, THE STRENGTH AND DISCIPLINE OF THE SOUL. Demy 8vo, cloth. 7/-

ULLATHORNE (Archbishop). THE ENDOWMENTS OF MAN, CONSIDERED IN THEIR RELATION WITH HIS FINAL END. Demy 8vo, cloth. 7/-

ULLATHORNE (Archbishop). GROUNDWORK OF THE CHRISTIAN VIRTUES, THE. Demy 8vo, cloth. 7/-

WISEMAN (H. E. Cardinal). A MONTH'S MEDITATIONS. From MS. left by His Eminence, and now first published. Cr. 8vo, leather back. 4/-

On the Life of Our Lord.

BAPTISM OF THE KING, THE. Considerations on the Sacred Passion. By Rev. H. J. Coleridge, S.J. 7/6

BLOOD OF THE LAMB, THE. By Rev. Kenelm Digby Best, of the Oratory. Cr. 8vo, cloth. 2/6 net (postage 3d.)

DOLOROUS PASSION OF OUR LORD JESUS CHRIST. From the Meditations of Anne Catherine Emmerich. Fcap. 8vo, cloth. 3/6

FABER (Rev. F. W.). BETHLEHEM. Cr. 8vo, cloth. 7/-

JESUS, THE ALL BEAUTIFUL. A Devotional Treatise on the Character and Actions of Our Lord. By the Author of "The Voice of the Sacred Heart." Edited by Rev. J. G. Macleod, S.J. Cr. 8vo, cloth. 6/6

THE LIFE OF OUR LORD. Written for Little Ones. By Mother M. Salome, of the Bar Convent, York. With Frontispiece. Cloth, gilt. 3/6

NATIVITY OF OUR LORD JESUS CHRIST, THE. From the Meditations of Anne Catherine Emmerich. Translated by George Richardson. 18mo, cloth, gilt. 2/6

WISEMAN (H. E. Cardinal). MEDITATIONS ON THE INCARNATION AND LIFE OF OUR LORD. Cr. 8vo, cloth. 4/-

WISEMAN (H. E. Cardinal). MEDITATIONS ON THE SACRED PASSION OF OUR LORD. With a Preface by H. E. Cardinal Vaughan. Cr. 8vo, cloth. 4/-

On the Sacred Heart.

IMITATION OF THE SACRED HEART OF JESUS. In Four Books. By Rev. Father Arnold, S.J. Fcap. 8vo, cloth, 4/6; Cloth, gilt, red edges, 5/-; leather, 8/6.

MANNING (H. E. Cardinal). THE GLORIES OF THE SACRED HEART. Cr. 8vo, cloth. 4/-

MANUAL OF THE SACRED HEART. Cloth, 2/- Cloth, red edges, with Portrait, 2/6. Leather, 4/6, 5/6, and 6/-

MEDITATIONS ON THE SACRED HEART. By the Rev. Joseph Egger, S.J. Cr. 8vo, cloth, gilt. 2/6.

SPIRIT OF THE SACRED HEART, THE. A Manual of Prayers and Devotions. Printed in bold black type, upon a fine white paper, making a handsome volume of over 700 pages. Cloth, red edges, 3/6. Leather, 5/6 to 12/6

On the Blessed Virgin.

BLESSED VIRGIN IN THE NINETEENTH CENTURY, THE. Apparitions, Revelations, Graces. By Bernard St. John. With Introduction by Rev. E. Thiriet, O.M.I. Cr. 8vo. Cloth, with six illustrations. 6/-

> The subject is treated from the point of view of a historian bent on a careful examination of facts that may be called contemporary. But while not aiming at being a devotional book properly so called, it is calculated by the facts which it puts forth to act as a powerful stimulus to devotion to Our Lady.
>
> In short, it is an admirable synthesis of the great apparitions of the Blessed Virgin in France in the Ninteenth Century.—*Extract from Preface*

BLESSED VIRGIN IN THE FATHERS OF THE FIRST SIX CENTURIES, THE. By Rev. Thomas Livius, M.A., C.SS R. Demy 8vo, xxvii., 481 pp., 12/-

FABER (Rev. F. W.). THE FOOT OF THE CROSS : or, The Sorrows of Mary. Cr. 8vo, cloth. 6/-

FATHER FABER'S MAY BOOK. A Month of May, arranged for daily reading, from the writings of Father Faber. 18mo, cloth, gilt edges. 2/-

GLORIES OF MARY, THE. By St. Alphonsus Liguori. Edited by Bishop Coffin, C.SS.R. Fcap. 8vo, cloth. 3/6

GRACES OF MARY, THE: or, Instructions and Devotions for the Month of Mary. New Edition. 32mo, cloth, gilt. 2/-

LIFE OF MARY FOR CHILDREN, THE. Translated from the German. By Mrs. Bennett Gladstone. With four Chromo-lithographs and forty-five Illustrations. 1/6

MADONNA : THE. A Pictorial Record of the Life and Death of the Mother of our Lord Jesus Christ by the Painters and Sculptors of Christendom in more than Five Hundred of their Works. The Text translated from the Italian of Adolfo Venturi, with an Introduction by Alice Meynell. Medium 4to. Bound in buckram. £1 11s. 6d.

MARY IN THE EPISTLES or, The Implicit Teaching of the Apostles concerning the Blessed Virgin contained in their Writings. By Rev. Thomas Livius, C.SS.R. 5/-

MARY MAGNIFYING GOD. By Rev. W. Humphrey, S.J. 2/6

MOMENTS WITH MARY. Being Selections from the Writings of St. Francis de Sales. By Rev. John Fitzpatrick, O.M.I. 18mo, cloth, gilt. 1/6

MONTH OF MARY. By Rev. Father Beckx. Cr. 8vo, 3/-

MONTH OF MARY. By St. Alphonsus Liguori. 32mo, cloth, gilt. 1/6

OUR LADY OF PERPETUAL SUCCOUR. A Manual of Devotion for every Day of the Month. Translated from the French by Rev. T. Livius, C.SS.R. 32mo, cloth, 1/- net; leather 2/- net, 2/6 net, and 4/6 net (postage on single copies 2d.)

OUR LADY OF PERPETUAL SUCCOUR, MANUAL OF. From the Writings of St. Alphonsus Liguori. By a Redemptorist Father. 18mo, cloth, 1/- net; leather, 2/- net. With Hymns: Cloth, 1/6 net; leather, gilt edges, 3/- net (postage on single copies 3d.)

OUR LADY'S MANUAL; or, Devotions to the Sacred Heart of Mary. Cloth, 2/-. Best Cloth, red edges, 2/6. Calf or morocco, 5/6 each

ROSARY, BOOK OF THE HOLY. By Rev. H. Formby. A Popular Doctrinal Exposition of the Fifteen Mysteries, with an Explanation of the corresponding Scripture Types. With Thirty-six full-page Engravings. Small 4to, handsome cloth. 3/6

THE HOLY ROSARY IN THE PRESENCE OF JESUS IN THE BLESSED SACRAMENT. Containing the Fifteen Mysteries illustrated in gold and colours, and aspirations suitable for each. Size 5½ by 3¼ inches; bound in leatherette, gilt, gilt edges, round corners, 1/- net (postage 1½d.).

TREATISE ON THE TRUE DEVOTION TO THE BLESSED VIRGIN MARY. By Blessed Grignon de Montfort. Father Faber's Translation. Edited by H. E. Cardinal Vaughan. Fcap. 8vo, cloth. 2/-

On the Holy Ghost.

DEVOTION TO THE HOLY GHOST FOR EACH DAY OF THE MONTH, SHORT READINGS ON. Being Extracts from the Works of Father Faber. Compiled by Rev. Fr. J. M., *Capuchin Franciscan*. Imperial 32mo, stiff wrapper, 3d. net. Cloth, 6d. net (postage 1d.) *Just Published*.

MANNING (H. E. Cardinal). THE INTERNAL MISSION OF THE HOLY GHOST. Cr. 8vo, cloth. 5/-

MANNING (H. E. Cardinal). THE TEMPORAL MISSION OF THE HOLY GHOST: or, Reason and Revelation. Cr. 8vo, 5/-

MANNING (H. E. Cardinal). THE HOLY GHOST THE SANCTIFIER. 32mo, cloth, gilt. 2/-

SUPPLIANT OF THE HOLY GHOST: a Paraphrase of the "Veni Sancte Spiritus." Composed by Rev. R. Johnson, of Louvain. Edited by Rev. T. E. Bridgett, C.SS.R. 32mo, cloth. 1/6

On the Blessed Sacrament and Holy Communion.

AT HOME NEAR THE ALTAR. By Rev. Matthew Russell, S.J. 18mo, cloth, gilt. 1/- net (postage 1½d.)

BANQUET OF THE ANGELS, THE. Preparation and Thanksgiving for Holy Communion. By Most Rev. Archbishop Porter, S.J. 18mo, blue cloth, gilt, 2/- Also in handsome leather bindings, suitable for First Communion memorial gifts, at 6/6 net. and 8/6 net.

CLOSE TO THE ALTAR RAILS. By Rev. Matthew Russell, S.J. 18mo, cloth, gilt. 1/- net (postage 1½d.)

CONFESSION AND COMMUNION. Intended for the use of Religious and those who communicate frequently. By the author of "First Communion." Edited by Rev. H. Thurston, S.J. 18mo, cloth. 1/6

DIVINE CONSOLER, THE. Little Visits to the Most Holy Sacrament. By J. M. Angéli, of the Lazarist Fathers. Translated by Geneviève Irons. 18mo, cloth, 2/6

EUCHARISTIC JEWELS. By Percy Fitzgerald. Fcap. 8vo. Fancy cloth, gilt. 2/6

FABER (Rev. F. W.). THE BLESSED SACRAMENT: or, the Works and Ways of God. Cr. 8vo, cloth. 7/6

FIRST COMMUNION. A Book of Preparation for First Communion. By Mother Mary Loyola. Edited by Father Thurston, S.J. Reset in new type. With some new Illustrations. Cr. 8vo, cloth. 3/6

"FIRST COMMUNION," QUESTIONS ON. By Mother Mary Loyola 1/-

LEGENDS OF THE BLESSED SACRAMENT: Gathered from the History of the Church and the Lives of the Saints by Emily Mary Shapcote. With numerous Illustrations. 4to, handsomely bound in cloth, gilt. 6/-

MANNING (H. E. Cardinal). THE BLESSED SACRAMENT THE CENTRE OF IMMUTABLE TRUTH. 32mo, cloth, gilt. 1/-

MOMENTS BEFORE THE TABERNACLE. By Rev. Matthew Russell, S.J. 18mo, cloth. 1/- net (postage 1d.)

REFLECTIONS AND PRAYERS FOR HOLY COMMUNION. Translated from the French. With Preface by H. E. Cardinal Manning. In Two Vols., each complete in itself. Fcap. 8vo, cloth, 4/6 each. Cloth, red edges, 5/- each. Leather 9/- and 10/- each

THE SACRIFICE OF THE MASS. An Explanation of its Doctrine, Rubric, and Prayers. By the Rev. M. Gavin, S.J. Crown 8vo, cloth, gilt. 2/-.

THE TREASURE OF THE CHURCH. By the Very Rev. J. B. Canon Bagshawe, D.D. Cr. 8vo, cloth, gilt. 3/6.

VISITS TO THE MOST HOLY SACRAMENT AND THE BLESSED VIRGIN Mary. By St. Alphonsus Liguori. Edited by Right Rev. Bishop Coffin, C.SS.R. 32mo, cloth, red edges, 1/-; leather 1/6, 2/6 and 4/6

On Purgatory.

DEVOTIONS FOR THE SOULS IN PURGATORY. By the Very Rev. Father Rawes, D.D. 32mo, cloth, red edges. 1/-

PRISONERS OF THE KING, THE. Thoughts on the Catholic Doctrine of Purgatory. By Rev. H. J. Coleridge, S.J. Fcap. 8vo, cloth. 4/-

PURGATORY: Illustrated by the Lives and Legends of the Saints. From the French of Rev. F. X. Schouppe, S.J. Cr. 8vo, cloth. 6/-

SOULS DEPARTED: Being a Defence and Declaration of the Catholic Church's Doctrine touching Purgatory and Prayers for the Dead. By Cardinal Allen. Edited by the Rev. T. E. Bridgett, C.SS.R. New and Cheaper Edition. Cloth. 3/6.

TREATISE ON PURGATORY. By St. Catherine of Genoa. With Preface by Cardinal Manning. New 32mo Edition, reset in plain type. Cloth, 1/-

On the Priesthood and on Religious Life.

A FEW FIRST PRINCIPLES OF RELIGIOUS LIFE. A Spiritual Instruction to Religious Men and Women. By Father H. Reginald Buckler, O.P. Wrapper. 6d net (postage 1d.).

CATECHISM OF THE VOWS, for the use of Persons Consecrated to God in the Religious State. By Rev. P. Cotel, S.J. 32mo, cloth. 1/-

MANNING (H. E. Cardinal). THE ETERNAL PRIESTHOOD. Cr. 8vo, cloth. 2/6

PARISH PRIEST'S PRACTICAL MANUAL, NEW. A Work useful also for other Ecclesiastics, especially for Confessors and for Preachers. By Very Rev. Joseph Frassinetti. Translated by Very Rev. Canon Hutch, D.D. 6/-

RELIGIOUS LIFE AND THE VOWS, THE. A Treatise by Right Rev. Mgr. Charles Gay, Bishop of Anthedon. Translated by O. S. B. Cr. 8vo, cloth. 5/-

SALVATORI'S PRACTICAL INSTRUCTIONS FOR NEW CONFESSORS, Edited by Father Anthony Ballerini, S.J., and Translated by Very Rev. William Hutch, D.D. 18mo. cloth, gilt. 4/-

Biography and Hagiology.

A SAINT OF THE ORATORY. Being the Life of the Blessed Anthony Grassi. By Lady Amabel Kerr. Cr. 8vo, cloth. 4/- net (postage 4d.)

ALEXIS CLERC, S.J. A Martyr from the Quarter-deck. By Lady Herbert of Lea. Cr. 8vo, cloth. 5/-

ARCHBISHOP ULLATHORNE, THE AUTOBIOGRAPHY OF. Edited by A. T. Drane. Demy 8vo, cloth. 7/6

ARCHBISHOP ULLATHORNE, THE LETTERS OF. Arranged by A. T. Drane. (Sequel to the "Autobiography.") Demy 8vo, cloth. 9/-

BIOGRAPHICAL HISTORY AND BIBLIOGRAPHICAL DICTIONARY OF THE ENGLISH CATHOLICS. From the Breach with Rome in 1534 to the present time. By Joseph Gillow. In Five Volumes, demy 8vo, cloth, £3 15s.; or separate volumes, 15/- each.

BUTLER (Rev. Alban) COMPLETE LIVES OF THE SAINTS FOR EVERY DAY OF THE YEAR. Popular Edition. Twelve Pocket Monthly Volumes and Index Volume, in neat cloth binding, gilt lettered, 1/6 each. Or the complete set of Thirteen Volumes, in handsome cloth case to match, 20/-

CURÉ D'ARS, LIFE OF THE. From the French of the Abbé Monnin. Edited by Cardinal Manning. Fcap. 8vo. 2/6

ENGLAND'S CARDINALS. By Dudley Baxter, B.A. With an appendix showing the reception of the Sacred Pallium by the Archbishops of Canterbury and Westminster. Cr. 8vo, cloth, gilt, with illustrations. 2/6.

FATHER JOHN MORRIS, S.J., THE LIFE AND LETTERS OF. 1826
—1893. By Rev. J. H. Pollen, S.J. Cr. 8vo, cloth. 6/-

FREDERICK WILLIAM FABER, D.D., THE LIFE AND LETTERS OF.
By Rev. John E. Bowden, of the Oratory. 6/-

FROM HEARTH TO CLOISTER in the Reign of Charles II.
Being a narrative of Sir John and Lady Warner's so-
much-wondered-at resolutions to leave the Anglican
Church and to enter the Religious Life. By Frances
Jackson. Crown 8vo, quarter leather, gilt top, price 5s.

IN HOLIEST TROTH. The Story of St. Encratida, one of the
Martyrs of Saragossa, A.D. 304. By Mother Mary Fidelis,
Author of "Growth in the Knowledge of our Lord," &c.
Crown 8vo, cloth, gilt. 3/6.

IRELAND AND ST. PATRICK. A Study of the Saint's Character
and of the Results of his Apostolate. By Rev. W. B.
Morris. Cr. 8vo, cloth. 5/-

MARGARET BEAUFORT, COUNTESS OF RICHMOND AND DERBY AND
MOTHER OF HENRY VII. (The King's Mother), MEMOIR
OF. By Lady Margaret Domvile. Cloth, gilt, gilt top.
With Portrait. 3/6

MARY WARD: A Foundress of the Seventeenth Century. By
Mother M. Salome, of the Bar Convent, York. With
an Introduction by the Bishop of Newport. Illustrated.
Crown 8vo, cloth, gilt. 5/-.

MINIATURE LIVES OF THE SAINTS, for every Day in the Year.
Edited by Rev. H. S. Bowden, of the Oratory. Two
Vols. 18mo, cloth, gilt. 4/-

MIRROR OF PERFECTION, THE. Being a record of St. Francis
of Assisi, ascribed to his Companion, Brother Leo of
Assisi. Translated by Constance, Countess De La
Warr, with an Introduction by Father Cuthbert,
O.S.F.C. Crown 8vo. Bound in buckram, gilt. 5/-
Popular Edition, Wrapper 1/- net (postage 3d.)

RECOLLECTIONS OF FOUR POPES (Pius VII.—Leo XII.—Pius
VIII.—Gregory XVI) And of Rome in their Times.
By Cardinal Wiseman. Crown 8vo, cloth. 3s. 6d.

ST. ALONSO RODRIGUEZ, LIFE OF. By Rev. F. Goldie, S.J.
Cr. 8vo, cloth. 7/6

ST. ALOYSIUS GONZAGA, S.J., LIFE OF. By Edward Healy
Thompson, M.A. Globe 8vo, cloth. 5/-

St. Benedict, Patriarch of the Monks of the West, The Life and Times of. Abridged and arranged from the German of the Very Rev. Dom Peter Lechner, by O. S. B. With 2 illustrations. Cr. 8vo, cloth. 5/-

St. Edmund of Abingdon, Archbishop of Canterbury, Life of. By Frances de Paravicini. Cr. 8vo, cloth, gilt. 6/-

St. Francis Xavier, The Life and Letters of. By Rev. H. J. Coleridge, S.J. Two Vols. Cr. 8vo, cloth. 10/6

St. Gertrude, Life and Revelations of. By the Author of "St. Francis and the Franciscans." Cr. 8vo, cloth. 7/6

St. Hugh of Lincoln, Life of. Translated from the French Carthusian Life, and Edited, with large additions, by Rev. Herbert Thurston, S.J. Cr. 8vo, cloth. 10/6

St. Ignatius Loyola and the Early Jesuits. By Stewart Rose. With more than 100 Illustrations, by H. W. and H. C. Brewer and L. Wain. Edited by the Rev. W. H. Eyre, S.J. Super royal 8vo. Handsomely bound in cloth, extra gilt. 15/- net (postage 8d.)

St. John the Evangelist : or, The Beloved Disciple. By Very Rev. H. A. Rawes, D.D. Fcap. 8vo, cloth. 2/6

St. Juliana Falconieri, Foundress of the Mantellate, or Religious of the Third Order of Servites, Life of. Edited, and with a Preface by the Rev. P. M. Soulier, O.S.M. Illustrated. 5/-

St. Patrick, Apostle of Ireland, Life of. By Rev. W. B. Morris. Cr. 8vo, green cloth. 5/-
The standard biography of Ireland's Apostle. For clear statement of facts and calm, judicious discussion of controverted points, it surpasses any work we know.—*American Catholic Quarterly.*

St. Philip Neri, Life of. Translated from the Italian of Cardinal Capecelatro by Rev. Thomas Alder Pope. Two Vols. Cr. 8vo, cloth. 12/6

St. Teresa, The Life and Letters of. By Rev. H. J. Coleridge, S.J. Three Vols. Cr. 8vo, cloth. 7/6 each

St. Thomas of Aquin, The Life and Labours of. By Archbishop Vaughan, O.S.B. Edited by Dom Jerome Vaughan, O.S.B. Cr. 8vo, cloth, gilt. 6/6

St. Thomas Aquinas, the Angelic Doctor, Life of. Edited by Rev. Pius Cavanagh, O.P. With Eleven Illustrations. Cr. 8vo, cloth. 4/6

VEN. MOTHER JEANNE ANTIDE THOURET, FOUNDRESS OF THE SISTERS OF CHARITY, LIFE OF. Adapted from the Italian, with additions by Blanche Anderdon (Whyte Avis). Fcap 8vo, with portrait. 1/6 net (postage 2d.)

Sermons and Discourses.

CHRISTIAN INHERITANCE, THE. Set forth in Sermons by Right Rev. J. C. Hedley, O.S.B., Bishop of Newport. Cr. 8vo, cloth, gilt. 6/-

LENTEN SERMONS ON THE SACRED PASSION AND DEATH OF OUR LORD. By Rev. P. Sabela. Cloth, gilt. 2/-

LIGHT OF LIFE, THE. Set forth in Sermons by the Right Rev. J. C. Hedley, O.S.B., Bishop of Newport. Cr. 8vo, cloth, gilt, gilt top. 6/-

LUKEWARM CHRISTIAN, THE. Two Sermons by Massillon. Arranged and abridged by Percy Fitzgerald. Fcap. 8vo, cloth, extra gilt, 2/-

MANNING (H. E. Cardinal). SERMONS ON ECCLESIASTICAL SUBJECTS. Cr. 8vo, cloth. 6/-

OUR DIVINE SAVIOUR, AND OTHER DISCOURSES. By Right Rev. Dr. Hedley, O.S.B., Bishop of Newport. Cr. 8vo, cloth, gilt. 6/-

SERMONS FOR THE SUNDAYS AND FESTIVALS OF THE YEAR. By Right Rev. Abbot Sweeney, O.S.B. Fifth and Cheaper Edition. Cr. 8vo, leather back. 7/6

Polemical and Historical.

ANSWERS TO ATHEISTS: or, Notes on Ingersoll. By Rev. L. A. Lambert. Cr. 8vo, wrapper, 6d. (postage 2d.); cloth, gilt lettered, 1/-

CATHOLIC CONTROVERSY. A Reply to Dr. Littledale's "Plain Reasons." By Very Rev. H. I. D. Ryder, of the Oratory. Fcap. 8vo, cloth. 2/6

CATHOLIC CONTROVERSY, THE. By St. Francis de Sales. Edited by Very Rev. Canon Mackey, O.S.B. Cr. 8vo, cloth. 6/-

CONTROVERSIAL CATECHISM. By Rev. Stephen Keenan. 2/-

THE DIVINE PLAN OF THE CHURCH: Where realized and where not. By the Rev. John MacLaughlin. Cr. 8vo. Wrapper, 1/6; cloth, 2/6

FORMATION OF CHRISTENDOM, THE. By T. W. Allies, K.C.S.G. New Popular Edition. Cr. 8vo. 5/- each volume.
Vol. I. The Christian Faith and the Individual. Vol II. The Christian Faith and Society. Vol. III. The Christian Faith and Philosophy. Vol. IV. As seen in Church and State.

IS ONE RELIGION AS GOOD AS ANOTHER? By Rev. John MacLaughlin. 50th Thousand. Wrapper, 6d. net (postage 2d.) Cloth, 1/6 net.

MANNING (H. E. Cardinal). WHY I BECAME A CATHOLIC. (RELIGIO VIATORIS.) Cr. 8vo, cloth. 1/-

MANNING (H. E. Cardinal). THE FOUR GREAT EVILS OF THE DAY. Cr. 8vo, cloth. 2/6

MANNING (H. E. Cardinal). THE WORKINGS OF THE HOLY SPIRIT IN THE CHURCH OF ENGLAND. Cr. 8vo, cloth. 1/6

ROME AND ENGLAND: or, Ecclesiastical Continuity. By Rev. Luke Rivington, D.D. Cr. 8vo, cloth. 3/6

ST. PETER, BISHOP OF ROME: or, The Roman Episcopate of the Prince of the Apostles. By Rev. T. Livius, M.A., C.SS.R. Demy 8vo, cloth, 12/-

Bibles and Prayer Books.

Messrs. Burns & Oates invite your inspection of the largest, the most varied, and the best selection of CATHOLIC BIBLES and PRAYER BOOKS in the United Kingdom. Each book—revised from time to time and brought down to date—bears the Episcopal Imprimatur, and is carefully printed on high-class paper. The binding, even of the Sixpenny Editions, is neat and tasteful, whilst the higher-priced Volumes are produced with all the elegance that modern handicraft secures. Illustrated Catalogues, giving full particulars of the various sizes, prices, and bindings, will be sent free on receipt of a post card.

HOLY BIBLE.
Octavo Edition (9 by 6in.) Cloth, red edges, 5/-; and in a great variety of leather bindings, at 8/- 10/-, 15/-, 18/-, 30/-, and 35/- each.
Pocket Edition (size $5\frac{1}{4}$ by $3\frac{1}{4}$ inches). Embossed cloth, red edges, 2/6; and in leather bindings at 4/6, 6/6, and 7/6

NEW TESTAMENT.
New Large-Type Edition. With annotations, references, and an historical and chronological index. Crown 8vo (size $7\frac{1}{2}$ by 5 inches). 500 pp. Cloth, 2/-, and in leather bindings at 4/6 and 8/6
Pocket Edition. Limp cloth, 6d. net (postage 2d.); cloth, red edges, leather bindings, 1/6, 3/- and 4/6

BIBLES AND PRAYER BOOKS

GARDEN OF THE SOUL. In Five Editions. 6d. to 17/6
KEY OF HEAVEN. In Three Editions. 6d. net to 5/-
PATH TO HEAVEN. New and enlarged Edition. (Over 1000 pages.) 2/- to 8/6.
MANUAL OF CATHOLIC PIETY. In Three Editions. 6d. net to 5/-
CATHOLIC'S VADE MECUM. 3/6 to 21/-
MANUAL OF PRAYERS FOR CONGREGATIONAL USE. New Pocket Edition with an enlarged Appendix, and the Epistles and Gospels. (5 by $3\frac{1}{4}$ inches). Cloth, 1/-; leather, 2/6, 5/-, and upwards.
FLOWERS OF DEVOTION. New Edition. With Ordinary of the Mass in large type. 1/6 to 6/-
GOLDEN MANUAL, THE. The most complete prayer book, 6/- to 30/-.
CATHOLIC'S DAILY COMPANION. 1/- to 5/-
MISSAL FOR THE LAITY. 6d. net to 5/-
ROMAN MISSAL. With all the New Offices, and the Propers for England, Ireland, Scotland, the Society of Jesus, and the Order of St. Benedict. Size $5\frac{7}{8}$ ins. by $3\frac{7}{8}$ ins. 5/- to 30/-
SPIRIT OF THE SACRED HEART. 3/6, 5/6, 8/6, and 12/6. 700 pages printed in large clear type.

Theological.

WHERE BELIEVERS MAY DOUBT; OR, STUDIES IN BIBLICAL INSPIRATION AND OTHER PROBLEMS OF FAITH. By the Very Rev. Vincent J. McNabb, O.P. Crown 8vo, cloth, gilt. 3s. 6d. (Just Published.) Contents:—
St. Thomas and Inspiration. Cardinal Newman and the Inspiration of Scripture. St. Thomas Aquinas on the Hexameron. "Scholasticism and the Modern Method." Mysticism. Imagination and Faith.

AQUINAS ETHICUS: or, The Moral Teaching of St. Thomas. A Translation of the principal portions of the Second Part of the "Summa Theologiæ," with notes. By Rev. Joseph Rickaby, S.J. Two Vols. Cr. 8vo, 12/-

DANTE'S DIVINA COMMEDIA: Its Scope and Value. From the German of Francis Hettinger, D.D. Edited by Rev. H. S. Bowden, of the Oratory. Cr. 8vo, cloth. 10/-

FOUNDATIONS OF FAITH: The Existence of God Demonstrated, From the German of Father Ludwig von Hammerstein, S.J. With an Introduction by Very Rev. W. L. Gildea, D.D. Cr. 8vo, cloth. 6/-

MANNING (H. E. Cardinal). SIN AND ITS CONSEQUENCES. 4/-

MANNING (H. E. Cardinal). THE FOURFOLD SOVEREIGNTY OF GOD. Cr. 8vo, cloth. 2/6

NATURAL RELIGION. Being Vol. I. of Dr. Hettinger's "Evidences of Christianity." Edited by Rev. H. S. Bowden. With an Introduction on "Certainty." Cr. 8vo. 7/6

REVEALED RELIGION. The Second Volume of Dr Hettinger's "Evidences of Christianity." Edited by Rev. H. S. Bowden. With an Introduction on the "Assent of Faith." Cr. 8vo, cloth. 5/-

Miscellaneous Works.

FAITH FOUND. A Tale of the Times. By Wilfrid Meynell. Wrapper 1/- net (postage 3d.)

GUIDE TO THE WESTMINSTER CATHEDRAL. A Brief Survey of its History from 1865 to 1903. With Illustrations. Price 6d. net. (postage 2d.).

LETTERS FROM THE HOLY LAND. By Lady Butler. With Sixteen Full page Illustrations in Colour by the Painter of "The Roll Call." Square demy 8vo, cloth, gilt top. 7/6 net (postage 4d.)

MANNING (H. E. Cardinal). MISCELLANIES. First and Second Series. 6/- each

MANNING (H. E. Cardinal). PASTIME PAPERS. Fcap. 8vo, cloth, gilt, with Portrait. 1/- net (postage 3d.)

MANNING (H. E. Cardinal). THE INDEPENDENCE OF THE HOLY SEE. Cr. 8vo, cloth. 2/6

THE CATHOLIC CHURCH FROM WITHIN. With Preface By H. E. Cardinal Vaughan. Second Edition. 6/6 net. (postage 4d.)

BURNS & OATES, LTD.,
28, ORCHARD STREET, LONDON, W.

www.ingramcontent.com/pod-product-compliance
Lightning Source LLC
Chambersburg PA
CBHW032123230426
43672CB00009B/1843